KENNIKAT PRESS SCHOLARLY REPRINTS
Ralph Adams Brown, Senior Editor

Series In
IRISH HISTORY AND CULTURE
Under the General Editorial Supervision of
Gilbert A. Cahill
Professor of History, State University of New York

A MEMOIR

ON

IRELAND NATIVE AND SAXON.

BY DANIEL O'CONNELL, M.P.

" On *our* side is VIRTUE AND ERIN—
On *theirs* is the SAXON AND GUILT."

MOORE.

KENNIKAT PRESS
Port Washington, N. Y./London

A MEMOIR ON IRELAND NATIVE AND SAXON

First published in 1843
Reissued in 1970 by Kennikat Press
Library of Congress Catalog Card No: 76-102622
SBN 8046-0799-0

Manufactured by Taylor Publishing Company   Dallas, Texas

KENNIKAT SERIES IN IRISH HISTORY AND CULTURE

THIS BOOK

IS

HUMBLY INSCRIBED

TO

HER MOST GRACIOUS MAJESTY

THE QUEEN

OF GREAT BRITAIN

AND

OF IRELAND.

"..................... .QUIS TALIA FANDO

* * * * * * *

TEMPERET A LACHRYMIS."

PREFACE.

I HUMBLY inscribe the following Memoir to Her most gracious Majesty the Queen; not in the shape of a dedication, or with the presumptuous hope of my being able to produce any work of sufficient interest to occupy the Royal mind. Yet, there is nothing more desirable than that the Sovereign of these realms should understand the real nature of Irish history; should be aware of how much the Irish have suffered from English misrule; should comprehend the secret springs of Irish discontent; should be acquainted with the eminent virtues which the Irish nation have exhibited in every phasis of their singular fate; and, above all, should be intimately acquainted with the confiscations, the plunder, the robbery, the domestic treachery, the violation of all public

faith, and of the sanctity of treaties, the ordinary
wholesale slaughters, the planned murders, the
concerted massacres, which have been inflicted
upon the Irish people by the English Governments.

It has pleased the English people in general to
forget all the facts in Irish history. They have
been also graciously pleased to forgive themselves
all those crimes! And the Irish people would
forgive them likewise, if it were not that much of
the worst spirit of the worst days still survives.
The system of clearance of tenants at the present
day, belongs to, and is a demonstration of, that
hatred of the Irish people which animated the
advice of Spenser and the conduct of Cromwell.

It is quite true that at the present day Judges
are not bribed with "*four shillings in the pound,*"
to be paid out of the property in dispute : but,
may not prejudice and bigotry produce unjust
judgments, as well as pecuniary corruption?—
And, are those persons free from reproach, or
from guilt, who are ready to select for the Bench
of justice, men whose sole distinguishing characteristic has been the exhibition of their animosity
to the religion and to the people of Ireland?

Did Stanley show none of the temper of Ireton in his Coercion Bill ? Is none of the spirit of Coote or of Parsons to be found (in a mitigated form) in those who refuse to the Catholic people of Ireland their just share of elective or municipal franchises ; and who insist that the Irish shall remain an inferior and a degraded caste, deprived of that perfect equality of civil and religious liberty, of franchises and privileges—which equality could alone constitute a Union, or render a Union tolerable ?

I wish to arouse the attention of the Sovereign and of the honest portion of the English people to the wrongs which Ireland *has* suffered, and which Ireland *is* suffering from British misrule. The Irish people are determined to preserve their allegiance to the Throne unbroken and intact ; but they are equally determined to obtain justice for themselves ; to insist on the restoration of their native Parliament, and to persevere in that demand without violating the law ; but also without remitting or relaxing their exertions, until the object is achieved and success attained.

What the Sovereign and the Statesmen of England should understand is, that the Irish people

feel and know, that there cannot happen a more
heavy misfortune to Ireland than the prosperity
and power of Great Britain. When Britain is
powerful, the anti-Irish faction in this country are
encouraged, fostered, promoted ; Irish rights are
derided; the grievances of Ireland are scoffed at ;
we are compelled to receive stinted franchises, or
none ; limited privileges, or none !—to submit to
a political inferiority, rendered doubly afflictive by
the contrast with the advantages enjoyed by the
people of England and the people of Scotland.
The Tory Landlord class—exterminators and all—
prime favourites at the Castle, countenanced and
sustained as the nucleus of that anti-Irish faction
which would once again transplant the Catholics
of Ireland to the remotest regions, if that faction
had the power to do so ; and which actually drives
those Catholics to transport themselves in multitudes to every country out of Ireland.

The worst result of British prosperity is, the
protection it gives to the hard-hearted and bigoted
class among the Irish Landlords.

It is also of the utmost importance that the
Sovereign and Statesmen of England should be

apprised that the people of Ireland know and feel that they have a deep and vital interest in the weakness and adversity of England. It was not for themselves alone that the Americans gained the victory over Burgoyne at Saratoga. They conquered for Irish as well as for American freedom. Nor was it for France alone that Dumourier defeated the Austrian army at Gemappe. The Catholics of Ireland participated in the fruits of that victory.

At the present day it would be vain to attempt to conceal the satisfaction the people of Ireland feel at the fiscal embarrassments of England. They bitterly and cordially regret the sufferings and privations of the English and Scotch artisans and operatives. But they do not regret the weakness of the English Government, which results from fading commerce and failing manufacture. For the woes of each suffering individual they have warm compassion and lively sympathy. From the consequent weakness of the Government party, they derive no other feelings than those of satisfaction and of hope.

Was ever folly—was ever fatuity so great, as is

xii PREFACE.

evinced in the system of governing such a country as Ireland in such a manner as to create and continue the sentiments and opinions which I have expressed, and feebly endeavoured to describe?

HER MAJESTY's most faithful,

most dutiful, and

most devoted Subject,

DANIEL O'CONNELL.

1ST FEBRUARY, 1843.

AN HISTORICAL MEMOIR

ON

IRELAND AND THE IRISH.

CHAP. I.

YEARS 1172—1612.

SEC. 1. THE English dominion in Ireland commenced in the year 1172. It was for some centuries extended over only an inconsiderable portion
of the island. From various causes the English
district or Pale sometimes augmented in size, sometimes diminished. It did not become generally
diffused over Ireland until the last years of Queen
Elizabeth, nor universally so, until shortly after
the accession of King James the First. The success of the forces of Queen Elizabeth was achieved
by means the most horrible ; treachery, murder,
wholesale massacre, and deliberately created Famine. Take the last instance : the growing crops
were year after year destroyed, until the fairest
part of Ireland, and in particular the province of
Munster, was literally depopulated. I give here
one quotation. It is from the English Protestant

historian Morrison :—" No spectacle was more
" frequent in the ditches of the towns, and espe-
" cially in wasted countries, than to see multitudes
" of these poor people, the Irish, dead, with their
" mouths all coloured green by eating nettles,
" docks, and all things they could rend above
" ground."

Mark ! Illustrious Lady—oh ! mark ! The most
frequent spectacle was, multitudes of dead—of
Irish dead—dead of hunger ! Lady, after having
endeavoured to sustain life by devouring, after the
fashion of the beasts of the field, the wild-growing
herbs. They were dead in multitudes and none to
bury them ! This was the consummation of the
subjugation of the Irish after a contest of 400
years.

Never was a people on the face of the globe so
cruelly treated as the Irish.

§ 2. The Irish people were not received into
allegiance or to the benefit of being recognized as
subjects until the year 1612, only 228 years ago,
when the Statute 11 James I. cap. 5, was enacted.
That Statute abolished all distinctions of race between English and Irish, " *with the intent that*,"
as the Statute expresses it, " *they may grow into*
" *one nation, whereby there may be an utter obli-*
" *vion and extinguishment of all former differ-*
" *ences and discorde betwixt them.*"

§ 3. During the four hundred and forty years,
that intervened between the commencement of the
English dominion in 1172 and its completion in

1612, the Irish people were known only as the
" Irish Enemies." They were denominated " Irish
Enemies" in all the Royal Proclamations, Royal
Charters, and Acts of Parliament, during that pe-
riod. It was their legal and technical description.

§ 4. During that period the English were prohibited from intermarrying with the Irish, from
having their children nursed by the wives of Irish
Captains, Chiefs, or *Lords ;* and what is still more
strange, the English were also prohibited from
sending goods, wares, or merchandizes for sale, or
selling them upon credit or for ready money to the
Irish.

§ 5. During that time any person of English descent might murder a mere Irish man or woman
with perfect impunity. Such murder was no more
a crime in the eye of the law, than the killing of a
rabid or ferocious animal.

§ 6. There was indeed this distinction, that if a
native Irishman had made legal submission and had
been received into English allegiance, he could no
longer be murdered with impunity, for his murder
was punishable by a small pecuniary fine: a punishment not for the moral crime of murdering a
man, but for the social injury of depriving the
State of a servant. Just as, at no remote period,
the white man in several of our West Indian Colonies was liable to pay a fine for killing a negro,
only because an *owner* was thereby deprived of a
slave.

CHAP. II.

YEARS 1612—1625.

" Residue of the reign of King James the First."

SEC. 1. I have traced the first period of Anglo-Irish History by a few of its distinctive characteristics. It comprised a period of 440 years of internal war, rapine, and massacre. The second period consists only of thirteen years, but possesses an interest of a different and a deeper character.

§ 2. Unhappily there had grown up during the first period another, and alas! a more inveterate source of *" differences and discorde "* between the people. I mean the Protestant Reformation. I am not now to give any opinion on the religious grounds of that all-important measure. I do not treat of it as a theologian. I speak of it merely historically, as a fact having results of a most influential nature.

§ 3. The native Irish universally, and the natives of English descent generally, rejected the Reformation. It was embraced but by comparatively few, and thus the sources of *" differences* and *discorde"* were perpetuated. The distinction of race was lost. Irish and English were amalgamated for the purpose of enduring spoil and oppression under the name of Catholics. The party which the English Government supported was composed of persons lately arrived in Ireland, men who, of course, took the name of " Protestants."

§ 4. The intent of the statute of 1612 was thus frustrated, the " *discorde* " between the Protestant and Catholic parties prevented the Irish from " growing into one nation," and still prevents them from being " one nation." The fault however has been and still is with the Government. Is it not time it were totally corrected ?

§ 5. The reign of James the First was distinguished by crimes committed on the Irish people under the pretext of Protestantism. The entire of the province of Ulster was unjustly confiscated, the natives were executed on the scaffold or slaughtered with the sword, a miserable remnant were driven to the fastnesses of remote mountains, or the wilds of almost inaccessible bogs. Their places were filled with Scotch adventurers, " aliens in blood and in religion." Devastation equal to that committed by King James in Ulster was never before seen in Christendom save in Ireland. In the Christian world there never was a people so cruelly treated as the Irish.

§ 6. The jurisdiction of Parliament being now extended all over Ireland, King James created in one day forty close boroughs, giving the right to elect two members of Parliament in each of these boroughs to thirteen Protestants, and this, in order to deprive his Catholic subjects of their natural and just share of representation.

CHAP. III.

YEARS 1625—1660.

SEC. 1. THE reign of Charles the First began under different auspices. The form of oppression and robbery varied—the substance was still the same. Iniquitous law took place of the bloody sword : the soldier was superseded by the judge ; and for the names of booty and plunder, the words forfeiture and confiscation were substituted. The instrument used by the Government was the " *Commission to enquire into defective titles.*" The King claimed the estates of the Irish people in three provinces. This commission was instituted to enforce that claim. It was a monstrous tribunal : an attempt was made to bribe juries to find for the Crown—that attempt failed. Then the Jurors, who hesitated to give verdicts against the people, were fined, imprisoned, ruined. The Judges were not so chary—they were bribed—aye, bribed, with four shillings in the pound of the value of all lands recovered from the subjects by the Crown before such Judges. And so totally lost to all sense of justice or of shame was the perpetrator of this bribery, STRAFFORD, that he actually boasted, that he had thus made the Chief Baron and other Judges " *attend to the affair as if it were their own pri-private business.*"

§ 2. By these unjust and wicked means the ministers of Charles the First despoiled for the use of the Crown, the Irish Catholic people of upwards of one million of arable acres, besides a considerably greater extent of land taken from the right owners, and granted to the rapacious individuals by whom the spoliation was effected.

§ 3. The civil war ensued. Forgetting all the crimes committed against them, the Irish Catholics adhered with desperate tenacity to the party of the King. The Irish Protestants, some sooner and others later, joined the usurping powers.

§ 4. During that civil war, the massacres committed on the Irish by St. Leger, Monroe, Tichbourne, Hamilton, Grenville, Ireton, and Cromwell, were as savage and as brutal, as the horrible feats of Attila or Ghengis Khan.

§ 5. In particular the history of the world presents nothing more shocking and detestable, than the massacres perpetrated by O'Brien, Lord Inchiquin in the Cathedral of Cashel; by Ireton, at Limerick, and by Cromwell in Drogheda and Wexford.

§ 6. When the war had ceased, Cromwell collected, as the first-fruits of peace, eighty thousand Irish in the southern parts of Ireland, to transplant them to the West India Islands. As many as survived the process of collection were embarked in transports for these islands. Of the eighty thousand, in six years, the survivors did not amount to

twenty individuals ! ! !   Eighty thousand Irish at
one blow deliberately sacrificed, by a slow but steady
cruelty, to the Moloch of English domination ! ! !
Eighty thousand—Oh God of mercy !

§ 7. Yet all these barbarities ought to be deemed
light and trivial, compared with the crowning
cruelty of the enemies of Ireland.   The Irish were
refused civil justice.   They were still more atrociously refused historical justice, and accused of
being the authors and perpetrators of assassina-
tions and massacres, of which they were only the
victims.

§ 8. No people on the face of the earth were
ever treated with such cruelty as the Irish.

CHAP. IV.

YEARS 1660—1692.

SEC. 1. WE are arrived at the Restoration—an
event of the utmost utility to the English and Scotch
royalists, who were justly restored to their properties.   An event, which consigned irrevocably
and for ever to British plunderers, and especially
to the soldiers of Ireton and Cromwell, the properties of the Irish Catholic people, whose fathers had
contended against the usurped powers to the last
of their blood and their breath.

§ 2. The Duke of York, afterwards James the

Second, took to his own share of the plunder, about eighty thousand acres of lands belonging to Irish Catholics, whose cause of forfeiture was nothing more than that they had been the friends and supporters of his murdered father, and the enemies of his enemies.

§ 3. Yet such was in the Irish nation the inherent love of principle,—a principle of honourable, but, in this instance, most mistaken loyalty—that when this royal plunderer was afterwards driven from the throne by his British subjects, he took refuge in Ireland, and the Irish Catholic nobility, gentry, and universal people, rallied round him, and shed their blood for him with a courage and a constancy worthy of a better cause.

§ 4. This section should be devoted to the treaty of Limerick. The Irish were not conquered, Lady, in the war. They had in the year preceding the treaty, driven William the Third with defeat and disgrace from Limerick. In this Irish victory the women participated. It is no romance. In the great defeat of William, the women of Limerick fought and bled and conquered. On the third of October, 1691, the treaty of Limerick was signed. The Irish army, 30,000 strong—the Irish nobility and gentry, and people, capitulated with the army and Crown of Great Britain. They restored the allegiance of the Irish nation to that Crown. Never was there a more useful treaty to England than this was under the circumstances. It was a most

deliberate and solemn treaty—deliberately confirmed by letters-patent from the Crown.   It extinguished a sanguinary civil war.   It restored the
Irish nation to the dominion of England, and secured that dominion in perpetuity over one of the
fairest portions of the globe.   Such was the value
given by the Irish people.

§ 5. By that treaty, on the other hand, the Irish
Catholic people stipulated for and obtained the
pledge of " *the faith and honour*" of the English
Crown, for the equal protection by law of their
properties and their liberties with all other subjects
—and in particular for the FREE AND UNFET-
TERED EXERCISE OF THEIR RELIGION.

CHAP. V.

YEARS 1692—1778.

SEC. 1. THE Irish in every respect performed
with scrupulous accuracy the stipulations on their
part of the Treaty of Limerick.

§ 2. That treaty was totally violated by the British government, the moment *it was perfectly safe*
to violate it.

§ 3. That violation was perpetrated by the enactment of a code, of the most dexterous but atrocious
iniquity that ever stained the annals of legislation.

§ 4. Let me select a few instances of the bar-

barity with which the treaty of Limerick was violated, under these heads :

First.—" PROPERTY."

" Every Catholic was, by Act of Parliament, de-
   " prived of the power of settling a jointure
   " on any Catholic wife—or charging his
   " lands with any provision for his daughters
   " —or disposing by will of his landed pro-
   " perty. On his death the law divided his
   " lands equally amongst all his sons.
" All the relations of private life were thus
   " violated.
" If the wife of a Catholic declared herself a
   " Protestant, the law enabled her not only
   " to compel her husband to give her a se-
   " parate maintenance, but to transfer to her
   " the custody and guardianship of all their
   " children.
" Thus the wife was encouraged and empowered
   " successfully to rebel against her husband.
" If the eldest son of a Catholic father at any
   " age, however young, declared himself a
   " Protestant, he thereby made his father
   " strict tenant for life, deprived the father
   " of all power to sell, or dispose of his estate,
   " and such Protestant son became entitled
   " to the absolute dominion and ownership
   " of the estate.

" Thus the eldest son was encouraged and, in-
   " deed, bribed by the law to rebel against
   " his father.
" If any other child beside the eldest son de-
   " clared itself, at any age, a Protestant,
   " such child at once escaped the controul
   " of its father, and was entitled to a main-
   " tenance out of the father's property.
" Thus the law encouraged every child to rebel
   " against its father.
" *If any Catholic purchased for money any*
   " *estate in land, any Protestant was em-*
   " *powered by law to take away that estate*
   " *from the Catholic, and to enjoy it without*
   " *paying one shilling of the purchase money*
" This was Law.—The Catholic paid the money,
   " whereupon the Protestant took the estate.
   " The Catholic lost both money and estate.
" If any Catholic got an estate in land by mar-
   " riage, by the gift, or by the will of a
   " relation, or friend, any Protestant could
   " by Law take the estate from the Catholic
   " and enjoy it himself.
" If any Catholic took a lease of a farm of land
   " as tenant at a rent for a life, or lives, or
   " for any longer term than thirty-one years,
   " any Protestant could by Law take the
   " farm from the Catholic and enjoy the
   " benefit of the lease.

" If any Catholic took a farm by lease for a
" term not exceeding thirty-one years, as
" he might still by Law have done, and by
" his labour and industry raised the value
" of the land so as to yield a profit equal
" to one-third of the rent, any Protestant
" might THEN by Law evict the Catholic,
" and enjoy for the residue of the term the
" fruit of the labour and industry of the
" Catholic.

" If any Catholic had a horse, worth more than
" five pounds, any Protestant tendering £5
" to the Catholic owner, was by law entitled
" to take the horse, though worth £50, or
" £100, or more, and to keep it as his own.

" If any Catholic being the owner of a horse
" worth more than five pounds, concealed his
" horse from any Protestant, the Catholic
" for the crime of concealing his own horse,
" was liable to be punished by an imprison-
" ment of three months, and a fine of three
" times the value of the horse, whatever
" that might be.

" So much for the Laws regulating by Act of
" Parliament, the property—or rather plun-
" dering by due course of Law, the property
" —of the Catholic.

" I notice—

Secondly.—EDUCATION.

" If a Catholic kept school, or taught any per-

" son, Protestant or Catholic, any species
" of literature, or science, such teacher was
" for the crime of teaching punishable by
" Law by banishment—and, if he returned
" from banishment, he.was subject to be
" hanged as a felon.

" If a Catholic, whether a child or adult, at-
" tended, in Ireland, a school kept by a
" Catholic, or was privately instructed by a
" Catholic, such Catholic, although a child
" in its early infancy, incurred a forfeiture
" of all its property, present or future.

" If a Catholic child, however young, was sent
" to any foreign country for education, such
" infant child incurred a similar penalty—
" that is, a forfeiture of all right to pro-
" perty, present or prospective.

" If any person in Ireland made any remittance
" of money or goods, for the maintenance
" of any Irish child educated in a foreign
" country, such person incurred a similar
" forfeiture.

Thirdly.—PERSONAL DISABILITIES.

" The Law rendered every Catholic incapable of
" holding a commission in the army, or
" navy, or even to be a private soldier, un-
" less he solemnly abjured his religion.

" The Law rendered every Catholic incapable of
" holding any office whatsoever of honour

" or emolument in the State. The exclusion
" was universal.

" A Catholic had no legal protection for life
" or liberty. He could not be a Judge,
" Grand Juror, Sheriff, Sub-sheriff, Master
" in Chancery, Six Clerk, Barrister, Attor-
" ney, Agent or Solicitor, or Seneschal of
" any manor, or even gamekeeper to a pri-
" vate gentleman.

" A Catholic could not be a member of any
" Corporation, and Catholics were precluded
" by Law from residence in some corporate
" towns.

" Catholics were deprived of all right of voting
" for members of the Commons House of
" Parliament.

" Catholic Peers were deprived of their right to
" sit or vote in the House of Lords.

" Almost all these personal disabilities were
" equally enforced by Law against any Pro-
" testant who married a Catholic wife, or
" whose child, under the age of fourteen,
" was educated as a Catholic, although
" against his consent.

Fourthly.—RELIGION.

" To teach the Catholic religion was a trans-
" portable felony ; to convert a Protestant
" to the Catholic faith, was a capital offence
" punishable as an act of treason.

" To be a Catholic regular, that is a monk or
" friar, was punishable by banishment, and
" to return from banishment an act of high-
" treason.

" To be a Catholic Archbishop or Bishop, or
" to exercise any ecclesiastical jurisdiction
" whatsoever in the Catholic Church in
" Ireland, was punishable by transportation
" —to return from such transportation was
" an act of high-treason, punishable by being
" hanged, embowelled alive, and afterwards
" quartered."

§ 5. After this enumeration, will you, Illustrious
Lady, be pleased to recollect that every one of these
enactments, that each and every of these laws, was
a palpable and direct violation of a solemn treaty
to which the faith and honour of the British Crown
was pledged, and the justice of the English nation
unequivocally engaged.

§ 6. There never yet was such a horrible code of
persecution invented, so cruel, so cold-blooded—
calculating—emaciating—universal—as this legislation, which the Irish Orange faction—the Shaws
—the Lefroys—the Verners of the day did invent
and enact. A code exalted to the utmost height of
infamy by the fact, that it was enacted in the
basest violation of a solemn engagement and deliberate treaty.

§ 7. It is not possible for me to describe that
code in adequate language—It almost surpassed

the eloquence of Burke to do so. "It had," as Burke describes it, " *It had a vicious perfection* " *—it was a complete system—full of coherence* " *and consistency; well digested and well dis-* " *posed in all its parts.* It was a machine of wise " *and elaborate contrivance, and as well fitted for* " *the oppression, impoverishment, and degrada-* " *tion of a people, and the debasement in them of* " *human nature itself, as ever proceeded from the* " *perverted ingenuity of man.*"

§ 8. This code prevented the accumulation of property, and punished industry as a crime. Was there ever such legislation in any other country, Christian or Pagan? But that is not all, because the party who inflicted this horrible code, actually reproached the Irish people with wilful and squalid POVERTY.

§ 9. This code enforced ignorance by Statute Law, and punished the acquisition of knowledge as a felony. Is this credible?—yet it is true. But that is not all; for the party that thus persecuted learning, reproached and still reproach the Irish people with IGNORANCE.

§ 10. *There;*—there never was a people on the face of the earth so cruelly, so basely, treated as the Irish. There never was a faction so stained with blood—so blackened with crime as that Orange faction, which, under the name of Protestant, seeks to retain the remnants of their abused power, by keeping in activity the spirit which created and

continued the infamous penal persecution of which
I have thus faintly traced an outline.

It would be worse than seditious, nay actually
treasonable, to suppose that such a faction can ever
obtain countenance from you, Illustrious Lady, destined, as I trust you are, at length to grant justice,
by an equalization of rights with your other subjects, to your faithful, brave, long oppressed, but
magnanimous, people of Ireland.

CHAP. VI.

Years 1778—1800.

§ 1. The persecution I have described—the persecution founded on a breach of national faith and
public honour—lasted for eighty-six long years of
darkness—of shame—and of sorrow.

It was intended to reduce the Catholic people of
Ireland to the state of the most abject poverty, and
by the same means to extirpate the Catholic religion.

Here a question of some interest arises :—What
was the success of the experiment? Before the
question is answered, let it be recollected that the
experiment had in favour of its success the Crown
—the Parliament—the Bishops and Clergy of the
established Church—the Judges—the Army, the
Navy—the Corporations—Mayors—Aldermen—
Sheriffs and Freemen—the Magistracy, the Grand

Jurors—the almost universal mass of the property and wealth of the Irish nation. It had besides the entire countenance, concurrence, and support of England and Scotland—not a tongue could utter in public one word against it, or if it so uttered even one word, it was stopped for ever—not a pen could write one word in opposition.

Yet with all these tremendous advantages, what was the success of the experiment?

Illustrious Lady—it failed—it totally failed. A just estimate would state that the Catholics went into the persecution about two millions in number; the Protestant persecutors—for, at that day, they were all persecutors—were about one million. The Catholics have increased to nearly seven millions —the Protestants still scarcely exceed the original million. The comparative increase of the one under persecution is enormous—the comparative decrease of the other whilst persecuting is astounding ; in the first instance the Catholics were at the utmost only two to one—in the second they are near seven to one :

" Thus captive Israel multiplied in chains."

Blessed be God ! So may persecution fail in every country until it shall universally be admitted to be as useless for conversion, as its exercise is debasing and degrading in those who employ it.

§ 2. The time for a relaxation of the " *Penal Code*"—that was the technical name given to the persecuting code—had at length arrived. In 1775 the obstinate refusal of the British Government to do "justice to America" was checked by blood. In 1777 a British army, in its "pride of place," surrendered at Saratoga to the once despised, insulted, and calumniated "Provincials." It was in 1778 too late to conciliate America. She proclaimed her independence, and America was for ever lost to the British crown.

§ 3. The ancient enemies of England in Europe armed, and assailed her. The English Government in their adversity learned one lesson from fatal experience; they for the first time tried conciliation to Ireland. The Penal Code was relaxed in 1778. Conciliation succeeded as it always will with the Irish people. America, it is true, was lost by refusing to conciliate—but Ireland was preserved to the British crown by conciliation.

§ 4. The relaxation of the " Penal Code" in 1778 was, in its own nature, a large instalment of the debt of "Justice to the Catholic people of Ireland." It restored to the Catholics the same power and dominion over the property they then held as the Protestants always enjoyed; and it enabled the Catholics to acquire as tenants, or as purchasers, any interest in lands for any terms or years, though they may be as long as one thousand years. But still they could not acquire by purchase, or as tenants, any freehold interests. The Catholics wisely accepted the instalment, and went on with increased

security and power to look for the rest of the debt
of justice.

§ 5. In 1782, England stood alone in a contest
with the greatest power in the world—the combined fleets of her enemies, as one of the rare instances in her naval annals, rode triumphant and
unopposed in the British channel. Accordingly
the " *Penal Code*" was once again relaxed—conciliated Ireland poured twenty thousand seamen
and active landsmen into the British navy—enabled
Rodney to pursue the French fleet to the West
Indies ; where, in his action with De Grasse, Irish
valour, emulating, and, if that were possible, exceeding British bravery, rendered the " meteor flag
of England" once more victorious—crushed the
naval power of the enemy—saved not only the
West Indian colonies, but also the honour of the
British crown, and strewed laurels over a peace
which would otherwise have been ignominious as
well as disastrous.

§ 6. The relaxation of the year 1782 was a second instalment of the debt of " Justice to Ireland."
It was a noble instalment. It enabled the Catholics
to acquire freehold property for lives, or of inheritance. But it did more ;—for the first time after
ninety years of persecuted learning, it enabled the
Catholics to open schools and to educate their youth
in literature and religion. The Catholics wisely
accepted that instalment, which restored in full

their rights of property, and gave them the inestimable right of education. They gratefully accepted
the instalment, and wisely and with increased
power, commenced a new struggle for the rest.

§ 7. The admission of the Catholics to the te-
nancy of lands in 1778, increased considerably the
rents of the Protestant landlords in Ireland. The
permission to the Catholics in 1782 to purchase
estates, enhanced enormously the value of the property of all the Protestants of Ireland. Conciliation and prosperity went hand in hand, and that
which benevolence alone would have suggested,
was proved by experience to be the best means to
increase the value of their property, which the most
rigid and the most selfish prudence would have
dictated to the Protestant proprietors of Ireland.

§ 8. There were other events in 1782, which
merit more than the passing glance I can now bestow upon them—events of the deepest, the most
soul-stirring interest. For the present, suffice it
to say, that the Irish Parliament which asserted
the legislative independence of Ireland was not
only the most advantageous to its constituents, but
was at the same time the most loyal to the British
crown, and the most useful to the British power.
It was that Parliament which voted and paid the
twenty thousand Irish Catholics who rushed to
man the British fleets, and contributed to Rodney's
victory. Ireland never had a Parliament more

attached to British connexion than the Irish Parliament which asserted Irish legislative independence.

§ 9. Ten years followed of great and increasing prosperity in Ireland—but they were years of peace and power in England, and there was no occasion to conciliate or court the Catholics of Ireland. Accordingly no further advance was made in their emancipation. The Catholics however shared in the universal prosperity of Ireland.

§ 10. The year 1792 found matters in this condition. The prosperity which the Catholics enjoyed in common with their other countrymen—the property which they were daily acquiring, made them impatient for political rights. They therefore petitioned the Irish House of Commons that the profession of the law might be opened to them, and for the elective franchise. It was with difficulty one member could be procured to move that the petition should be laid upon the table, and another to second it. The motion was opposed by the member for Kildare, Mr. Latouche; he moved that the petition should be rejected—there was no danger apprehended from its rejection. It was accordingly rejected, all the members of the Government voting for that rejection.

§ 11. But before the close of 1792, a new scene was opened.—The French armies defeated their enemies at every point. The Netherlands were conquered, and a torrent of republicanism, driven

on by military power, threatened every state in
Europe. The cannon of the battle of Gemappe were
heard at St. James's—the wisdom of conciliating
the Catholics was felt and understood ; and in the
latter end of that same year 1792—in the early part
of which the Government had ignominiously rejected
the Catholic petition with contempt—that same
Government brought in a bill still further to relax
the "Penal Code ;" and early in the next year
brought in another bill, granting, or I should rather
say restoring, greater privileges to the Catholics.

§ 12. By the effect of both these bills, the bar
was opened to the Catholics—they might become
barristers, but not King's counsel—they could be
attorneys and solicitors—they could be freemen of
the lay corporations—the Grand Jury box and the
magistracy were opened to them—they were allowed to attain the rank of Colonel in the army—
and still greater than all, they were allowed to
acquire the elective franchise, and to vote for
members of Parliament. This was the third great
instalment of public justice obtained by the Catholics of Ireland.

§ 13. But it should be recollected that these
concessions were made more in fear than in friendship. The revolutionary war was about to commence—the flames of republicanism had spread
far and near. It was eagerly caught up amongst
the Protestant and especially among the Presbyterian population of the north of Ireland. Belfast

was its warmest focus; it was the deep interest of
the British Government to detach the wealth and
intelligence of the Catholics of Ireland from the
republican party. This policy was adopted. The
Catholics were conciliated. The Catholic nobility,
gentry, mercantile, and other educated classes, almost to a man, separated from the republican party.
That which would otherwise have been a revolution,
became only an unsuccessful rebellion. The intelligent and leading Catholics were conciliated, and
Ireland was once again, by the wise policy of concession and conciliation, saved to the British
crown.

§ 14. Illustrious Lady—the Rebellion of 1798
itself was, almost avowedly, and beyond a doubt
proveably, fomented to enable the British Government to extinguish the Irish legislative independence and to bring about the Union.—But the
instrument was nearly too powerful for the unskil-
ful hands that used it, and if the Catholic wealth,
education, and intelligence, had joined the rebellion, it would probably have been successful.

§ 15. One word upon the legislative independence of Ireland—that which is now called a " Repeal of the Union." It is said to be a severance
of the empire—a separation of the two countries.
Illustrious Lady, these statements are made by men
who know them to be unfounded. An Irish legislative independence would, on the contrary, be the

strongest and most durable connexion between
your Majesty's Irish and your British dominions.
It would, by conciliating your Irish subjects and
attending to their wants and wishes, render the
separation of Ireland from the lawful dominion of
your crown, utterly impossible.

§ 16. No country ever rose so rapidly in trade,
manufactures, commerce, agricultural wealth, and
general prosperity, as Ireland did from the year
1782 until the year 1798, when the "fomented
Rebellion" broke out, and for a space, a passing
and transitory space, marred the fair prospects of
Ireland.

CHAP. VII.

The Year 1800.

§ 1. This year would justify a volume to itself.
It was the year that consummated the crimes
which, during nearly seven centuries, the English
Government perpetrated against Ireland. It was
the year of the destruction of the Irish legislature.
It was the fatal, ever to be accursed year of the
enactment of the Union.

§ 2. The Union was inflicted on Ireland by the
combined operation of terror, torture, force, fraud,
and corruption.

§ 3. The contrivers of the Union kept on foot
and fomented the embers of a lingering rebellion.
They hallooed the Protestant against the Catholic,
and the Catholic against the Protestant. They
carefully kept alive domestic dissensions, for the
purposes of subjugation.

§ 4. Whilst the Union was in progress, the Ha-
beas Corpus act was suspended—all constitutional
freedom was annihilated in Ireland—MARTIAL
LAW WAS PROCLAIMED—the use of torture was
frequent—liberty, life, or property, had no protection—public opinion was stifled—trials by court-
martial were familiar—meetings legally convened
by sheriffs and magistrates were dispersed by military violence—the voice of Ireland was suppressed
—the Irish people had no protection. Once again,
I repeat, MARTIAL LAW WAS PROCLAIMED—thus
the Union was achieved in total despite of the Irish
nation.

§ 5. But this was not all—the most enormous
and the basest corruption was resorted to. Lord
John Russell is reported to have stated some time
ago at a public dinner, that the Union was carried
at an expense of £800,000. He was much mistaken, speaking as he did merely from a vague recollection. The parliamentary documents will
show him that the one item of the purchase money
of rotten and nomination boroughs, cost no less a
sum than one million, two hundred and forty-
five thousand pounds.—The pecuniary corruption

amounted altogether to about three millions of
pounds sterling.

§ 6. But this was not all—the expenditure of
patronage was still more open, avowed, and profligate; Peerages were a familiar staple of traffic—
the command of ships of the line and of regiments
—the offices of Chief and Puisne Judges, the sta-
tions of Archbishops and Bishops, Commissioner-
ships of the Revenue, and all species of Collector-
ships—in short, all grades of offices—the sanctuary
of the law and the temples of religion, were traf-
ficked upon as bribes, and given in exchange for
votes in parliament in favour of the Union.

§ 7. But this was not all. Notwithstanding all
the resources of intimidation and terror—of martial law and military torture—of the most gigantic
bribery ever exhibited—the Union could not be
carried until several of the nomination boroughs
were purchased, to return a number of Scotchmen
and Englishmen, all of whom held rank in the
army or navy, or other offices under Government,
removeable at pleasure. The number of such
" Aliens" was almost as great as the majority by
which the Union was carried.

§ 8. The Union was not a treaty or compact,
Illustrious Lady. It was not a bargain, or agreement. It had its origin in, and was carried by
force, fraud, terror, torture, and corruption. It
has to this hour no binding power but what it de-
rives from force. It is still a mere name. The

countries are not united. The Irish are still treated as " Aliens in blood and in religion."

§ 9. Thus was the legislative independence of Ireland extinguished. Thus was the greatest crime ever perpetrated by the English Government upon Ireland consummated.

§ 10. The atrocity of the manner of carrying the Union was equalled only by the injustice of the terms to which Ireland was subjected.

§ 11. I hate to dwell on this detestable subject. I will put forward only two of the features of the injustice done to Ireland. The one relates to finance—the other to representation.

§ 12. The epitome of the financial fraud perpetrated against the Irish is just this. At the time of the Union Ireland owed twenty millions of funded debt. England owed four hundred and forty-six millions. If the Union were a fair and reasonable treaty, the debts of the two countries should continue to bear the same proportions. Perhaps even that arrangement would, under all the circumstances, be harsh towards Ireland. But what is the consequence to Ireland of the Union? It is this, that all the land, houses, and other property, real and personal, of Ireland, are now pledged to the repayment equally with England of eight hundred and forty millions of pounds sterling!!! At the utmost the Irish ought to owe a sum not exceeding forty millions. By the Union we are made to owe eight hundred and forty millions. But for the Union, the entire Irish debt would have been long since paid off, and Ireland, like Norway, would have no national debt. Never was there a people so unjustly treated as the Irish!

§ 13. The gross injustice done to Ireland in the matter of representation in the united Parliament was this : The ingredients to entitle either country to representation were said by the fabricators of the Union to be—population and property. The only evidences of property that Lord Castlereagh would allow, were exports, imports, and revenue. He totally omitted rental—yet, upon his own data, Ireland was entitled to 108—out of a total of 658 representatives.

He took off eight, of his own will and pleasure, and left Ireland but 100 members.

But in truth he ought to have taken into calculation the relative rental of each country, and then the right of Ireland to 169 members would appear. Still more, had the ingredients of a relative representation consisted, as they ought to have consisted, solely of population and revenue, the right of Ireland to 176 members would be demonstrated.

§ 14. If the Union had been a fair treaty, no chicanery could have deprived Ireland of at the least 150 members. Yet one-third were struck off at the despotic will and pleasure of the English Government. This is indeed a grievous injustice, and much of the insecurity of the Union rests upon it. Substantial justice in this respect has ever been withheld. Thus we are degraded and insulted by the Union.

CHAP. VIII.

YEARS 1800—1829.

§ 1. The alleged object of the Union was to consolidate the inhabitants of both islands into one nation—one people. The most flattering hopes were held out, the most solemn pledges were vowed —Ireland was no longer to be an alien and a stranger to British liberty. The religion of the inhabitants was no longer to be a badge for persecution—the nations were to be identified—the same privileges—the same laws—the same liberties.

They trumpeted, until the ear was tired and all good taste nauseated, the hackneyed quotation, the " *Paribus se legibus*"—the " *Invictæ gentes*" —the " *Eterna in federa.*"

§ 2. These were words—Latin or English, they were mere words—*Ireland lost everything and got nothing by the Union.* Pitt behaved with some dignity when he resigned the office of Prime Minister, on finding that George the Third refused to allow him to redeem the Union pledge of granting Catholic Emancipation. But that dignity was

dragged in the kennel, when he afterwards consented to be Minister with his pledge broken and
his faith violated.   Yet there are still " Pitt Clubs"
—are there not ?—in England ! ! !

§ 3. *Ireland lost everything and gained nothing
by the Union.*   There is one great evil in the political economy of Ireland.   There is one incurable
plague-spot in the state of Ireland.   It is, that
nine-tenths of the soil belong to absentees.   This
evil was felt as a curse pregnant with every possible woe even before the Union.   It has enormously increased since—the Union must inevitably
have increased, and must continue to increase ab-
senteeism.   Even all the establishments necessary
to carry on the Government save one—that of the
Lord Lieutenant—have become absentees.

§ 4. *Ireland lost all and gained nothing by the
Union.*   Every promise was broken, every pledge
was violated.   Ireland struggled, and prayed, and
cried out to friends for aid, and to Parliament for
relief.

§ 5. At length a change came over the spirit of
our proceedings.   The people of Ireland ceased to
court patronage, or to hope for relief from their
friends.   They became "friends to themselves," and
after twenty-six years of agitation, they forced the
concession of Emancipation.   They compelled the
most powerful as well as the most tricky, the most
daring as well as the most dexterous, of their enemies, to concede Emancipation.

§ 6. WELLINGTON and PEEL—blessed be heaven—we defeated you. Our peaceable combination, bloodless, unstained, crimeless, was too strong
for the military glory—bah! of the one, and for
all the little arts, the debasing chicanery, the
plausible delusions, of the other. Both at length
conceded, but without dignity, without generosity,
without candour, without sincerity. Nay, there
was a littleness in the concession almost incredible,
were it not part of public history. They emancipated a people, and by the same act they proscribed
an individual. PEEL and WELLINGTON, we defeated and drove you before us into coerced liberality, and you left every remnant of character
behind you, as the spoil of the victors.

§ 7. There was an intermediate period in which
Emancipation could have been conceded with a
good grace, and would have been accepted as a
boon. It was the year 1825. In that year, when
everything favoured the grant of Emancipation—
when it could have been granted with grace and
dignity—when it could have been bestowed as the
emanation of the mighty minds of statesmen and
conquerors,—in 1825, Wellington and Peel successfully opposed Emancipation, and thus preserved that,
which might have been their glorious triumph, to
become the instrument of their own degradation.

§ 8. Let it not be forgotten that the House of
Commons three times during these twenty-nine

years passed an Emancipation bill; but that bill was, each of those times, rejected by the House of Lords. The Lords however yielded to the fourth assault, backed as it was by the power of the Irish nation. We at length defeated the perpetual enemy of Ireland—the British House of Lords.

§ 9. Let it be recollected that our struggle was for "freedom of conscience." Oh how ignorant are the men who boast of Protestant tolerance, and declaim on Catholic bigotry! This calumny was one of the worst evils we formerly endured. At present we laugh it to scorn. The history of the persecutions perpetrated by the Protestant Established Church of England, upon Catholics on the one hand, and upon Presbyterians and other Protestant dissenters on the other, is one of the blackest in the page of time.

§ 10. The Irish Catholics, three times since the Reformation restored to power, never persecuted a single person—blessed be the great God!

CHAP. IX.
YEARS 1829—1840.

§ 1. There never was a people on the face of the earth, so cruelly, to basely, so unjustly treated as the people of Ireland have been by the English Government.

§ 2. The Catholics being emancipated, the people of England had leisure to awaken to a sense of the delusions practised upon them by false alarms on the score of religion and loyalty. The delusion was most valuable to the deluders. At length the monstrous nature of what was called Parliamentary representation stared the British people in the face. It was, perhaps, the greatest and most ludicrous farce that had ever been played on the great stage of the world. Luckily a blunder, such as no man out of a madhouse had ever before committed—a blunder of the Duke of Wellington—brought the absurdity and oppression of this farce into so glaring a point of view, as to render it impossible to be continued. He, as a Prime Minister of England, declared his conviction that the nomination and rotten-borough system of England, WAS THE ACTUAL PERFECTION OF POLITICAL SAGACITY—NAY, HE ALMOST EXALTED IT INTO AN EMANATION OF A DIVINER MIND.

This was irresistible—common sense revolted—Reform was inevitable.

§ 3. Again, the most gross and glaring injustice was done to Ireland. It is admitted that, without the aid of the Irish members, Reform could not have been carried. Even the most malignant of our enemies, Stanley, has admitted that fact. To the Irish, therefore, a deep debt of gratitude was due from the British Reformers. But how have we been

requited? We have been treated with the basest
and most atrocious ingratitude.

§ 4. We are still suffering under the ingratitude
of the British Reformers—under the consistent injustice of the British Tories.

Under four heads I will, as briefly as possible,
sketch our complaints ;—not the abject complaint
of those who have no hope in, and no reliance upon,
their own virtue. I make the complaint in the
language of a freeman. I make it on behalf of a
people who have made others free, and who deserve to be free themselves. As my only preface,
I desire these four facts to be remembered.

1st. That the Irish Representatives turned the
scale of victory, and carried the English Parliamentary Reform Bill.

2nd. They equally, and by the same Act, carried
the Scotch Reform Bill.

3rd. They equally, and by inevitable consequence,
carried the English Municipal Reform Bill.

4th. They equally carried the Scotch Municipal
Reform Bill.

§ 5. Even if they had not these merits, they were
entitled, unless the Union be an insulting mockery,
they were—the Irish were—on the plainest principles of common sense, entitled to equal measures
of Reform with England and Scotland. This the
Union entitled them to. But their case has this
glorious adjunct to its right—namely, that they

had principally contributed to obtain Reform for the two other countries.

§ 6. The complaints of the Irish people are these: My first complaint is, that the Irish did not get an equal Parliamentary Reform Bill with Scotland or with England.

" 1st. Ireland did not get the proper portion of
" representatives. Wales got an increase
" of six members upon a population of
" 800,000. Scotland, upon a population of
" 2,300,000, got an increase of eight. Ire-
" land, upon a population of 8,000,000, got
" an increase of five.

" Scotland increased her representatives by one
" in five—Wales by one in six—Ireland by
" one in ten ! ! ! and even one of these was
" given *against* not *for* Ireland—the second
" member for the University of Dublin. But
" let it be one in ten.

" Thus the original iniquity of the Union in re-
" spect to representation was enhanced by
" the Reform Bill. Ireland, upon the score
" of population and property, was entitled
" to 176 members out of 658—we offered
" to take 125.

" 2nd. The next and still greater injustice done
" to Ireland was in the nature of the fran-
" chise.

" In the towns, though the franchise is nomi-

" nally the same, yet it is substantially and
" really infinitely greater in Ireland than
" in England.   A house worth ten pounds
" a-year, gives the franchise in London and
" in Liverpool.   How few, how very few
" houses are there in either not worth ten
" pounds a-year ?

" A house worth ten pounds a-year gives the
" franchise in Ennis or in Youghal.   How
" few houses are there in these towns, or
" similar towns in Ireland, worth ten pounds
" a-year?   To be just, this franchise should,
" for a ten pound house in England, allow
" a five pound house in Ireland.   I com-
" plain of the injustice thus done us, by
" making that nominally the same which is
" substantially different.

" In the county constituencies the injustice was
" still more glaring.   We have, in fact, but
" two franchises for *the people*—they are
" both of ten pounds *clear* annual value,
" *ruled* to be above rent—an enormously
" high rate of franchise—the one of a free-
" hold tenure, the other for a term of
" twenty years.

" Contrast this with England ; which, by her
" Reform Bill, multiplied her franchises to
" nine different and distinct species.

" England, a rich country, has nine different

" species of franchise, to meet every grada-
" tion of property, including in them the
" more ancient 40s. freehold franchise.

" Ireland, infinitely the poorer country, has, in
" fact, for her people, only two franchises,
" and these so enormously high as ten
" pounds clear annual value.

" Perhaps the annals of history never displayed
" a more disgusting injustice than was thus
" committed by the Irish Reform Bill upon
" the Irish people.

" The THIRD base act of ingratitude committed by
" the English Reformers upon the people of
" Ireland, was the 'base and bloody' Coercion
" Act, in the very spirit in which Cromwell
" and Ireton acted.   In that very spirit the
" first reformed Parliament passed the atro-
" cious Coercion Act, as the reward of the
" Irish people for their successful efforts in
" the cause of Reform :   yes—Anglesey,
" Stanley, Lord Grey, Brougham, all, all
" joined in recompensing us for our patriotic
" exertions in their behalf, by abolishing all
" constitutional liberty, by annihilating the
" trial by jury, and leaving the lives, liber-
" ties, and properties of the people of Ire-
" land, at the mercy of military caprice,
" violence, or passion.

" Sacred Heaven !—were there ever a people so

" cruelly, so vilely treated as the people of
" Ireland? Here, indeed, was a specimen
" of the gratitude of British Reformers!!!
" The FOURTH complaint I have to make affects
" only the British Tories. This injustice
" is done to the people of Ireland by the
" House of Lords. England has reformed
" Municipal Corporations—Scotland has re-
" formed Municipal Corporations.
" Ireland was for several years pertinaciously re-
" fused reformed Municipal Corporations.
" Ireland has been still more outrageously in-
" sulted by the Corporate Reform Bill, which
" has been at length—I will not say con-
" ceded, but flung to her—as one would
" fling offal to a dog.
" Ireland has been insulted by the Irish Corpo-
" rate Reform Bill, flung to her after so
" many years of refusal ;
" Firstly—Because by the Irish Corporate Re-
" form Bill the new Corporations are evisce-
" rated of all the real power and authority
" necessary to enable them to give protection
" to the people in the corporate towns and
" cities ; to enable them to watch over the
" administration of justice ; to introduce
" economy in the expenditure, and modera-
" tion in the levying, of local taxes. In
" short, the Irish Corporate Reform Act has

"produced a mongrel species of Corpora-
"tion more dead than alive; powerless and
"paralyzed.

" Secondly—The Irish Corporate Reform Bill is
" an insult to the people of our towns and
" cities by the contrast of the municipal
" franchise in England compared with that
" in Ireland. In the English towns and
" cities every man rated to the poor, no
" matter at how low an amount, is entitled
" to the municipal franchise, and to be
" placed accordingly on the Burgess Roll.
" In Ireland, on the contrary, no man is en-
" titled to the municipal franchise or to be
" placed on the Burgess Roll, unless he is
" rated to the full amount of ten pounds.
" The law thus includes all the English who
" are rated at all; and excludes at the same
" time all the Irish who are rated at any
" sum under ten pounds, and who form a
" most numerous class. And this insult is
" aggravated by those who say that there is
" a *union* between England and Ireland!—
" Bah!

" Thirdly—Another contrast renders the Irish
" Corporate Reform Bill a yet more aggra-
" vated insult to the Irish people. It is
" this :—In the English towns and cities
" each person on the Burgess Roll has his

"right to vote qualified by the condition of
"paying only one tax; namely, the poor
"rate, including (if any) the Burgess rate:
"whereas in Ireland, (for example in the
"city of Dublin,) every person on the
"Burgess Roll has his right to vote qualified
"by the necessity of paying *at least* NINE—
"and, almost in all instances *no less than*
"ELEVEN different taxes: a necessity which
"reduces the number of persons actually
"entitled to make use of the municipal
"franchise by at least one-third."

There are other points of inferiority in the Irish
Corporate Reform Bill which I scorn to take the
trouble of noticing. The complaint I make is sufficiently intelligible to justify our indignation and
utter disgust.

With this complaint I close the catalogue of
actual wrongs perpetrated upon Ireland since the
passing of the Emancipation Bill.

§ 7. There remains the question of tithes, now
called Tithe Rent Charge. Ireland feels the ancient and long continued injustice to the heart's
core. The Catholic people of Ireland support and
maintain a perfect hierarchy in their own Church.
—They support four Archbishops—twenty-five Bishops—many Deans—Vicars-general—with more
than three thousand parish Priests and Curates, to
administer to the spiritual wants of about seven

millions of Christians. Can they—ought they to be content to be compelled to contribute anything to the support of a hierarchy with which they are not in communion? No!—they are not—they cannot—they ought not to be content whilst one atom of the present tithe system remains in existence.

If tithes be public property—and what else are they?—alleviate the burthen on the public, and appropriate the residue to public and national purposes, especially to education. This is common sense and common honesty. • We can never settle into contentment with less.

CONCLUSION.

THESE pages contain a faint outline of the sad story of the woes and miseries of Ireland. The features of that story are characterized by the most odious crimes committed by the English rulers on the Irish people. Rapine, confiscation, murder, massacre, treachery, sacrilege,—wholesale devastation, and injustice of every kind, continued in many of its odious forms to the present hour.

The form of persecution is altered—the spirit remains the same. Those who heretofore would have used the dagger, or the knife of the assassin, employ now only the tongue, or the pen of the calum-

niator—and instead of murdering bodies, exhaust
their energies in assassinating reputation. Calumny
has been substituted for murder, and the faction
which has so long rioted in Irish blood, consoles
its virulent and malignant passions by indulging
in ever varying, never-dying falsehood and truculent slander.

What is the present condition of the Irish mind
—what ought to be the designs of the patriots of
Ireland?

We feel and understand that, if the Union was
not in existence—if Ireland had her own Parliament, the popular majority would have long since
carried every measure of salutary and useful reform. Instead of being behind-hand with England
and Scotland, we should have taken the lead, and
achieved for ourselves all and more than we have
contributed to achieve for them.

If there were no Union—Ireland would be the
part of the British dominions in which greater progress would have been made in civil and religious
liberty, than in any other part subject to the British
crown. If the Union had not been carried, Ireland
would have long since paid off her national debt,
and been now almost entirely free from taxation.

The Union, and the Union alone, stands in the
way of our achieving for ourselves every political
blessing.

Injustice—degradation—comparative weakness,

wide spreading poverty, unendurable political inferiority,—these are the fruits of the Union.

Of its effects on the people of Ireland, I will state but one fact—that, upon a population of eight millions, there are two millions, three hundred thousand individuals, dependant for subsistence on casual charity ! ! ! And this in one of the most abundantly fertile countries on the globe.

The Irish insisted and do insist that nothing can be a greater outrage than to make them submit to the degradation and burthen of a Union with another country, and, at the same time, to withhold from them a full equalization of privileges and franchises with that other country. Such equalization is the meaning of the word "Union;" any other Union is a permanent falsehood—a living lie.

FIRSTLY. The Union entitled the Catholics of Ireland—that is, emphatically the people of Ireland—to religious equality with the English and Scotch. It was thus distinctly and in writing avowed by Pitt in his negotiation with Catholic Peers and others who called themselves the leaders of the Catholic people. But what is better, that right was essential to the very nature of the Union.

In this respect the Union was for twenty-nine years "a living lie."

The partial realization of the Union in this respect, after a struggle of twenty-nine years, is entirely due to the virtue of the Irish people; and not to the good sense or the honesty of the English government.

But, as long as the people of Ireland are compelled to do that which neither the people of England, nor the people of Scotland do—that is, to support the Church of the minority; so long will the Union continue to be in that respect "a living lie."

SECONDLY. The Union entitled the people of Ireland to the same elective franchise with the people of England. In this respect the Union entitled the people of Ireland to a perfect equality, not only in name, but in substance, in the enjoyment of the elective franchise.

In this regard, the Union is to the present day "a living lie;" a lie aggravated by base ingratitude and vile injustice.

THIRDLY. The Union entitled the people of Ireland to an adequate portion of the representation in Parliament. But such proportion has been scornfully and contemptuously refused. The Union is therefore in this essential respect, " a living lie."

FOURTHLY. The Union entitled the people of Ireland to an identity of relief with England, from corporate monopoly, bigotry, plunder, and abuse of every other kind. I have already shown how insulting is the contrast between the Corporate Reforms of England and of Ireland; the

Union therefore is again, in this respect, "a living lie."

In respect to the Municipal Reform; in respect to the Elective Franchise; in respect to the Representation in Parliament—but, above all and before all, in respect to the accursed Tithe System—the Union is "a living lie."

The people of Ireland therefore demand the Repeal of the Union and the restoration of their domestic Parliament.

The Precursor Association declared in the name and with the assent of the Irish people, that they *might* have consented to the continuance of the Union, if justice had been done them;—if the franchise had been simplified and much extended—if the Corporations had been reformed and continued—if the number of Irish members had been augmented in a just proportion—and if the tithe system had been abolished and conscience left completely free.

But on the other hand, these just claims being rejected—these just demands being refused—our just rights being withheld, the Irish people are too numerous, too wise, and too good, to despair, or to hesitate on the course they should adopt. The restoration of the national legislature is therefore again insisted upon, and no compromise, no pause, no cessation of that demand shall be allowed until Ireland is herself again.

One word to close. No honest man ever despaired of his country. No wise enemy will place his reliance on the *difficulties* which may lie in the way between seven millions of human beings and that liberty which they feel to be their right. FOR THEM THERE CAN BE NO IMPOSSIBILITY.

I repeat it—that as surely as to-morrow's sun will rise, Ireland will assert her rights for herself, preserving the golden and unonerous link of the crown—true to the principles of unaffected and genuine allegiance, but determined, while she preserves her loyalty to the British throne, to vindicate her title to constitutional freedom for the Irish people.

In short, Ireland demands that faction should no longer be encouraged ; that the Government should be carried on *for* the Irish people, and not *against* them. She is ready and desirous to assist the Scotch and English reformers to extend their franchises and consolidate their rights—but she has in vain insisted on being an equal sharer in every political advantage. She has vainly sought EQUALITY—IDENTITY. She has been refused— contemptuously refused. Her last demand is free from any alternative—

IT IS THE REPEAL !

OBSERVATIONS,
PROOFS, AND ILLUSTRATIONS.

CHAPTER I. Years 1172—1612.

TO THE FIRST SECTION.

I have long felt the inconvenience resulting from the ignorance of the English people generally of the history of Ireland. Why should they not be ignorant of that history? The story itself is full of no other interest than a painful one, disgusting from its details of barbarous infliction on the one hand, and partial and therefore driftless resistance on the other. To the English it seems enough to know, that one way or the other Ireland had become subject to England. It was easily taken for granted that the mode of subjugation was open war and honourable conquest; and finally that the Union was nothing more than the raising up of a vassal-people to a participation in the popular rights and political condition of the conquerors, brought about by identifying both nations.

We are come to a period in which it is most important to have these matters inquired into and understood. To provoke the inquiry, and to facilitate the comprehension of the facts of Irish history, I have drawn up the foregoing memoir. I have arranged it by its chronology, in such a manner as to bring out in masses the iniquities practised by the English Government upon the Irish, with the full approbation, or at least entire acquiescence, of the British people. I am very desirous to have it unequivocally understood, that one great object of mine is to involve the people of England in much —in very much of the guilt of their Government. If the English people were not influenced by a bigotry, violent as it is unjust, against the Catholic religion on the one hand, and strong national an- tipathy against the Irish people on the other, the Government could not have so long persevered in its course of injustice and oppression. The bad passions of the English people, which gave an evil strength to the English Government for the op- pression of the Irish, still subsist, little diminished, and less mitigated.

My purpose to rouse the attention of the British nation to the sad story of Ireland, is only partially and indeed in small part satisfied by the foregoing memoir. It will be more fully answered by con- firming the general assertions of that memoir by means of particular details—details taken almost exclusively from English and Protestant historians, and given in the very words of these writers.

He who reads my extracts from authors adverse in every sense of the word to Ireland, will enter-

CHAP. I.] PROOFS, ETC. 47

tain no doubt of the accuracy of my statements, as they are supported by such testimony.

The first writer whom I quote, Sir John Davies, was for many years Attorney-General in Ireland, to that pragmatical and despicable tyrant James the First. I think the nature of the English *acquisition* of Ireland, and the mode in which the supposed conquerors disposed of the country, will be best understood from him.

The first specimen of the flippancy with which the English disposed of Ireland, after Henry II. had been but a few weeks in Ireland, is thus described *(Davies' Historical Relations)* :—

"All Ireland was, by Henry II., cantonized among
"ten of the English nation : (viz., the Earl
"Strongbow, Robert Fitz-Stephens, Miles
"de Cogan, Philip Bruce, Sir Hugh de Lacy,
"Sir John Courcey, William Burke Fitz-
"Andelm, Sir Thomas de Clare, Otho de
"Grandison, and Robert Le Poer,) and
"though they had not gained possession of
"*one third part of the kingdom*, yet IN
"TITLE they were owners and lords of all, so
"AS NOTHING WAS LEFT TO BE GRANTED
"TO THE NATIVES ! ! ! And *therefore* we
"do not find in any record, or history, for
"the space of three hundred years after
"these adventurers first arrived in Ireland,
"that any Irish lord obtained a grant of his
"country from the Crown, but only the

"King of Thomond, who had a grant, but
"only during King Henry the Third's mi-
"nority; and Roderick O'Connor, King of
"Connaught, to whom King Henry II., be-
"fore this distribution was made, did grant
"that he should be king under him, and
"keep his kingdom of Connaught in the
"same GOOD AND PEACEABLE STATE, in
"which he kept it before his invasion of
"Ireland."

This first act of English domination is quite characteristic. It is an epitome of all the subsequent
history. With a precarious possession, through the
grant of an Irish chieftain, M'Morrough, of less
than one-third of Ireland, they at once "*leave
nothing for the natives ! ! !*"

It is true, indeed, that Henry afterwards granted
a special charter, conceding the benefit of the
English laws—and, of course, the right of property
—to five Irish families. They were called, in
pleading, persons "of the five bloods"—"*de quinque sanguinibus.*"

     "These were the O'Nials of Ulster, O'Melach-
     "linsof Meath, the O'Connors of Connaught,
     "the O'Briens of Thomond, and the Mac
     "Murroughs of Leinster."—*Davies' Hist.
     Rel.* p. 45.

Henry II. also granted a charter to the "Ostmen,
or Esterlings,"—that is, the Danes of Waterford,
who were inhabitants of that city long before his

coming to Ireland,—" that they should have and
enjoy in Ireland the laws of England, and according to that law be judged and inherit." This appears from the following passage in *Davies*, page 80.

" Among the pleas of the crown, 4 Edward II,
 " we find a confirmation made by Edward
 " I, of a charter of denization, granted by
 " Henry II, to certain Ostmen or Ester-
 " lings, who were inhabitants of Waterford,
 " long before Henry II attempted the con-
 " quest of Ireland :
 " ' Edwardus Dei gratia, etc. Justitiario suo
 " Hiberniæ salutem : quia per inspectionem
 " Chartæ Dom. Hen. Reg. filii Imperatricis
 " quondam Dom. Hiberniæ proavi nostri
 " nobis constat, quod Ostmanni de Water-
 " ford legem Anglicorum in Hibernia habere
 " et secundem ipsam legem judicari et de-
 " duci debent :' "

Nor was this a barren privilege. These Danes,
by that charter, obtained protection for their lives
and properties, which none of the Irish save the
above-named five families obtained. The Irish
could not sue as plaintiffs in any court of law.
They were not treated as conquered enemies,
bound to accept the laws of the conqueror, but
entitled to the protection of those laws. They
were treated as perpetual enemies, whom it was
lawful to rob or kill, at the pleasure or caprice

of an English subject.   Let the Attorney-General,
Sir John Davies, speak.   *Hist. Tracts*, p. 78.

" That the mere Irish were reputed aliens, ap-
" peareth by sundry records, wherein judg-
" ments are demanded, if they shall be
" answered in actions brought by them.

" In the Common Plea Rolls of 28 Edward III
" (which are yet preserved in Bermingham's
" Tower,) this case is adjudged.   Simon
" Neale brought an action against William
" Newlagh, for breaking his close in Clon-
" dalkin, in the county of Dublin : the
" defendant doth plead that the plaintiff is
" Hibernicus et non de quinque sanguinius :
" ['an Irishman, and not of the five bloods;']
" and demandeth judgment, if he shall be
" answered.   The plaintiff replieth : That
" he is of the five bloods—to wit, of the
" O'Neiles of Ulster, who, by the grant of
" the progenitors of our Lord the King, ought
" to enjoy and use the English liberties,
" and for freemen to be reputed in law.*

" The defendant rejoineth : that the plaintiff is
" not of the O'Neiles of Ulster—nec de
" quinque sanguinibus, [nor of the five

---

* The record runs thus in the original : " Quod ipse est de
" quinque sanguinibus, viz. De les O'Neiles de Ulton, qui per
" concessionem progenitorum Domini Regis, libertatibus Anglicis
" gaudere debent et utuntur, et pro liberis hominibus reputantur."

" bloods]. And thereupon they are at issue.
" Which being found for the plaintiff, he
" had judgment to recover his damages
" against the defendant.

" Again, in the 29 Edward I., before the Justices
" in Oyer, at Drogheda, Thomas Le Botteler
" brought an action of déténue against
" Robert de Almain, for certain goods. The
" defendant pleadeth : That he is not bound
" to answer the plaintiff for this—that the
" PLAINTIFF IS AN IRISHMAN, *and not of*
" *free blood.*

" And the aforesaid Thomas says that he is an
" Englishman, and this he prays may be
" enquired of by the country. Therefore
" let a jury come, and so forth :

" And the jurors on their oath, say that the afore-
" said Thomas is an Englishman. THERE-
" FORE it is adjudged that he do receive
" his damages."*

Thus these records demonstrate, that the Irishman had no protection for his property ; because,
if the plaintiff, in either case, had been declared
by the jury to be an Irishman, the action would be

---

* In the record thus : " Quod non tenetur ei inde respondere,
" eo quod est Hibernicus, et non de libero sanguine.

" Et prædictus Thomas dicit, quod Anglicus est, et hoc petit
" quod inquiratur per patriam. Ideo fiat inde Jurat, &c. Jurati
" super Sacramentum suum dicunt ; quod prædictus Thomas
" Anglicus est ; ideo consideratum est, quod recuperet," &c.

barred ; though the injury was not denied upon
the record to have been committed. The validity
of the plea in point of law was also admitted ; so
that, no matter what injury might be committed
upon the real or personal property of an Irishman,
the courts of law afforded him no species of remedy.

But this absence of protection was not confined
to property ; the Irishman was equally unprotected
in his person and in his life. The following quotation, from Sir John Davies, puts this beyond a
doubt. *Hist. Tracts*, p. 82.

" The mere Irish were not only accounted *aliens*,
  " but *enemies*, and altogether out of the
  " protection of the law ; so as it was no
  " capital offence to kill them : and this is
  " manifest by many records. At a gaol de-
  " livery at Waterford, before John Wogan,
  " Lord Justice of Ireland, the 4th of Edward
  " the Second, we find it recorded among
  " the pleas of the crown of that year,* *That*

---

* The original record runs thus : " Quod Robertus le Wayleys,
" rectatus de morte Johannis filii Juor Mac Gillemory felonice per
" ipsum interfecti, &c., venit et bene cognovit quod prædictum
" Johannem interfecit : dicit tamen quod per ejus interfecionem
" feloniam committere non potuit, quia dicit quod prædictus
" Johannes fuit purus Hibernicus, et non de libero sanguine, etc.
" Et cum Dominus dicti Johannis (cujus Hibernicus idem Johannes
" fuit) die quo interfectus fuit, solutionem pro ipso Johanne Hiber-
" nico suo sic interfecto petere voluerit, ipse Robertus paratus erit
" ad respondend. de solutione prædict. prout justitia suadebit. Et

" *Robert Wallace being arraigned of the*
" *death of John, the son of Juor Mac Gil-*
" *lemory, by him feloniously slain, and so*
" *forth, came and well-acknowledged that*
" *he slew the aforesaid John, yet he said,*
" *that by his slaying he could not commit*
" *felony, because he said, that the afore-*
" *said John was a mere Irishman, and not*
" *of the five bloods, and so forth; and he*
" *further said, that inasmuch as the Lord*
" *of the aforesaid John, whose Irishman*
" *the said John was, on the day on which*
" *he was slain, had sought payment for*
" *the aforesaid slaying of the aforesaid*
" *John as his Irishman, he the said*
" *Robert was ready to answer for such*
" *payment as was just in that behalf. And*
" *thereupon a certain John Le Poer came,*
" *and for our Lord the King said, that*
" *the aforesaid John, the son of Juor Mac*
" *Gillemory, and his ancestors of that sur-*
" *name, from the time in which our Lord*
" *Henry Fitz-Empress, heretofore Lord*

" super hoc venit quidam Johannes Le Poer, et dicit pro Domino
" Rege, quod prædict. Johannes filius Juor Mac Gillemory, et
" antecessores sui de cognomine prædict. a tempore quo Dominus
'' Henricus filius Imperatricis, quondam Dominus Hiberniæ, tri-
" tavus Domini Regis nunc, fuit in Hiberniâ, legem Anglicorum
" in Hiberniâ usque ad hunc diem habere, et secundum ipsam
" legem judicari et deduci debent."

" *of Ireland, the ancestor of our Lord the*
" *now King, was in Ireland, the law of*
" *England in Ireland thence to the pre-*
" *sent day, of right had and ought to have,*
" *and according to that law ought to be*
" *judged and to inherit.* And so pleaded
" the charter of denization granted to the
" Oostmen recited before; all which ap-
" peareth at large in the said record:
" wherein we may note, that the killing of
" an Irishman was not punished by our law,
" as manslaughter, which is felony and
" capital, (for our law did neither protect
" his life nor avenge his death), but by a
" fine, or pecuniary punishment, which is
" called anericke, according to the Brehon,
" or Irish law."

The following record speaks still more distinctly
the perfect right claimed and enjoyed by the
English in Ireland, of slaughtering with impunity
the "mere Irish." It records a case tried at Limerick, before the same Lord Chief Justice Wogan,
in the fourth year of Edward the Second, and is
as follows :

* " *William Fitz Roger being arraigned for*

---

* The original record is in these words :
" Willielmus filius Rogeri rectatus de morte Rogeri de Cantelon
" felonice per ipsum interfecti, venit et dicit, quod feloniam per
" interfectionem prædictam committere non potuit, quia dicit quod
" prædict. Rogerus fuit purus Hibernicus et non de libere san-

" *the death of Roger de Cantelon, by him*
" *feloniously slain, comes and says that he*
" *could not commit felony by means of such*
" *killing; because the aforesaid Roger*
" *was an Irishman, and not of free blood.*
" *And he further says that the said Roger*
" *was of the surname of O'Hederiscal,*
" *and not of the surname of Cantelon; and*
" *of this he puts himself on the country,*
" *and so forth. And the jury upon their*
" *oath say, that the aforesaid Roger was*
" *an Irishman of the surname of O'Hede-*
" *riscal, and for an Irishman was reputed*
" *all his life;* AND THEREFORE *the said*
" *William, as far as regards the aforesaid*
" *felony, is acquitted. But inasmuch as*
" *the aforesaid Roger O'Hederiscal was*
" *an Irishman of our Lord the King, the*
" *aforesaid William was re-committed to*
" *jail, until he shall find pledges to pay*

" guine etc.; et ulterius dicit quod prædict. Rogerus fuit de cog-
" nomine de Ohederiscal et non de cognomine de Cantelon, et de
" hoc ponit se super patriam, etc.   Et jurati dicunt super sacram.
" suum quod prædictus Rogerus Hibernicus fuit et de cognomine
" de Ohederiscal et pro Hibernico habebatur tota vita sua.   IDEO
" prædict. Willielmus quoad feloniam prædict. quietus.   Sed quia
" prædictus Rogerus Ohederiscal fuit Hibernicus Domini Regis,
" prædict. Willielmus recommittatur gaolæ, quosque plegios in-
" venerit de quinque marcis solvendis Domino Regi pro solutione
" prædicti Hibernici."

"*five marks to our Lord the King, for the*
"*value of the aforesaid Irishman.*"

One more quotation from Sir John Davies, will
place in the clearest light the spirit in which the
English party governed Ireland, and the results of
such misgovernment. It will also serve to show
that there is nothing new under the sun ; as the
pretence of the modern faction that *they* are able
to root out the Irish, is but the repetition of the
factious cry of former days. The only difference
is this : that in the olden day it *might* have been
realized ; at the present, it is utterly impossible it
should be successful.

The following quotation is from p. 85 of *Davies's
Tracts :*

" In all the Parliament Rolls which are extant,
" from the fortieth year of Edward the
" Third, when the statutes of Kilkenny were
" enacted, till the reign of King Henry the
" Eighth, we find the degenerate and dis-
" obedient English called rebels ; but the
" Irish, which were not in the King's peace,
" are called enemies. Statute Kilkenny, c.
" 1, 10 and 11 ; 2 Henry the Fourth, c. 24 ;
" 10 Henry the Sixth, c. 1, 18 ; 18 Henry
" the Sixth, c. 4, 5 ; Edward the Fourth, c.
" 6 ; 10 Henry the Seventh, c. 17. All
" these statutes speak of English rebels and
" Irish enemies ; as if the Irish had never
" been in the condition of subjects, but

" always out of the protection of the law,
" and were indeed in worse case than aliens
" of any foreign realm that was in amity
" with the crown of England. For by divers
" heavy penal laws, the English were for-
" bidden to marry, to foster, to make gos-
" sips with the Irish, or to have any trade
" or commerce in their markets or fairs;
" nay, there was a law made no longer since
" than the twenty-eighth year of Henry the
" Eighth, that the English should not marry
" with any person of Irish blood, though he
" had gotten a charter of denization ; unless
" he had done both homage and fealty to
" the King in the Chancery, and were also
" bound by recognizance with sureties, to
" continue a loyal subject. Whereby it is
" manifest, that such as had the govern-
" ment of Ireland under the crown of Eng-
" land, did intend to make a perpetual se-
" paration and enmity between the English
" and the Irish, pretending, no doubt, that
" the English should in the end root out the
" Irish ; *which the English not being able*
" *to do*, caused a perpetual war between
" the nations, which continued four hun-
" dred and odd years, and would have
" lasted to the world's end, if in the end
" of Queen Elizabeth's reign the Irish had
" not been broken and conquered by the

" sword, and since the beginning of his
" Majesty's reign, been protected and go-
" verned by the law."

The compliment included in the last phrase to
the then reigning monarch, James I, was naturally
enough to be expected from Sir John Davies, who
was his Attorney-General; but it will soon appear
that the law was scarcely less destructive than the
sword, and that the Irish had very little cause to
rejoice at the transition.

It is not, however, to be taken for granted that
it was the sword alone which had been used against
the Irish during the preceding reigns. The vexa-
tions of law were superadded to the cruelty of
open violence ; and the statutes passed by the Parliament of the English Pale afforded specimens of
the senseless, and indeed ludicrous, malignity of
the English party against the Irish. I think it
right to add the following specimens :—

" 10th Henry the Sixth. This was an act en-
" titled, *An Act, that no person, liege or
" alien, shall take merchandize or things
" to be sold, to faire, market, or other place,
" amongst the Irish enemies,* &c., whereby
" it was enacted, ' That no merchant, nor
" other person, liege or alien, should use,
" in time of peace nor warre, to any manner
" of faire, market, or other place amongst
" the Irish enemies, with merchandise or
" things to be sold, nor send them to them,

" if it were not to acquite any prisoner of
" them that were the King's liege men ; and
" if any liege man did the contrary, he
" should be holden and adjudged a felon,
" and that it should be lawful for every
" liege man to arrest and take such mer-
" chants and persons, with their merchan-
" dize and things, and to send them to the
" next gaole, there to remain until they
" should be delivered as law requireth, and
" the King to have one halfe of the said
" goods, and he or they that should take
" them the other halfe,'—as by the said act
" more at large appeareth."

It is quite impossible in the annals of English
history to meet such another specimen of legislation as that which made an English merchant a
felon, for no other crime than that of selling his
goods at the best profit he could get. There was,
however, another statute passed, in the same 10th
year of Henry VI, which shows that there was to
be no peace nor truce with the Irish ; but that they
were in time of truce, or even of peace, to be
slaughtered as enemies. It was an act, intituled,—

" *An Act, that every liege man shall take the*
" *Irish conversant as espialls amongst the*
" *English, and make of them as of the*
" *King's enemies ;* whereby it was enacted,
" ' That it should be lawfull for every liege
" man, to take all manner of Irish enemies,

" which in time of peace and truce should
" come and converse amongst the English
" lieges, to spie their secresies, force, wayes,
" and subtilties, and to make of them as of
" the King's enemies.' "

It will be observed that these Acts of Parliament
were passed in the year 1432, that is, 260 years
after the English invasion of Ireland by Henry II.
It appears that the latter of these acts was not considered sufficiently sanguinary, for the same English party passed another law in the year 1465, the
fifth year of Edward IV, intituled,—

" *An Act, that it shall be lawfull to kill any*
" *that is found robbing by day or night,*
" *or going or coming to rob or steal, having*
" *no faithfull man of good name or fame in*
" *their company in English apparel :*"

Whereby it was enacted,—

" That it shall be lawfull to all manner of men
" that find any theeves robbing by day or
" by night, or going or coming to rob or
" steal, in, or out, going, or coming, having
" no faithfull man of good name in their
" company in English apparrel, upon any of
" the liege people of the King, that it shall
" be lawfull to take and kill those, and to
" cut off their heads, without any impeach-
" ment of our Sovereign Lord the King, his
" heirs, officers, or ministers, or of any
" others."

Thus, in truth, the only fact necessary to be ascertained, to entitle an Englishman to cut off the head of another man, was, that such other should be an Irishman.   For if the Irishman was not robbing, or coming from robbing, who could say but that he might be *going* to rob ; " in, or out," as the statute has it.   And the Englishman—the cutter off of the head, was made sole judge of where the Irishman was going, and of what he intended to do.   The followers of Mahomet, with regard to their treatment of their Grecian subjects, were angels of mercy when compared with the English in Ireland.   Care was also taken, that no part of the effect of the law should be lost, by the mistaken humanity of any individual Englishman ; for an additional stimulant was given by the following section of the Act :

" And that it shall be lawful by authority of the
    " said Parliament to the said *bringer* of the
    " said head, and his *ayders* to the same, for
    " to destrain and levy by their own hands,
    " of every man having one plow-land in the
    " barony where the said thief was so taken,
    " two-pence, and of every man having half
    " a plow-land in the said barony, one-penny,
    " and every other man having one house
    " and goods to the value of fourty shillings,
    " one-penny, and of every other cottier
    " having house and smoak, one half-penny."

After such statutes as these, it is matter of little

surprise that so late as the 28th year of the reign
of Henry VIII.—that is, in the year 1537—an act
was passed, intituled, " *An Act against marrying,*
" *or fostering with, or to, Irishmen.*" By this
act, it was prohibited under the severest penalties,
to marry an Irishman, but the Legislature was not
so ungallant as to prohibit marriage with Irish
women. *That* would have been inflicting the severest possible punishment upon themselves; and
considering the natural antipathy that the English
in those days entertained against everything Irish,
it furnishes the strongest proof that the Irish
women at that time afforded the same models of
beauty and goodness for which they are celebrated
at the present day.

Even in the reign of Queen Elizabeth, the spirit
of hatred and contempt of the Irish animated the
Legislature. So late as the year 1569, an act was
passed, (in the 11th year of her reign,) intituled,
" *An Act prohibiting any Irish lord or captaine*
" *of this realme, to foster to any of the lords of*
" *the same realme ;*" whereby it was enacted—

    " That no lord nor captaine of the Irish of Ire-
    " land, should from henceforth foster to
    " any earl, viscount, baron, or lord of the
    " same realm ; and that what Irish lord or
    " captaine soever, that from henceforth
    " should receive or take to foster the child
    " *mulier*, or BASTARD of any of the said
    " earls, viscounts, barons, or lords, the same

" should be deemed and adjudged high-
" treason in the taker, and also felony in
" the giver, according to the taxation and
" discretion of the lord-deputie, governour,
" or governours, and councell of this realm
" for the time being."

Such were the laws made by the Parliament of
the English settlers in Ireland, in the spirit of contempt and hatred of the Irish people. Yet the extent of territory which belonged to the English,
was, during all this time, extremely limited. How
ignorant is the present generation of the fact, that
for centuries England claimed the actual dominion
of only twelve of our counties ; and, even in these,
the English laws were only in force, in the parts
actually occupied by men of English descent. Upon
this point the authority of Davies is distinct and
decisive.—*Hist. Tract.* p. 93.

" True it is, that King John made twelve shires
" in Leinster and Munster, namely Dublin,
" Kildare, Meth, Uriel, Catherlogh, Kil-
" kenny, Wexford, Waterford, Cork, Lime-
" rick, Kerry, and Tipperary. Yet these
" counties stretched no farther than the
" lands of the English colonies extended.
" In them only were the English laws pub-
" lished and put in execution ; and in them
" only did the itinerant judges make their
" circuits and visitations of justice, and not
" in the countries possessed by the Irish,

" which contained two-thirds of the kingdom
" at least : and therefore King Edward the
" First, before the court of Parliament was
" established in Ireland, did transmit the
" statutes of England in this form."

Davies then sets forth the writ for the promulgation of the statutes in Ireland : it is in Latin of
course, and is stated to be for the common utility
of our people ; but that promulgation is confined
to " *the several places belonging to us in our
land of Ireland.*" Davies then proceeds thus :—
" By which writ, and by all the pipe-rolls of
" that time, it is manifest that the laws of
" England were published and put in execu-
" tion only in the counties which were then
" made and limited, and not in the Irish
" countries, which were neglected and left
" wild."

It appears, however, that although there were
twelve counties thus nominally under English dominion, yet, before the reign of Henry the Eighth,
they had shrunk into four : at least, that in not
more than four were the English laws obeyed and
executed. For Davies, in speaking of the Acts
called Poyning's Laws, after alleging that they were
intended for all Ireland, is forced to confess that
they were executed only within a very limited portion of that country. His words, at p. 177, are :
" And that the execution of all these laws had
" no greater latitude than the Pale, is ma-

"nifest by the statute of 13th Henry the
" Eighth, c. 3, which recites, ' that at that
" time the King's laws were obeyed and
" executed in the four shires only ;' and
" yet the Earl of Surrey was then Lieute-
" nant of Ireland, a governor much feared
" of the King's enemies, and exceedingly
" honoured and beloved of the King's sub-
" jects. And the instructions given by the
" State of Ireland to John Allen, Master
" of the Rolls, employed in England near
" about the same time, do declare as much ;
" wherein, among other things, he is required
" to advertise the King that his land of
" Ireland was so much decayed, that the
" King's laws were not obeyed twenty miles
" in compass. Whereupon grew that by-
" word used by the Irish, viz., ' That they
" dwelt by west the law, which dwelt beyond
" the river of the Barrow ;' which is within
" thirty miles of Dublin. The same is tes-
" tified by Baron Finglas, in his discourse
" of the decay of Ireland, which he wrote
" about the twentieth year of King Henry
" the Eighth."

It will not be a matter of astonishment that the
English dominion had shrunk into the narrow limits
of four counties, to any person acquainted with
the hideous system of daily recurring misrule and

tyranny which was constantly practised towards
the Irish, as well as towards the weaker portion
of the English settlers, by the more powerful of the
English lords and proprietors. These proprietors
adopted and exaggerated the most oppressive portions of the English feudal system, and they added
to that every injustice committed by the more
powerful upon the weak amongst the natives. The
following passage from Davies (p. 131) will show
what must have been the effects of such accumulated
oppressions ; especially as they were practised with
little intermission for more than four centuries :

" The most wicked and mischievous custom of
" all, was that of *Coin* and *Livery*, which
" consisted in taking of man's meat, horse
" meat, and money, of all the inhabitants of
" the country, at the will and pleasure of the
" soldier; who, as the phrase of the Scripture
" is, *did eat up the people as it were bread ;*
" for that he had no other entertainment.
" This extortion was originally Irish ; for
" they used to lay *bonaght** upon their peo-
" ple, and never gave their soldier any other
" pay. But when the English had learned
" it, they used it with more insolence, and
" made it more intolerable ; for this oppres-

---

* " Bonaght" was the Irish term for billeting of soldiers, with
a right to be maintained in food.

" sion was not temporary, nor limited either
" to place or time ; but because there was
" everywhere a continual war, either offen-
" sive or defensive, and every lord of a
" country, and every marcher, made war
" and peace at his pleasure, it became uni-
" versal and perpetual; and indeed was the
" most heavy oppression that ever was used
" in any Christian or heathen kingdom.
" And therefore, *vox oppressorum*, this cry-
" ing sin did draw down as great, or greater
" plagues upon Ireland, than the oppression
" of the Israelites did draw upon the land
" of Egypt. For the plagues of Egypt,
" though they were grievous, were but of
" a short continuance ; but the plagues
" of Ireland lasted FOUR HUNDRED YEARS
" TOGETHER."

The natural consequences followed; they may
as well, and cannot be better described, than in the
words of Davies :

" This extortion of *Coin* and *Livery* produced
" two notorious effects : first, it made the
" land waste; next, it made the people idle;
" for when the husbandman had laboured
" all the year, the soldier in one night con-
" sumed the fruits of all his labour, *longique*
" *perit labor irritus anni.* Had he reason
" then to manure the land for the next

"year? Or rather, might he not complain
"as the shepherd in Virgil:

" 'Impius hæc tam culta novalia miles habebit?
Barbarus has segetes? En quo discordia cives
Perduxit miseros? En queis consevimus agros?'

" And hereupon of necessity came depo-
"pulation, banishment, and extirpation of
"the better sort of subjects; and such as
"remained became idle and lookers on,
"expecting the event of those miseries and
"evil times: so as their extreme extortion
"and oppression hath been the true cause
"of the idleness of this Irish nation; and
"that rather the vulgar sort have chosen
"to be beggars in foreign countries, than to
"manure their fruitful land at home." (pp.
132, 133.)

The same result is produced by the oppression
of the present day. The Irish for four centuries
suffered the miseries of "Coin and Livery," as
they now suffer from tithes and absentee rents.
They are still driven, not as beggars, but as labourers, to foreign lands, and to cultivate every
soil but their own.

Thus, during four centuries, the property of the
Irish had no protection. An Irishman could not
maintain an action in the English courts of law,
no matter what injury might be done to his property. An Irishman had no protection for his

person or his life. It was not, in point of law, a
trespass, or punishable as such in any action or
civil suit, to beat or wound or imprison. To murder him by the basest mode of assassination was
no felony nor crime in the eye of the law. We
have seen with what perfect impunity he could be,
and *was* plundered, under the names of " Coin and
Livery."

It might be supposed by some, that the Irish
were unwilling to receive the English laws, or to
be received into the condition of subjects. The
Attorney-General, Davies, however, tells us the
contrary. At p. 87, he puts the question thus :—

" But perhaps the Irish in former times did
" wilfully refuse to be subject to the laws
" of England, and would not be partakers of
" the benefit thereof, though the crown of
" England did desire it ; and therefore they
" were reputed aliens, outlaws, and enemies.
" ASSUREDLY THE CONTRARY DOTH APPEAR."
And in page 101, he expressly declares,—

" That for the space of two hundred years at
" least, after the first arrival of Henry the
" Second in Ireland, the Irish would have
" gladly embraced the laws of England, and
" did earnestly desire the benefit and pro-
" tection thereof; which, being denied them,
" did of necessity cause a continual border-
" ing war between the English and Irish."

It does, indeed, appear, that the reason why that wise monarch, King Edward III., did not extend the benefit of English protection and English law to the Irish people, was, that the great Lords of Ireland, the Wicklows, the Stanleys, and the Rodens of the day, certified to the King,—

" That the Irish might not be naturalized, with-
" out being of damage or prejudice to them,
" the said Lords, or to the Crown."

This appears by a writ, directed by that monarch to the Lord Justice of Ireland, commanding him to consult and take the opinion of the great Lords of Ireland, with the return thereon, amongst the rolls in the Tower of London, quoted at length by Davies, at p. 88.

I will refer, for the present, only to one passage more in the *Tracts* of that Attorney-General, in further illustration of the text of my first chapter. It is to be found at page 90 :—

" This, then, I note as a great defect in the civil
" policy of this kingdom ; in that for the
" space of three hundred and fifty years at
" least after the conquest first attempted,
" the English laws were not communicated
" to the Irish, nor the benefit and protection
" thereof allowed unto them, though they
" earnestly desired and sought the same :
" for as long as they were out of the protec-
" tion of the law, so as every Englishman

" might oppress, spoil, and kill them without
" control, how was it possible they should
" be other than outlaws and enemies to the
" Crown of England ?   If the King would
" not admit them to the condition of sub-
" jects, how could they learn to acknow-
" ledge and obey him as their sovereign ?
" When they might not converse or com-
" merce with any civil man, nor enter into
" any town or city without peril of their
" lives ; whither should they fly, but into
" the woods and mountains, and there live
" in a wild and barbarous manner ?" (p. 90.)
The passages which I have already quoted, show
that the Irish sought for, but could not obtain, any
species of legal protection.   It would be too tedious
to enter into a detail of all the horrors inflicted
upon them by the lawless power and treachery of
the English settlers.   Nothing could be more
common than scenes of premeditated slaughter—
massacres perpetrated under the guise of friendly
intercourse, into which the natives permitted themselves to be betrayed.   No faith was kept with the
Irish : no treaty nor agreement was observed any
longer than it was the interest of the English settlers to observe it,—or whilst they were not strong
enough to violate it with safety.

It would be equally shocking and tedious to re-
cite all the well-attested acts of cruelty and perfidy

which were perpetrated on the Irish people by the
order or connivance of the English government.
There is in the College of Dublin, a State Paper
of considerable importance. It is a memorial presented by a Captain Thomas Lee, drawn up with
great care and with very singular ability; written
about the year 1594, and addressed to Queen Elizabeth, giving her a detailed account of the real
state of Ireland. It was a confidential document,
for the personal information of the Queen. I shall
have occasion to extract many passages of it. In
the meantine, I will give, from other authors, two
or three instances only, of the horrible cruelty
exercised towards the Irish by the English Governors.

My first quotation is from Leland's *History of
Ireland*, Book IV. He tells us, chap. 2, that when
in the year 1579 the garrison of Smerwick in Kerry
surrendered *upon mercy* to Lord Deputy Gray, he
ordered upwards of seven hundred of them to be
put to the sword or hanged.

" That mercy for which they sued, was rigidly
" denied them; Wingfield was commissioned
" to disarm them; and when this service
" was performed, *an English company was
" sent into the fort, and the garrison was
" butchered in cold blood : nor is it without
" pain that we find a service so horrid, so de-
" testable, committed to Sir Walter Raleigh.*"

It also appears that for this, and such other exploits, Sir Walter Raleigh had 40,000 acres of land bestowed upon him in the county of Cork, which he afterwards sold to Richard, first Earl of Cork.

The next instance is almost contemporaneous. It introduces another historic name. Shortly before the same year, 1579,—

" Walter Earl of Essex, on the conclusion of a " peace, invited Brian O'Nial of Claneboy, " with a great number of his relations, to " an entertainment, where they lived together " in great harmony, making good cheer for " three days and nights; when, on a sudden, " O'Nial was surprised with an arrest, toge- " ther with his brother and his wife, by the " Earl's orders. *His friends were put to* " *the sword before his face, nor were the* " *women and children spared.* He was, " himself, with his brother and wife, sent " to Dublin, WHERE THEY WERE CUT IN " QUARTERS. This increased the disaffec- " tion, and produced the detestation of all " the Irish; for this chieftain of Claneboy " was the senior of his family, and as he " had been universally esteemed, so he was " now as universally regretted."—*MS. Trinity College, Dublin.*

The next instance I shall mention, occurred in

the year 1577.   It is thus introduced by Morrisson
the historian (folio edition, p. 3) :—

" After the 19th year of Queen Elizabeth, vide-
   " licit anno 1577, the Lords of Connaught
   " and O'Rooke," says Morrisson, " made a
   " composition for their lands with Sir Ni-
   " cholas Malby, governor of that province;
   " wherein they were content to yield the
   " Queen so large a rent and such services,
   " both of babourers to work upon occasion
   " of fortifying, and of horse and foot to
   " serve upon occasion of war, that their
   " minds seemed not yet to be alienated
   " from their wonted awe and reverence to
   " the Crown of England.   Yet, in the same
   " year *a horrible* MASSACRE *was committed*
   " *by the English at Mulloghmaston on some*
   " *hundreds of the most peaceable of the*
   " *Irish gentry, invited thither on the public*
   " *faith and under the protection of Govern-*
   " *ment.*"

The manner of this massacre appears to have
been this (the spot is now part of the King's
County) :—

   " The English published a proclamation, inviting
   " all the well-affected Irish to an interview
   " on the Rathmore, at Mulloghmaston, en-
   " gaging at the same time for their security,
   " and that no evil was intended.   In conse-

"quence of this engagement, the well-
"affected came to Rathmore aforesaid; and
"soon after they were assembled, they
"found themselves surrounded by three or
"four lines of English horse and foot com-
"pletely accoutred, by whom they were un-
"generously attacked and cut to pieces;
"and not a single man escaped."

This seems to be one of the massacres particularly alluded to by Captain Lee in his memorial.
Speaking of the treachery and cruelty of the English Governors of Ireland, he says,—

"They have drawn unto them by protection,
"three or four hundred of these country
"people, under colour to do your Majesty's
"service, and brought them to a place of
"meeting, where your garrison soldiers
"were appointed to be, who have there
"most dishonourably put them all to the
"sword; and this hath been BY THE CON-
"SENT AND PRACTICE OF THE LORD DEPUTY
"FOR THE TIME BEING."

Perhaps the instances of cruelty to individuals
and to private families are more heart-rending than
the wholesale massacres to which I have referred.
The following quotation is from Morrisson's *History of Ireland*, folio 10 :—

"About the year 1590 died M'Mahon, chieftain
"of Monaghan, who, in his lifetime, had

" surrendered his country into her Majesty's
" hands, and received a re-grant thereof
" under the broad seal of England, to him
" and to his heirs male ; and in default of
" such, to his brother Hugh Roe M'Mahon,
" with other remainders.   And this man
" dying without issue male, his said brother
" came up to the state, that he might be
" settled in his inheritance, hoping that he
" might be countenanced and cherished as
" her Majesty's patentee.   But he found,
" as the Irish say, he could not be admitted
" until he promised six hundred cows ; for
" such, and no other, were the Irish bribes.
" He was afterwards imprisoned for failing
" in part of his payment ; and in a few days
" enlarged, with promise that the Lord
" Deputy himself would go and settle him
" in his county of Monaghan ; whither his
" lordship took his journey shortly after,
" with M'Mahon in his company.   At their
" first arrival the gentleman was clapt into
" bolts ; and in two days after he was in-
" dicted, arraigned, and executed at his own
" door ; all done, as the Irish said, by such
" officers as the Lord Deputy carried with
" him for that purpose from Dublin.   The
" treason for which he was condemned, was,
" because two years before, he, pretending

" a rent due unto him out of Fearney, levied
" forces and made a distress for the same,
" which, by the English law, adds my au-
" thor, may perhaps be treason ; but in that
" country, never before subject to law, it
" was thought no rare thing nor great of-
" fence. The marshal, Sir Henry Bagnal,
" had part of the country ; Captain Hens-
" flower was made seneschal of it, and had
" M'Mahon's chief house and part of the
" land ; and to divers others, smaller por-
" tions of land were assigned ; and the Irish
" spared not to say that these men were all
" the contrivers of his death, and that every
" one was paid something for his share."

Another instance I select from a multitude of
similar cases mentioned by Lee in his memorial.

" The Irish who have once offended," says Lee
    in his memorial to Elizabeth, " live they
    " never so honestly afterwards, if they grow
    " into wealth, are sure to be cut off by one
    " indirect way or other."

Of this he gives the following melancholy instance :—

" In one of her Majesty's civil shires, there lived
    " an Irishman peaceably and quietly as a
    " good subject, many years together, where-
    " by he grew into great wealth ; which his
    " landlord thirsting after, and desirous to

" remove him from his land, entered into
" practice with the sheriff of the shire to
" dispatch this simple man, and divide his
" goods between them.   Whereupon they
" sent one of his own servants for him, and
" he coming with him, *they presently took*
" *the man and hanged him ;* and, keeping
" the master prisoner, they went immediately
" to his dwelling and shared his substance,
" which was of great value, between them,
" turning his wife and many children to
" begging.   After they had kept him (the
" master) fast for a season with the sheriff,
" they carried him to the castle of Dublin,
" where he lay bye the space of two or three
" terms ; and he, having no matter objected
" against him whereupon to be tried by law,
" they, by their credit and countenance,
" being both English gentlemen, and he who
" was the landlord the chiefest man in the
" shire, informed the Lord Deputy so hardly
" of him, as that, without indictment or
" trial, they executed him, to the great
" scandal of her Majesty's state, and the
" impeachment of her laws.   Yet this, and
" the like exemplary justice," adds he, " is
" ministered to your Majesty's poor subjects
" there."

Individual instances of this kind, make oppres-

sion more familiar to the human mind, and leave a
stronger impression on the recollection, from their
individuality.   They also illustrate the *working* of
the system.   They, in fact, bring it home more
pointedly and distinctly to the eye of reason and
common sense.   But we must not lose sight of the
more general description of crimes perpetrated by
the Government, and with the sanction of the persons who from time to time acted as the Sovereign's
deputies at the head of that Government.

Here is a passage of this description from the
same memorial :—

" There have also been divers others pardoned
    " by your Majesty, who have been held very
    " dangerous men, and after their pardon
    " have lived very dutifully and done your
    " Majesty great service ; yet upon small
    " suggestions to the Lord Deputy that they
    " should be spoilers of your Majesty's sub-
    " jects, notwithstanding their pardon, *there*
    " *have been bonds demanded of them for*
    " *their appearance at the next sessions.*
    " They, knowing themselves guiltless, have
    " most willingly entered into bonds, and
    " appeared ; and there (no matter being
    " found to charge them) they have been
    " arraigned only for being in company with
    " some of your Majesty's servitors, at the
    " killing of notorious known traitors, and

"*for that only* have been condemned of
"treason, and lost their lives! And this
"dishonest practice hath been by the con-
"sent of your deputies."

But it was not treachery alone, however hideous
and sanguinary, which formed, as it were, the
principal ingredient in the English Government
of Ireland. *Direct assassination* — WHOLESALE
ASSASSINATION—was another instrument of that
Government! In short, there were no crimes that
man ever perpetrated against man, or that fiends
of hell, in their satanic malignity, ever invented,
which were not actually made portion of the familiar mode by which the English managed the
government of Ireland during the period alluded
to in the first chapter, and to which these illustrations refer.

Let me give one specimen more, from the same
memorial, of wholesale villany :—

" When there have been notable traitors in arms
    "against your Majesty, and sums of money
    "offered for their heads, yet could by no
    "means be compassed, they have in the end
    "(of their own accord) made means for
    "their pardon, offering to do great service,
    "which they have accordingly performed,
    "to the contentment of the State, and there-
    "by received pardon, and have put in sure-
    "ties for their good behaviour, and to be

" answerable at all times at assizes and ses-
" sions, when they should be called; *yet,*
" *notwithstanding, there have been secret*
" *commissions given for the murdering of*
" *these men !!!*"
It is scarcely credible these things should be done,
by a Government calling itself Christian, and by a
people calling themselves Christians.

Yet, they are FACTS—recorded of an English
Protestant Government and people; not by Catholic, or inimical writers; but by Protestant historians and Protestant officers, high in command
and authority under the Protestant Crown of England: such documents being addressed in general
to the Sovereign; and being, as to the statement
of facts, of the most unimpeachable authenticity.

Here is another specimen :
" When upon the death of a great lord of a
" country there hath been another nomi-
" nated, chosen, and created, he hath been
" entertained with fair speeches, taken down
" into his country, *and for the offences of*
" *other men indictments have been framed*
" *against him, whereupon he hath been*
" *found guilty, and so lost his life ;* which
" hath bred such terror in other great
" lords of the like measure, as maketh them
" stand upon those terms which they now
" do."

Another specimen :

"A great part of that unquietness of O'Donnell's
 " country, came by Sir William Fitzwilliams
 " his placing of one Willis there to be she-
 " riff; who had with him three hundred of
 " THE VERY RASCALS AND SCUM OF THAT
 " KINGDOM, WHICH DID ROB AND SPOIL THAT
 " PEOPLE, RAVISH THEIR WIVES AND DAUGH-
 " TERS, AND MAKE HAVOC OF ALL, which
 " bred such a discontentment, as that the
 " whole country was up in arms against
 " them, so as if the Earl of Tyrone had not
 " rescued and delivered him and them out
 " of the country, they had all been put to
 " the sword."

The savages of New Zealand never were, nor
could have been, guilty of such barbarities, as were
the monsters who administered the English Government in Ireland. Here is another description of
the state of Ireland in the reign of Edward the
Second. I insert it to show that at the distance of
centuries the British policy in Ireland was the same.
It is taken from the History of Ireland written by a
distinguished Protestant Clergyman named Leland.
These are his words :—

" The oppression exercised with impunity in
 " every particular district; the depredations
 " everywhere committed among the inferior
 " orders of the people, not by open enemies

" alone, but by those who called themselves
" friends and protectors; and who justified
" their outrages on the plea of lawful autho-
" rity; *their avarice and cruelty; their*
" *plundering and* MASSACRES, *were still*
" *more ruinous than the defeat of an army or*
" *the loss of a city!*   The wretched sufferers
" had neither power to repel, nor law to
" restrain or vindicate their injuries.   In
" times of general commotion, laws the most
" wisely framed, and most equitably admi-
" nistered, are but of little moment.   But
" now the very source of public justice
" was corrupted and poisoned."—*Le-*
land, Book II. chap. 3.

In a previous passage, Leland had given us the
real cause why this horrible state of misgovernment
was continued : and we find the very same principle
in existence, which actuates the conduct of the
great Orange leaders of the present day.

" The true cause which for a long time fatally
" opposed the gradual coalition of the Irish
" and English race, under one form of go-
" vernment, was, that the great English set-
" tlers found it more for their immediate
" interest, that a free course should be left
" to their oppressions; *that many of those*
" whose lands they coveted *should be*
" *considered as* ALIENS; that they should

" be furnished for their petty wars by arbi-
" trary exactions ; *and in their rapines and*
" MASSACRES, *be freed from the terrors*
" *of a rigidly impartial and severe tribu-*
" *nal.*"—*Leland*, Book II. chap. 1.

I give another passage from the same Protestant
Clergyman, Leland ; — because it describes the
modus agendi in the oppression of the Irish, by
giving power and authority to persons resident in
Ireland, who affected to be the only friends of the
English interest. It is just the story of the Orange-
ists of the present day. Power was given, and the
administration of affairs committed to the persons
whose *only* attachment to English connexion was,
that it gave them the means of committing crime
with impunity. These persons *fabricated* outrages ;
or exaggerated any crimes that might have been
really committed. They were accordingly entrusted
with authority, to put down disturbances and preserve the peace. That power they naturally, and,
indeed, necessarily abused. But I had better use
the words of Leland himself :—

" Riot, rapine, and MASSACRE, and all the
    " tremendous effects of anarchy, were the
    " natural consequences. Every inconsider-
    " able party, who, *under pretence of loyalty*,
    " received the King's commission to repel
    " the adversary in some particular district,
    " BECAME PESTILENT ENEMIES TO THE

" INHABITANTS.   Their properties, *their*
" *lives,* THE CHASTITY OF THEIR
" FAMILIES, were all exposed to barba-
" rians, who sought only to glut their brutal
" passions ; and by their horrible excesses,
" saith the annalist, purchased the curse of
" God and man."—*Leland,* Book II. ch. 3.
That these disorders and crimes were encouraged, or at least not discountenanced, either in
the words, or by the example of the English Viceroys, is a melancholy fact, that appears in every
page of Irish history. They could not, without
arrant hypocrisy, discourage in others, that which
they practised on a larger scale themselves. The
following is the general account given of the Irish
Viceroys, by the same Protestant historian whom I
have so often quoted :—

" At a distance from the supreme seat of power,
" and with the advantage of being able to
" make such representations of the state of
" Ireland as they pleased, the English Vice-
" gerents acted with the less reserve. They
" were generally tempted to undertake the
" conduct of a disordered State, for the sake
" of private emolument, and their object was
" pursued WITHOUT DELICACY OR INTEGRITY;
" SOMETIMES WITH INHUMAN VIOLENCE."—
Leland, Book III. chap. 1.
Speaking of the departure of one of them, in the

reign of Henry the Sixth, Leland has a short passage, which, with a small variation in phrase, might
serve as the general character of the English
Governors of Ireland :—

> " Furnival" (chief governor) " departed with the
> " execration of all those, clergy and laity
> " alike, *whose lands he had ravaged, whose*
> " *castles he had seized, whose fortunes had*
> " *been impaired by his extortion* and exac-
> " tions, or who had shared in the distress
> " arising from the debts he left undis-
> " charged."—*Leland*, Book III. chap. 1.

It will be perceived that the English Governors
behaved with the same impartial and indiscriminate
treachery and cruelty to the descendants of the
English, and to the native Irish themselves. Nothing can exceed the baseness of the means which
were unblushingly resorted to by the monster
Government of Ireland. I select as an instance
from Hollinshed's Chronicles, the mode in which,
in the reign of Henry the Eighth, the insurrection
of Lord Thomas Fitzgerald was terminated. Perjury, murder, and blasphemy so richly concur in
capping the climax of atrocity and baseness, that it
may alone serve to demonstrate the spirit in which
Ireland was governed. The passage from Hollinshed is this :—

> " With Fitzgerald, Sir William Brereton skir-
> " mished so fiercelie, as both the sides were

" rather for the great slaughter disadvan-
" taged, than either part by anie great vic-
" tory furthered. Master Brereton, there-
" fore, perceiving that rough nets were not
" the fittest to take such peart birds, gave his
" advice to the Lord Deputie to grow with
" Fitzgerald by faire means to some rea-
" sonable composition. The Deputie liking
" of the motion, craved a parlie, sending
" certayne of the English as hostages to
" Thomas his campe, with a protection di-
" rected unto him, to come and go at will
" and pleasure. Being upon this securitie
" in conference with Lord Greie, he was
" persuaded to submit himselfe unto the King
" his mercie, *with the Governour's faithfull*
" *and undoubted promise that he should be*
" *pardoned upon his repaire into England.*
" And to the end that no treachery might
" be misdeemed of either side, THEY BOTH
" RECEIVED THE SACRAMENT OPENLIE IN
" THE CAMPE, as an infallible seale of the
" covenants and conditions of either part
" agreed !   Heerupon Thomas Fitzgerald,
" sore against the willes of his councellors,
" dismist his armie, and rode with the De-
" putie to Dublin, where hee made short
" abode, when he sailed to England with the
" favourable letters of the Governour and

" the councell. And as he would have taken
" his journeie to Windsore where the Court
" laie, he was intercepted contrarie to his
" expectation in London waie, and conveied
" without halt into the towre! and before
" his imprisonment was bruited, letters were
" posted into Ireland, streictlie commanding
" the Deputie upon sight of them, to appre-
" hend Thomas Fitzgerald his uncles, and
" to see them with all convenient speed
" shipt into England, which the Lord Deputie
" did not slacke. *For, having feasted*
" *three of the gentlemen at Kilmainan, im-*
" *mediately after their banket, (as it is*
" *nowe and then seene that sweet meate will*
" *have sowre sauce,)* HE CAUSED THEM TO
" BE MANACLED, AND LED AS PRISONERS TO
" THE CASTELL OF DUBLIN! and the other
" two were so roundlie snatcht up in vil-
" lages hard by, as they sooner felt their own
" captivitie, than they had notice of their
" brethren's calamitie! The next wind that
" served into England, these five brethren
" were embarked, to wit, James Fitzgerald,
" Walter Fitzgerald, Oliver Fitzgerald,
" John Fitzgerald, and Richard Fitzgerald.
" *Three of these gentlemen, James, Walter*
" *and Richard, were knowne to have crossed*
" *their nephue Thomas, to their power, in*

" *his rebellion ; and therefore were not oc-*
" *casioned to misdoubt anie danger !*   But
" such as in those daies were enemies to the
" house, incensed the King so sore against it,
" persuading him, that he should never con-
" quer Ireland as long as anie Geraldine
" breathed in the countrie : as for making
" the pathwaie smooth, *he was resolved to*
" *lop off as well the good and sound grapes*
" *as the wild and fruitlesse berries ;* whereby
" appeareth how dangerous it is to be a rub,
" when a king is disposed to sweepe an
" alley."—*Hollinshed*, VI. 302.

  " Thomas Fitzgerald, the third of February, and
  " these five brethren his uncles, were hanged,
  " drawne, and quartered at Tyburne, which
  " was incontinently bruited as well in Eng-
  " land and Ireland, as in foreign soiles."—
  Idem, 303.

One incident during the war with Lord Thomas
Fitzgerald, is worth recording :—

  " One hundred and forty of his (viz. Lord Thomas
    " Fitzgerald's) gallowglasses had the mis-
    " fortune to be intercepted and made pri-
    " soners ; and as intelligence was received
    " that the rebels advanced and prepared to
    " give battle, Skeffington," (the Governor)
    " with a barbarous precaution, *ordered these*
    " *wretches to be slaughtered ; an order so*

" effectually executed, that but one of all
" the number escaped the carnage."—Le-
land, Book III. chap. 6.

It should be kept in mind that during the period
of four hundred years and upwards, the usual
mode of governing both English and Irish within
the jurisdiction of the Anglican Government, was
by Martial Law; which was treated as if it really
formed part of the Common Law of Ireland. The
abstract of a commission to execute Martial Law,
as given by Hollinshed, is worth recording :—

" The Lord Justice from Waterford, upon notice
" of the trouble dailie increasing, sent a
" commission of the eleventh of Februarie,
" to Sir Warham Sentleger to be provost
" marshall, *authorising him to proceed ac-*
" *cording to the course of marshall law*
" *against all offenders,* as the nature of his
" or their offences did merit and deserve ;
" so that the partie offender bee not able to
" dispend fortie shillings by the yeare in
" land, or annuitie, or be not woorth ten
" pounds in goods ; also that upon good
" cawses he maie parlie and talke with anie
" rebell, and grant him a protection for ten
" daies : that he shall banish all idlers and
" sturdy beggars : that he shall apprehend
" aiders of outlaws and theeves, AND EXECUTE
" ALL IDLE PERSONS TAKEN BY NIGHT! that

he shall give in the name and names of such
" as shall refuse to aid and assist him; that in
" doing of his service *he shall take horse-*
" *meat and man's-meat where he list, in*
" *anie man's house for one night;* that
" everie gentleman and nobleman doo deliver
" him a book of all the names of their ser-
" vants and followers; that he shall put in
" execution all statutes against merchants
" and other penal laws, and the same to see
" to be read and published in every church
" by the parson and curate of the same : and
" that he doo everie month certifie the Lord
" Justice *how manie persons,* and of their
" offences and qualities, that he shall execute
" and put to death! with sundrie other ar-
" ticles, which generallie are comprised in
" every commission for the marshall law."—
Hollinshed, VI. 429.

This is given only as a specimen. It is mentioned as a common practice, and is spoken of thus,
by one of the Chief Governors. He talks, it will
be seen, of "giving this power to *sundrie ;*" so that
he was not at all scrupulous as to the persons to
whom he committed it :—

" *I also granted unto sundrie, power to execute*
" *the martiall lawe,* and left authoritie with
" Sir Edmond Butler, and Patrick Sherlock,
" to levie and entertayne men to prosecute

" the outlawes, and such as no man would
" answere for. I have herde, that since
" that tyme some have been executed."—
Sydney, I. 21.

That persons were executed by Martial Law in
time of profound peace, is indisputable.

" The Lord Dillon affirmed that martial law had
" been practiced, and men hanged by it in
" times of peace."—*Nalson*, II. 60.

I shall make one quotation more to establish the
fact that it was considered in Ireland that the
officers of the Crown could supersede the Common
Law whenever they pleased ; by substituting trial
by Court Martial.

" *Martial Law is so frequent and ordinary in*
" *Ireland that it is not to be denied ;* and
" so little offensive there, that the Common
" Law takes no exception at it ! ! !"—*Rushworth*, VIII. 198.

The manner in which the execution of the Martial Law worked, we can discover from the following
instance,which I find in Cox's *History of Ireland :*—

" The Earl of Ormond's officers made a complaint
" against Lovell, Sheriff of the county of
" Kilkenny, that he had executed Martial
" Law on several felons that had lands and
" goods, which would be forfeited to the
" Earl by their attainders, *and that the*
" *Sheriff took those lands and goods to his*
" *own use.*"—*Cox*, 395.

The result of all these grievances and oppressions was the almost total secession from English power, even of the parts of Ireland that had been overrun by the English and submitted to English authority.

There has been lately published a document, from which a few extracts will give a thorough insight into the real state of Ireland so late as the reign of Henry the Eighth. The document I allude to is to be found in the 2nd Volume of the State Papers lately published under the authority of a Commission from the Crown; containing State Papers of the reign of Henry VIII.; and appears to have been a representation made to that monarch of the state of Ireland; and a plan for its reformation. It shows that there were no less than eight counties, which, though shire land, yet did not recognize the authority of England : and five other counties, one half of each of which equally disclaimed the English authority; including in these counties, even the county of Dublin itself. There were, besides, no less than sixty districts, called " Regions," which were altogether under the dominion and authority of Irish Chieftains; and, what will seem still more surprising to those who are unacquainted with the history of Ireland, there were no less than thirty other " Regions," or Districts, under the sway and authority of Chieftains of pure English descent; but who did not acknowledge or submit to the authority of the English government. It is

better to give the very words of the document;
and first, as relates to the Irish " Regions," we find
the following passage :—

" And fyrst of all, to make His Grace under-
" stande that there byn more than 60 coun-
" trys, called Regyons, in Ireland, inhabyted
" with the king's Irish enemies : some region
" as big as a shire, some more, some less
" unto a little ; some as big as halfe a shire,
" and some a little less ; where reigneth
" more than 60 chief captains, whereof some
" calleth themselves Kings, some King's
" Peers in their language, some Princes,
" some Dukes, some Archdukes, that liveth
" only by the sword, and obeyeth to no
" other temporal person, but only to himself
" that is strong : and every of the said cap-
" tains maketh war and peace for himself,
" and holdeth by sworde, and hath imperial
" jurisdiction within his rome, and obeyeth
" to no other person English or Irish, ex-
" cept only to such persons as may subdue
" him by the sworde."

Next, with regard to the English Chieftains,
there is this passage :

" Also, there is more than 30 great captains of
" the English noble folk, that followeth the
" same Irish order, and keepeth the same
" rule, and every of them maketh war and

" peace for himself without any licence of the
" king, or of any other temporal person,
" save to him that is strongest, and of such
" that may subdue them by the sword."
Next, as to the counties that had thrown off the
English authority, we have this passage :—
" Here followeth the names of the counties that
" obey not the King's laws, and have nei-
" ther Justice, neither Sheriffs, under the
" King :
    " The county of Waterfford.
    " The county of Corke.
    " The county of Kilkenny.
    " The county of Lymeryk.
    " The county of Kerry.
    " The county of Conaught.
    " The county of Wolster.*
    " The county of Carlagh.†
    " The county of Uryell.‡
    " The county of Meathe.§
    " Halfe the county of Dublin.
    " Halfe the county of Kildare.
    " Halfe the county of Wexford.
" All the English folke of the said counties
" be of Irish habit, of Irish language, and
" of Irish conditions, except the cities and
" the walled towns."

---

* *i. e.* Ulster.   † Carlow.   ‡ Monaghan.   § Westmeath.

It will be observed that the entire of Connaught was considered at that time as but one county, though it now contains several; and the entire of Ulster was named but as one county, though it has now many. From the next passage we see what a miserably small portion of Ireland acknowledged the authority of the English monarch :—

> " Here followeth the names of the counties sub-
> "ject unto the King's laws :
>> " Halfe the county of Uryell,* by estima-
>> " tion.
>> " Halfe the county of Meath.†
>> " Halfe the county of Dublin.
>> " Halfe the county of Kildare.
>> " Halfe the county of Wexford.
>> " All the common people of the said halfe
>> " counties, that obeyeth the King's laws,
>> " for the more part be of Irish birth, of
>> " Irish habit, and of Irish language."

It will be seen from another extract, how completely the independence of the Irish Chieftains was recognized by all the English constituted authorities, such as they were :—

> " Here followeth the names of the English coun-
> " ties, *that bear tribute to the wylde Irish :*
>> " The barony of Lecchahill in the county
>>> " of Wolster, to the Captain of Clan-

---

* Louth.   † The present county of Meath.

" huboy, payeth yearly £40 ; or else to
" Oneyll, whether of them be strongest.
" The county of Uryell payeth yearly to
" the great Oneyll, £40.
" The county of Meathe payeth yearly to
" O'Conor, £300.
" The county of Kyldare payeth yearly
" to the said O'Conor, £20.
" The King's Exchequer payeth yearly
" to M'Morough, 80 marks.
" The county of Wexford payeth yearly
" to M'Morough and to Arte Oboy,
" £40.
" The county of Kilkenny and the county
" of Tipperary, pay yearly to O'Car-
" roll, £40.
" The county of Limerick payeth yearly
" to O'Brien Arraghe, in English money,
" £40.
" The same county of Limerick payeth
" yearly to the great O'Brien, in Eng-
" lish money, £40.
" The county of Cork to Cormac M'Teyge
" payeth yearly, in English money,
" £40.
" *Summa.* £740."
The following passage is very characteristic :—
" Also there is no folke daily subject to the King's
" lawes, but half the county of Uryell ; half

" the county of Meath; half the county of
" Dublin; half the county of Kildare; and
" there be as many Justices of the King's
" Bench, and of the Common Pleas, and as
" many Barons of the Exchequer, and as
" many Officers, Ministers, and Clerks in
" every of the said countyes, as ever there
" was, when all the lande for the more parte
" was subject to the lawe." (P. 9.)

It will thus be seen that the spirit of jobbing was
as vivacious in Ireland in the reign of Henry the
Eighth, as it is at the present moment.

The document from which I have taken these extracts, contains a plan for reforming the abuses of
the system of government in Ireland, which appears
to have been dictated by a very impartial spirit.
It is altogether a very curious document. The
reader will perhaps smile at such a passage as this:—

" Also it is a proverbe of olde date, ' The pride
    " of Fraunce, the treason of Inglande, and
    " the warre of Irelande, shall never have
    " ende.' Which proverbe, touching the
    " warre of Irelande, is like alwaie to con-
    " tinue, without God sette in men's breasts
    " to finde some new remedy that never was
    " found before."

The reduction of Ireland to a civil state, was the
object of the writer of the document in question:
and the quaint manner in which he concludes his

argument in favour of the adoption of his plans for
the conciliation of Ireland, runs thus :—

"The prophecy is, that the King of Ingland
"shall put this land in such order, that all
"the warres of the lande, whereof groweth
"all the vices of the same, *shall cease for*
"*ever ;* and, AFTER THAT, God shall give
"suche grace and fortune to the same King,
"that he shall, with the army of Ingland
"and of Ireland, subdue the realme of
"Fraunce to his obeisance for ever, and shall
"rescue the Greeks, and recover the great
"city of Constantinople, and shall vanquish
"the Turkes, and win the Holy Crosse,
"and the Holy Lande, and shall die Em-
"peror of Rome, and eternall blisse shall
"be his ende."   (P. 31.)

How expressive of the impolicy of misgoverning
Ireland, is the concluding paragraph of the paper
in question !   The writer says,—

"That if this lande were put once in order as
"aforesayd, it would be none other but a
"very Paradise, *delicious of all pleasaunce,*
"*to respect and regard of any other lande*
"*in this worlde ;* inasmuch as there never
"was straunger ne alien person, greate or
"small, that would avoyde therefro by his
"will, notwithstanding the said misorder,
"if he might the meanes to dwell therein,

" his honesty saved ; much more would be
" his desire if the land were once put in or-
" der."   (P. 31.)

I have dwelt the more at length upon the State
Paper from which I have taken the foregoing extracts, because it serves to show the real cause why
the English Government continued to hold the possession of any part of Ireland.   It has often been
asked, why the Irish, who deprived the English Government of so much of the island, and reduced them
within such narrow limits, did not totally expel that
Government, and establish one of their own?   This
document at once clearly shows the causes that
prevented such a desirable result.   It shows that
the Irish had no point of union, or centralization ;
that they were totally divided among themselves—
the enemies of one another.   The same cause that,
in a more mitigated form, *now* prevents Ireland
from being a nation, did at that time preclude,
in a more rude and savage manner, the establishment of nationality.   The Irish Chieftains had the
power, and seldom wanted either the inclination or
the incitement to make war upon each other.   Mu-
tual injuries, reciprocal devastations, created and
continued strife and hate amongst them.   The
worst elements of continued dissension subsisted.
When upon particular occasions some universal or
fgeneral oppression made them combine, their con-
ederacy was but of short duration.   When the

English party was strong, it endeavoured by force
to put down such confederacy. But the *forcible*
attempts were in general successfully resisted by
the Irish; who gained the futile glory of many a
victory over some of the most accomplished commanders of the English forces. But these defeats
taught the English officers that cunning which is
called political wisdom.   They assailed the avarice,
or fomented the resentments of particular chieftains;
and succeeded in detaching them from the general
cause. These chieftains betrayed their companions
in arms ; joined their forces with those of the English ; and participated in the councils, and united
with the force, which by degrees broke down the
power of the other chieftains. But the traitors obtained no permanent profit ; and no length of fidelity
to the English commanders secured them the confidence or the kindness of their unprincipled seducers.

There is a remarkable instance of this, recorded
as having occurred after a battle fought at Knocktow,
in Connaught, in the reign of Henry the Seventh ;
in which the Irish were totally defeated by the combined army of English, and of royalist Irish, who
aided them under the command of the Lord Gormanstown.   I take the following quotation from
Leland (vol. 2, p. 120) :—

"Immediately after the victory of Knocktow,
"Lord Gormanstown turned to the Earl of
"Kildare, in the utmost insolence of suc-

" cess, ' *We have slaughtered our enemies,*
" said he ; '*but to complete the good deed,*
" *we must proceed yet further,—cut the*
" *throats of those Irish of our own party.*' "
I shall now proceed with extracts of equal authority and authenticity, showing the mode in which
English authority in the reign of Queen Elizabeth
became predominant.   What arms were unable to
achieve, was brought about by the most horrible
and persevering cruelties.   The Irish, who could
not be subdued by *force*, were compelled to yield
to *famine*.   The harvests were destroyed year after
year ; the cattle were taken away and slaughtered ;
provisions of every kind were destroyed ; the
country was devastated—the population perished
for want of food ; famine and pestilence were the
irresistible arms used by England to obtain the
dominion.

It is horrible to think that this mode of subjugation was suggested in detail by the Poet Spenser ;
a man who, though affected by the quaintness of
his time, was endowed with the most poetic genius ;
but his imagination, which might have been inflamed by fictitious woe, exhausted itself in devising
real horrors for Ireland.   He had his plan for the
pacification of Ireland.   It was no other than that
of *creating famine, and ensuring pestilence!* and
he encouraged the repetition of these diabolical
means, by his own evidence of their efficacy.   He

recommended, indeed, that twenty days should be given to the Irish to come in and submit ; after the expiration of which time they were to be shown no mercy.   But let me quote his own words :—

    " The end will (I assure mee) bee very short,
      " and much sooner than it can be in so
      " greate a trouble, as it seemeth, hoped for :
      " altho' there should none of them fall by
      " the sword, nor be slaine by the soldiour :
      " yet thus being kept from manurance, and
      " their cattle from running abroad, by this
      " hard restraint THEY WOULD QUI-
    " ETLY CONSUME THEMSELVES,
    " AND DEVOURE ONE ANOTHER!"
—*Spenser's Ireland*, p. 165.

These counsels of Spenser were carried into effect.   The war with Desmond, who was in fact forced into rebellion—that is, into a contest with the Queen, afforded the pretext and opportunity for exercising these cruelties.   Take these specimens from Hollinshed, who thus describes the progress of the English army through the country :—

    " As they went, they drove the whole country
      " before them into the Ventrie, and by that
      " means they preyed and took all the cattle
      " in the country, to the number of eight
      " thousand kine, besides horses, garrons,
      " sheep, and goats : *and all such people as*
      " *they met, they did without mercy put to*

" *the sword ;* by these means, the whole
" country having no cattle nor kine left,
" they were driven to such extremities, that
" *for want of victuals they were either to die*
" *and perish for famine,. or to die under the*
" *sword.*"—*Hollinshed,* VI. 427.

" The soldiers, likewise, in the camp, were so
" hot upon the spur, and so eager upon the
" vile rebels, that that day *they spared nei-*
" *ther man, woman, nor child, but ALL*
" *was committed to the sword.*"—*Hollinshed,* VI. 430.

I give the next quotation to show how trivial it
was considered to slaughter four hundred unarmed
people in a single day.   It was thought an insuffi-
cient day's service :—

" The next daie following being the twelfe of
" March, the Lord Justice and the Earle
" divided their armie into two severall com-
" panies by two ensigns and three together,
" the Lord Justice taking the one side, and
" the other taking the side of Sleughlogher,
" and so they *searched the woods, burned*
" *the towne, and killed that daie about foure*
" *hundred men, and returned the same*
" *night with all the cattel which they found*
" *that day.*   And the said lords, being *not*
" *satisfied with his daie's service,* they did
" likewise the next daie divide themselves,

" spoiled and consumed the whole countrie
" until it was night."—Hollinshed, VI. 430.
This is but a specimen of the mode in which the
war was carried on. I give a few more instances,
and I could multiply them by hundreds :—
   " They passed over the same into Conilo, where
      " the Lord Justice and the Earl of Ormond
      " divided their companies, and, as they
      " marched, *they burned and destroyed the*
      " country."—Hollinshed, VI. 430.
   " He divided his companies into foure parts, and
      " they entred into foure severall places of
      " the wood at one instant; and by that
      " means they scoured the wood throughout,
      " *in killing as mannie as they tooke,* but
      " the residue fled into the mountains."—
      Hollinshed, VI. 452.
   " There were some of the Irish taken prisoners,
      " that offered great ransomes ; but presently
      " upon their bringing to the campe, *they*
      " were hanged."—Pacata Hibernia, 421.
It will be seen that the troops were thus employed,
not in attacking any armed or resisting enemy, for
there was none ; but in killing unarmed men, and
destroying provisions. The Queen's army was in
Munster ; and here are some specimens of the way
in which they were working out Spenser's plan :—
   " By reason of the continuall persecuting of the
      " rebells, who could have no breath nor rest

" to releeve themselves, but were alwaies by
" one garrison or other hurt and pursued ;
" and by reason the harvest was taken from
" them, their cattells in great numbers
" preied from them, and the whole countrie
" spoiled and preied : the poore people, who
" lived onlie upon their labors, and fed by
" their milch cowes, were so distressed that
" they would follow after the goods which
" were taken from them, *and offer them-*
" *selves, their wives, and children, rather*
" *to be slaine by the armie, than to suffer*
" *the famine wherewith they were now*
" *pinched."—Hollinshed*, VI. 433.   Also
Leland, Book IV. chap. 2.

Again ; take the following from Sir George
Carew :—

" The President having received certaine infor-
" mation, that the Mounster fugitives were
" harboured in those parts, *having before*
" *burned all the houses and corne*, and taken
" great preyes in Owny Onubrian and
" Kilquig, a strong and fast countrey, not
" farre from Limerick, diverted his forces
" into East Clanwilliam and Muskery-quirke,
" where Pierce Lacy had lately beene suc-
" coured ; and *harassing the country*, KILLED
" ALL MANKIND THAT WERE FOUND THEREIN,
" *for a terrour to those as should give re-*

"*leefe to runagate traitors.* Thence wee
" came into Arleaghe woods where wee did
" the like, *not leaving behind us man or*
" *beast,* corne or cattle, except such as had
" been conveyed into castles."—*Pacata Hibernia,* 189.

" *They wasted and forraged the country, so as*
" *in a small time it was not able to give the*
" *rebells any reliefe ; having spoiled and*
" *brought into their garrisons the most part*
" *of their corne, being newly reaped."—*
Pacata Hibernia, 584.

" Hereupon Sir Charles, with the English regi-
" ments, overran all Beare and Bantry, *de-
" stroying all that they could find meet for*
" *the reliefe of men, so as that country was*
" *wholly wasted."—Pacata Hibernia,* 659.

But it was not in Munster only, that the horrors
of this system were practised. I may observe that
it was in the reign of Elizabeth that the general
practice commenced of calling the Irish *rebels* instead of *enemies,* the reason of which is sufficiently
obvious. For it was under the name of rebels that
the people, who for the greater part were living in
peaceable submission to English authority, were
deprived of the produce of their harvests, and consumed by famine. The following extracts will show
how this system was acted upon in Leinster, and in
part of Ulster. I quote from Leland :—

" The Leinster rebels, by driving the royalists
" into their fortified towns, AND LIVING LONG
" WITHOUT MOLESTATION, HAD CULTIVATED
" THEIR LANDS, AND ESTABLISHED AN UNU-
" SUAL REGULARITY AND PLENTY IN THEIR
" DISTRICTS. But now they were exposed
" to the most rueful havoc from the Queen's
" forces. The soldiers, encouraged by the
" example of their officers, EVERY WHERE
" CUT DOWN THE STANDING CORN WITH THEIR
" SWORDS, and devised every means to de-
" prive the wretched inhabitants of all the
" necessaries of life ! ! *Famine was judged*
" *the speediest and most effectual means of*
" *reducing them ;* AND THEREFORE THE
" DEPUTY WAS SECRETLY NOT DISPLEASED
" WITH THE DEVASTATIONS MADE EVEN IN
" THE WELL-AFFECTED QUARTERS BY THE
" IMPROVIDENT FURY OF THE REBELS.

" The like melancholy expedient was
" practised in the northern provinces. The
" Governor of Carrickfergus, Sir Arthur
" Chichester, issued from his quarters, and
" for twenty miles round, reduced the coun-
" try to a desert. Sir Samuel Bagnal, the
" Governor of Newry, proceeded with the
" same severity, and laid waste all the adja-
" cent lands. All the English garrisons
" were daily employed in pillaging and

" wasting : while Tyrone, with his dispirited
" party, shrunk gradually within narrower
" bounds. THEY WERE EFFECTUALLY PRE-
" VENTED FROM SOWING AND CULTIVATING
" THEIR LANDS."—*Leland*, Book IV. ch. 5.

To give some variety to these horrors, I will
quote an incident that occurred in the year 1574.
Pour varier les agrémens, as the French would
say.

" —' Anno 1574.   A solemn peace and concord
" ' was made between the Earl of Essex and
" ' Felim O'Nial.   However, at a feast
" ' wherein the earl entertained that chief-
" ' tain, and at the end of their good cheer,
" ' O'Nial and his wife were seized, and
" ' their friends who attended *were put to*
" ' *the sword before their faces.   Felim,*
" ' *together with his wife and brother, were*
" ' *conveyed to Dublin, where they were cut*
" ' *up in quarters.*'   This execution gave
" universal discontent and horror.   In like
" manner, a few years after, the Irish chief-
" tains of the King's and Queen's counties,
" were invited by the English to a treaty of
" accommodation.   *But when they arrived*
" *at the place of conference, they were in-*
" *stantly surrounded by troops, and all*
" *butchered on the spot.*"—*Leland*, Book
IV. ch. 2 *(note).*

As these individual instances of cruelty and treachery give a more vivid interest to the general tale of all species of atrocious crimes, I will just give one example more of individual depravity, in no less a person than the Lord President of Munster. It is in truth, a fact of a family! being part of the general system.

> " Carew still descended to more dishonourable
> " practices.   One Nugent, a servant of Sir
> " Thomas Norris, had deserted to the rebels,
> " and by the alacrity of his services he
> " acquired their confidence.   In a repenting
> " mood he submitted to the President,"
> (Carew,) " and to purchase his pardon,
> " promised to destroy either the titular earl*
> " or his brother John.   *As a plot was*
> " *already laid against the former*, and as
> " his death could only serve to raise up new
> " competitors for his title, THE BRAVO WAS
> " DIRECTED TO PROCEED AGAINST JOHN. He
> " seized his opportunity, and attempted to
> " despatch him ; but as his pistol was just
> " levelled, he was seized, condemned to die,
> " and at his execution confessed his design :
> " *declaring that many others* HAD SWORN
> " TO THE LORD PRESIDENT *to effect what he*
> " *intended.*"—*Leland,* Book IV. ch. 5.

---

* Viz., the Earl of Desmond.

Carew's description of the policy adopted in his own day, might serve for a much later period :—

"IT WAS THOUGHT NO ILL POLICY TO MAKE THE "IRISH DRAW BLOOD UPON ONE ANOTHER, "WHEREBY THEIR PRIVATE QUARRELS MIGHT "ADVANCE THE PUBLIC SERVICE."—*Pacata Hibernia*, 650.

I now come back to the systematic plan of destroying property ; especially the harvests. We find the following incidental notices, among the repetitions of more detailed destruction :—

A. D. 1600.   " On the 12th of August, Mount- "joy with 560 foot and 60 horse, and some "volunteers, marcht to Naas, and thence "to Philipstown, and in his way tooke 200 "cows, 700 garrons, and 500 sheep, and so "*burning the country.*"—*Cox,* 428.

1600. " Sir Arthur Savage, Governor of Connagh, "designed to meet the Lord Lieutenant, "but could not accomplish it, *though he "preyed and spoil'd the country as far as "he came.*"—*Cox,* 428.

1600.   " Mountjoy staid in this country till the "23rd of August, *and destroyed* £10,000 "*worth of corn, and slew more or less "of the rebels every day.* One Lenagh, a "notorious rebel, was taken and hanged, "and a prey of 1000 cows, 500 garrons, "and many sheep, was taken by Sir Oliver

" Lambert in Daniel Spany's countrey, *with*
" *the slaughter of a great many rebels.*"—
Cox, 428.

1600. " About the 18th of December, Sir
" Francis Barkley having notice that many
" rebels were relieved in Clanawley, marcht
" thither and got a prey of 1000 cows, 200
" garrons, many sheep, and other booty,
" *and had the killing of many traytors.*"—
Cox, 434.

" The next morning being the fourth of January,
" 1602, Sir Charles Wilmot coming to seeke
" the enemy in their campe, hee entered
" into their quarter without resistance, where
" *hee found nothing but hurt and sicke men,*
" *whose paines and lives by the soldiers were*
" *both determined.*"—*Pacata Hibernia*, 659.

" Greate were the services these garrisons per-
" formed ; for Sir Richard Pearce and Cap-
" tain George Flower, with their troopes,
" *left neither corne nor horne, nor house*
" *unburnt between Kinsale and Ross.* Cap-
" tain Roger Harvie, who had with him his
" brother, Captain Gawen Harvie, Captain
" Francis Slingsby, Captain William Staf-
" ford, and also the companies of the Lord
" Barry and the treasurer, with the Presi-
" dent's horse, *did the like between Ross*
" *and Bantry.*"—*Pacata Hibernia*, 645.

The result of all these proceedings is described
by so many of the English historians, in terms of
such complicated horror, that volumes might be
filled with the particular instances of cruelty and
barbarity. I give these quotations :—
" Repeated complaints were made of the inhuman
    " rigour practised by Grey" (the Deputy)
    " and his officers. The Queen was assured
    " that he tyrannized with such barbarity,
    " THAT LITTLE WAS LEFT IN IRELAND FOR
    " HER MAJESTY TO REIGN OVER, BUT ASHES
    " AND CARCASSES !"—*Leland*, Book IV.
    chap. 2.
" The southern province seemed to be totally
    " depopulated, and, except within the cities,
    " exhibited an *hideous scene of famine and*
    " *desolation.*"—*Leland*, Book IV. chap. 3.
It might be supposed that the progress of destruction would now have been arrested ; that
enough in the demoniacal labour of massacre and
spoliation had been done ; and that the kingdom
might have at last been permitted to enjoy some
respite from the atrocities of fiends in human form.
But this was forbidden by the active anti-Irish
spirit—the national antipathy to, and jealousy of,
this country ; which spirit then, as well as now,
exercised its evil and malignant influences on our
destiny. We have seen already, that where the
Irish had driven the royalists into their fortified

towns, and freed themselves from English molestation, "THEY HAD CULTIVATED THEIR LANDS, AND
ESTABLISHED AN UNUSUAL REGULARITY
AND PLENTY IN THEIR DISTRICTS."—
(Leland, Book IV. chap. 5.) But Irish peace,
plenty, and prosperity formed no part of English
policy. It appears from Leland that the oppression
and plunder of Ireland, the butchery of her inhabitants, and the perpetuation of social discord, were
regularly systematized, reasoned on, and, despite
some opposition, adopted and established as a measure of state policy. Here are Leland's words :—

"Some of her" (Elizabeth's) "counsellors, ap-
"pear to have conceived an odious jealousy
"which reconciled them to the distractions
"and miseries of Ireland.

"'Should we exert ourselves,' said they,
"'in reducing this country to order and
"'civility, *it must soon acquire power, con-*
"'*sequence, and riches.* The inhabitants
"'will thus be alienated from England; they
"'will cast themselves into the arms of some
"'foreign power, or perhaps erect them-
"'selves into an independent and separate
"'state. LET US RATHER CONNIVE AT
"'THEIR DISORDERS; for a weak and dis-
"'ordered people never can attempt to de-
"'tach themselves from the Crown of Eng-
"'land.' We find Sir Henry Sydney and

" Sir John Perrot, who perfectly understood
" the affairs of Ireland, and the dispositions
" of its inhabitants, both expressing the ut-
" most indignation at this horrid policy,
" which yet had found its way into the
" English Parliament."—*Leland,* Book IV.
chap. 3.

This policy was incessantly and vigorously acted
upon. The " disorders" were perpetuated. There
was no pause. The efficient manner in which the
army performed the service of destruction, was
boasted of by many of the English historians. Let
any man who chooses, read in cold blood the following extract :—

" They performed that service effectually, and
" brought the rebels to so low a condition,
" *that they saw three children eating the*
" *entrails of their dead mother*, upon whose
" flesh they had fed many days, and roasted
" it by a slow fire."—*Cox*, 449.

Nor did the entire conquest and death of Desmond, and the total suppression of any resistance,
satiate the English commanders or their soldiers :
let the following description of their conduct, by a
contemporary historian, suffice for our present
purposes :—

" After Desmond's death, and the entire sup-
" pression of his rebellion, unheard of cru-
" elties were committed on the provincials

" of Munster (his supposed former ad-
"herents) by the English commanders.
" GREAT COMPANIES OF THESE
" PROVINCIALS, MEN, WOMEN,
" AND CHILDREN, WERE OFTEN
" FORCED INTO CASTLES AND
" OTHER HOUSES, WHICH WERE
" THEN SET ON FIRE. And if any of
" them attempted to escape from the flames,
" they were shot or stabbed by the soldiers
" who guarded them. *It was a diversion to*
" *these monsters of men to take up infants*
" *on the point of their spears, and whirl them*
" *about in their agony ;* apologising for their
" cruelty by saying, that 'if they suffered
" them to live to grow up, they would be-
" come popish rebels.' Many of their women
" were found hanging on trees, with their
" children at their breasts, strangled with the
" mother's hair."—*Lombard. Comment. de
Hibern.* p. 535 ; apud *Curry, Hist. Review,*
p. 27 (note).

All the Irish, and persons of the English race
who had resisted the Queen's authority, having
been destroyed by the sword or famine, the subjugation of the country became complete. There is
in Hollinshed's Chronicle a quaintness of expression
that gives an additional interest to the details he
has preserved ; but they have, from their own na-

ture, a deeper interest still.   If these details had been given of cruelties towards wretched and infidel barbarians in the remotest extremity of the globe, they would excite great compassion, and heartfelt commiseration in any human being.   But let it be recollected that these are authentic and unimpeachable narratives of crimes which Christian Englishmen committed upon Christian Irish.   The historians who have recorded these facts, had every motive to palliate, and none to exaggerate, the English barbarity and cruelty.   Yet the wildest flights of imagination, could scarcely suppose anything in fiction equal to the horrors of the reality. The following passage describes the closing scene of the conquest of the southern provinces of Ireland :—

" And as for the great companies of souldiers,
" gallowglasses, kerne, and the common
" people who followed this rebellion, *the*
" *numbers of them are infinite whose bloods*
" *the earth drank up, and whose carcasses*
" *the beasts of the field and the ravening*
" *fowls of the air did consume and devoure.*
" After this followed an extream famine ;
" and such whom the sword did not destroy,
" the same did consume and eat out ; *very*
" *few or none remaining alive* excepting
" such as were fled over into England ; and
" yet the store in the towns was far spent

" and they in distress, albeit nothing like in
" comparison to them who lived at large ;
" *for they were not onelie driven to eat*
" *horses, dogs, and dead carrions ; but also*
" *did devoure the carcasses of dead men,*
" whereof there be sundrie examples; namely,
" one in the county of Cork, where, when a
" malefactor was executed to death, and his
" body left upon the gallows, certain poor
" people did secretly come, took him down,
" and did eat him ; likewise in the bay
" of Smeerweeke, or St. Marieweeke, the
" place which was first seasoned with this
" rebellion, there happened to be a ship to
" be there lost through foul weather, and
" all the men being drowned, were there
" cast on land. The common people, who
" had a long time lived on limpets, orewads,
" and such shell-fish as they could find, and
" which were now spent; as soon as they
" saw these bodies, they took them up, and
" most greedily did eat and devoure them ;
" and not long after, death and famine did
" eat and consume them. The land itself,
" which *before* those wars was populous,
" well inhabited, and rich in all the good
" blessings of God, BEING PLENTEOUS
" OF CORNE, FULL OF CATTEL,
" well stored with fish and sundrie other

" good commodities, is now become waste
" and barren, yielding no fruits, the pastures
" no cattel, the aire no birds ; the seas,
" (though full of fish,) yet to them yielding
" nothing. Finally, every waie the curse of
" God was so great, *and the land so barren*
" *both of man and beast,* that whosoever did
" travell from the one end to the other of
" all Munster, even from Waterford to the
" head of Smeerweeke, *which is about six*
" *score miles, he would not meet anie man,*
" *woman, or child,* saving in towns and
" cities ; nor yet see any beast, but the very
" wolves, the foxes, and other like ravening
" beasts, many of them laie dead, being fa-
" misht, and the residue gone elsewhere."—
Hollinshed, VI. 459.

But let me refer again to Spenser. His description relates even to an earlier period of the war.
He is speaking of the province of Munster ; these
are his words :—

" Notwithstanding that the same was a most rich
" and plentiful country, full of corne and
" cattel, yet, ere one yeare and a half, they
" were brought to such wretchedness as
" that any stony heart would rue the same.
" Out of every corner of the woods and
" glynns, they came creeping forth upon
" their hands, for their legs could not bear

"them ; they looked like anatomies of
"death ; they spake like ghosts crying out
"of their graves ; *they did eate the dead*
"*carrions, happy where they could finde*
"*them ;* yea, and one another soone after ;
"insomuch as the very carcasses they spared
"not to scrape out of their graves, and,
"if they found a plot of watercresses or
"shamrocks, there they flocked as to a feast
"for the time ; yet, not able to continue
"there withal ; that in shorte space, there
"was none almost left, AND A MOST
"POPULOUS AND PLENTIFUL
"COUNTREY SUDDAINELIE LEFT
"VOYDE OF MAN AND BEAST."
—*Spenser's State of Ireland,* p. 165.

I pray attention to these two passages.   The first
from Morrisson's History of Ireland, folio 272 ; it
is thus abstracted by Curry in his Review :—

"Because," says Morrisson, "I have often made
"mention formerly of our destroying the
"rebel's corne, and using all means to
"famish them, let me now, by two or three
"examples, show the miserable estate to
"which they were thereby reduced."   He
then, after telling us that Sir Arthur Chichester, Sir Richard Morrisson, and other
commanders, saw a most horrid spectacle of
three children, whereof the eldest was not

above ten years' old, feeding on the flesh of
their dead mother, with circumstances too
shocking to be repeated ; and that the common sort of rebels were driven to unspeakable
extremities, beyond the records of any his-
tories that he had ever read in that kind ;
he mentions a horrid stratagem of some of
these wretched people, to allay the rage of
hunger, in the following manner : " Some
" old women," says he, " about the Newry,
" used to make a fire in the fields, and di-
" vers little children driving out the cattle
" in the cold mornings and coming thither
" to warm themselves, were by these women
" surprised, killed, and eaten ; which was
" at last discovered, by a great girl breaking
" from them by the strength of her body ;
" and Captain Trevor sending out soldiers
" to know the truth, they found the chil-
" dren's skulls and bones, and apprehended
" the old women, who were executed for the
" fact.   No spectacle," adds Morrisson,
" was more frequent in the ditches of towns,
" and especially in the wasted countries,
" than to see multitudes of these poor people
" dead, with their mouths all coloured green
" by eating nettles, docks, and all things
" they could rend up above ground."
Such were the means by which the final subju-

gation of Ireland was produced. Such were the
preparations made for the reign of James the
First. And I might close the proofs and illustrations of my first chapter, in the words of Sir
John Davies :—

"Thus had the Queen's army under Lord
"Mountjoy, broken and absolutely subdued
"all the lords and chieftains of the Irishry.
"Whereupon, *the multitude being brayed,*
"*as it were, in a mortar, with sword,*
"*famine, and pestilence together,* submitted
"themselves to the English Government,
"received the laws and magistrates, and
"most gladly embraced the King's* pardon
"and peace in all parts of the realm, with
"demonstrations of joy and comfort."

Yes, Sir John Davies. The Irish people were
brayed as in a mortar ; and the process of "braying
as in a mortar" has been continued from that day
to this. It has, in fact, been the leading principle
in the government of Ireland. Never was any
people on the face of the globe, so cruelly treated
as the Irish !

I cannot conclude my selections illustrating the
reign of Queen Elizabeth, without bringing out of
the obscurity of the Statute Book, and giving pub-
licity to the nature of the title by which Elizabeth

---

* James I.

claimed the province of Ulster. It will be found
embalmed with most ludicrous solemnity in an Act
of the Irish Parliament, entitled " *An Act for the
attainder of Shane O'Neill, and the extinguishment of the name of O'Neill, and the entitling of
the Queen's Majesty, her heirs and successors, to
the country of Tyrone, and other countries and territories in Ulster.*" This Act was passed in the year
1569 ; it is the eleventh of Elizabeth, sess. 3,
chap. 1 :—

" And now, most deere sovereign Ladie, least
" that any man which list not to seeke and
" learn the truth, might be ledd eyther of
" his own fantasticall imagination, or by the
" sinister suggestion of others, to thinke
" that the sterne or lyne of the O'Neyles
" should or ought by priority of title, to hold,
" and possess annie part of the dominion or
" territories of Ulster before your Majestie,
" your heirs, and successors, wee, your
" Grace's said faithful and obedient subjects,
" for avoyding of all such scruple, doubt, and
" erroneous conceyt, doo intend here (par-
" don first craved of your Majestie for our
" tedious boldness) to disclose unto your
" Highness *your auncient and sundrie strong*
" *authentique titles*, conveyed farr beyond
" the said lynage of the O'Neyles and all
" other of the Irish, to the dignitie, state,

" title, and possession of this your realm of
" Ireland.

" And therefore it may like your most excellent
" Majestie to be advertized, that the auncient
" chronicles of this realm, written both in
" the Latine, English, and Irish tongues,
" alledged sundrie auncient titles for the
" kings of England to this lande of Irelande.
" And first, that at the beginning, afore the
" comming of Irishmen into the sayd lande,
" they were dwelling in a province of
" Spayne, the which is called Biscan,
" whereof Bayon was a member, and the
" chief citie. And that, at the said Irish-
" men's comming into Ireland, one King
" Gurmond, son to the noble King Belan,
" King of Great Britaine which is now called
" England, was Lord of Bayon, as many of
" his successors were to the time of King
" Henry the Second, first conquerour of
" this realm ; AND THEREFORE THE IRISH-
" MEN SHOULD BE THE KING OF ENGLAND
" HIS PEOPLE, AND IRELAND HIS LAND.

" Another title is, that at the same time that
" Irishmen came out of Biscay as exhiled
" persons, in sixty ships, they met with the
" same King Gurmond upon the sea at the
" ysles of the Orcades, then comming from
" Denmark with great victory. Their cap-

" tains, called Hebrus and Hermon, went
" to this King, and him tolde the cause of
" their comming out of Biscay, and him
" prayed, with greate instance, that he
" would graunt unto them that they might
" inhabit some lande in the west. The King
" at the last, by the advice of his councell,
" *granted them Ireland to inhabite*, and as-
" signed unto them guides for the sea, to
" bring them thither; AND THEREFORE THEY
" SHOULD AND OUGHT TO BE THE KING OF
" ENGLAND'S MEN.

" Another title is, as the Clerke Geraldus Cam-
" brensis writeth at large the historie of the
" conquest of Ireland by King Henry the
" Second, your famous progenitor, how
" Dermot Mac Morch, Prince of Leinster,
" which is the first part of Ireland, being a
" tyrant or tyrants, banished, went over the
" sea into Normandie, in the parts of France,
" to the said King Henry ; and him basely
" besought of succour which he obtained,
" and thereupon became liegeman to the
" said King Henry, through which he
" brought power of Englishmen into the
" land, and married his daughter, named
" Eve, at Waterford, to Sir Richard Fitz-
" Gilbert, Earle of Stranguile in Wales, and
" to him granted the reversion of Leinster,

" with the said Eve his daughter. And af-
" ter that the said Earle granted to the said
" King Henry the citie of Dublin, with cer-
" tain cantreds of lands next to Dublin, and
" all the haven towns of Leinster, to have
" the rest to him in quiet with his Grace's
" favour.

" Another title is, that in the year of our Lord
" God one thousand one hundred sixtie two,
" the aforesay'd King Henry landed at the
" citie of Waterford within the realm of
" Ireland ; and there came to him Dermot,
" King of Corke, which is of the nation of
" the M'Carties, and of his own proper will
" became liege, tributarie for him and his
" kingdom, and upon that made his oathe
" and gave his hostages to the king. Then
" the King roade to Cashell, and there came
" to him Donald, King of Limerick, which
" is of the nation of the O'Brienes, and be-
" came his liege, as the other did. Then
" came to him Donald, King of Ossorie,
" Mac Shaglin, King of Ophaly, and all the
" princes of the south of Ireland, and became
" his liegemen as aforesaid. Then went the
" said King Henry to Dublin, and there
" came to him O'Kirnill, King of Uriel,
" O'Rourke, King of Meth, and Rotherick,
" King of all Irishmen of the land, and of

" Connaught ; with all the princes, and men
" of value of the land, and became liege
" subjects, and tributaries, by great oaths
" for them, their kingdoms and lordships
" to the said King Henry ; and that of their
" own good wills, as it should seem ; for
" that THE CHRONICLES MAKE NO MENTION
" OF ANY WARRE OR CHIVALRY DONE BY THE
" SAID KING, ALL THE TIME THAT HE WAS
" IN IRELAND."

This, to be sure, is a most ludicrous piece of
legislation : absurd to a degree that will make any
man stare with astonishment who reads it at the
present day.   The only rational title which it makes
out being one of compact, giving the people of Ireland a right to the benefit of British laws ; a right
which is a dead letter even unto the present day !

OBSERVATIONS, PROOFS, AND ILLUSTRATIONS.

CHAPTER II.—PART I.

Years 1612—1625.

THE extracts which I have given from Irish history, in corroboration of the text of my first chapter, will have given the reader some idea of the multiplied and variegated cruelties, horrors, treacheries, and massacres by which the English dominion was extended and maintained in various parts of Ireland; and at length spread all over the entire land by means of provoked famine and pestilence. Queen Elizabeth did not live long enough to enjoy the consummation of this fiendish policy, nor to reign amidst the tranquillity of the grave. It remained for her unworthy successor to reap the fruits of her cruelties. The people being " brayed as in a mortar"—I like to repeat the phrase of Sir John Davies—the survivors readily acquiesced in any alteration of law, and very gratefully received that alteration which in the year 1612 acknowledged for the first time the Irish as subjects, and admitted them under the protection of the Crown.

It affords an inquiry of some interest to ascertain what was the genius and the disposition, what the social and moral character of the people who had endured such hideous cruelties, and who were now made citizens of the State. I will not draw that character in the glowing colours in which it has been painted by Irish writers, or by any favourers or partizans of the Irish. I will take that character from Englishmen and Protestants; and from persons who themselves were participators in the crimes which I have mentioned, and in those which remain to be described.

The following is from an English Protestant writer, by no means favourable to the Irish; on the contrary, a man disposed to speak ill of, and to calumniate, them and their clergy. Here is the worst he could say of them :—

" The people are thus inclined, religious, frank,
" amorous, irefull, sufferable of infinite
" paines, verie glorious, manie sorcerers,
" excellent horsemen, delighted with warres,
" great almsgivers, passing in hospitality.
" The lewder sort, both clerkes and laiemen,
" are sensuall and ouer loose in liuing. The
" same being vertuouslie bred up or re-
" formed, are such mirrors of holinesse and
" austeritie, that other nations retain but a
" shadow of devotion in comparison of them.
" As for abstinence and fasting, it is to

"them a familiar kind of chastisement."—
Stanihurst, apud *Hollinshed,* VI. 67.

But as character is best shown by individual
traits, especially when the writer is one adversely
inclined, I select a passage descriptive of the fidelity
that existed between foster brothers amongst the
Irish ; and it is not going too far to say, that a
people capable of such high and generous attachment to each other, and to their duty, ought to
rank high in the estimation of good men. Mark
the following extract :—

" You cannot find one instance of perfidy, deceit,
   " or treachery among them ; nay, they are
   " ready to expose themselves to all manner
   " of dangers *for the safety of those who*
   " *sucked their mother's milk.* You may
   " beat them to a mummy ; you may put
   " them on the rack ; you may burn them
   " on a gridiron ; you may expose them to
   " the most exquisite torture that the cruellest
   " tyrant can invent ; yet you will never re-
   " move them from that innate fidelity which
   " is grafted in them ; you will never induce
   " them to betray their duty."—*Ware,* II. 73.

I will now add more favourable testimony of
other English Protestant writers. Take this passage from a decided enemy of the Irish name and
nation :—

" The Irish themselves were a people *peaceable,*

"*harmless, and affable to strangers, and*
"*to all, pious and good, whilst they re-*
"*tained the religion of their forefathers.*"
—*Borlase,* 14.

Baron Finglas, who was Chief Baron of the Exchequer under Henry VIII., places the Irish character on far higher ground than the English, so far as concerns submission to law and justice. He says :—

"It is a great abusion and reproach, that the
"laws and statutes made in this land are
"not observed ne kept, after the making of
"them, eight days : which matter is one of
"the destructions of Englishmen of this
"land : *and divers Irishmen doth observe*
"*and keepe such laws and statutes which*
"*they make upon hills in their country,*
"FIRM AND STABLE, WITHOUT BREAKING
"THEM FOR ANY FAVOUR OR REWARD."—
Baron Finglas's Hibernica, 51.

The next is from Lord Coke, who cannot be suspected of any undue leaning in favour of the Irish :—

"I have been informed by many of those that
"had judicial places in Ireland, and [know]
"partly of my own knowledge, THAT THERE
"IS NO NATION OF THE CHRISTIAN WORLD
"THAT ARE GREATER LOVERS OF JUSTICE
"THAN THE IRISH ARE : *which virtue must*

" *of course be accompanied by many others.*"
—*Coke*, IV. Inst. 349.

The next is a passage which has often been
quoted from the celebrated Sir John Davies :—

" They will gladly continue in this condition of
" subjects, without defection, or adhering
" to any other lord or king, *as long as they*
" *may be protected and justly governed,*
" *without oppression on the one side, or*
" *impunity upon the other.* FOR THERE IS
" NO NATION OF PEOPLE UNDER THE SUN
" THAT DOTH LOVE EQUAL AND INDIFFERENT
" JUSTICE BETTER THAN THE IRISH ; *or will*
" *rest better satisfied with the execution*
" *thereof, although it be against themselves.*
—*Davies's Hist. Tract*, 213.

There has been lately published by the Irish
Archæological Society in the first volume of their
Tracts relating to Ireland, a small work entitled
" A BRIEFE DESCRIPTION OF IRELAND, MADE IN
THE YEAR 1589 BY ROBERT PAYNE ;" from which I
select two extracts that confirm strongly the praises
bestowed upon the Irish love of justice :—

" Nothing is more pleasing unto them, than to
" heare of *good Justices* placed amongst
" them. They have a common saying which
" I am persuaded they speake unfeinedly,
" which is, *Defend me and spend me :*
" meaning from the oppression of the worser

"sorte of our countriemen : they are obe-
" dient to the laws ; *so that you may travel*
" *through all the land without any danger*
" *or injurie offered of the verye worst Irish,*
" AND BE GREATLY RELEEVED OF THE BEST."
—Page 4.

My next quotation is peculiarly interesting at the
present moment. It shows what the Corporations
of Ireland were in Catholic times, before Protestantism and Exclusion were the ruling impulses :—

"BUT AS TOUCHING THEIR GOVERN-
" MENT IN THEIR CORPORATIONS
" WHERE THEY BEARE RULE, IS
" DONE   WITH   SUCH   WISDOME,
" EQUITY,   AND   JUSTICE,   AS DE-
" MERITS   WORTHY   COMMENDA-
" TIONS.   For I myself divers times have
" seene in severall places within their juris-
" dictions wel near twenty causes decided at
" one sitting, with such indifferencie that for
" the most parte both plaintife and defendant
" hath departed contented : *yet manie that*
" *make show of peace, and desireth to live*
" *by blood, doe utterly mislike this or any*
" *good thing that the poore Irish man*
" *dothe."—Ibid.*

There is nothing new under the sun. The tranquillity which existed in Ireland, whilst the disposition of the Melbourne Government was evinced,

to administer the laws impartially, had been
found at former periods to arise from precisely
a similar cause. Sir John Perrot had endeavoured
to show the Irish impartial justice, and Hooker,
who in some of his writings, bestows on the
Irish unmeasured vituperation and abuse, yet
says, that at the close of Sir John Perrot's administration—

"Everie man with a white sticke only in his
"hands, and with great treasures, might
"and did travell without feare or danger
"where he woulde, (as the writer heerof by
"triall knew it to be true,) and the white
"sheepe did keepe the blacke, and all the
"beasts lay continually in the fields, without
"stealing or preieing."—*Hooker;* apud *Hollinshed,* VI. 370.

Let us listen to Sir John Davies upon this subject, and one will imagine it is the Attorney-General
of the Melbourne Government who speaks :—

"I dare affirm, that in the space of five years
"last past, there have not been found so
"many malefactors worthy of death, in all
"the six circuits of this realm, which is now
"divided into thirty-two shires at large, as
"in one circuit of six shires, namely, the
"western circuit in England! *For the
"truth is, that in time of peace, the Irish
"are more fearful to offend the law than*

" *the English, or any other nation what-*
" *soever.*"—*Davies,* p. 200.

As to the bravery of the Irish, it may be super-
fluous to give any proof of it from Protestant and
inimical testimony; since friends and foes alike
admit the chivalrous gallantry of the Irish people;
and the Scotch philosophers have lately demonstrated the superiority of their physical powers.
I cannot, however, refrain from inserting the following quotation from Edmund Spenser :—

" I have heard some great warriors say, that in
" all the services which they had seen abroad
" in foreign countries, THEY NEVER SAW A
" MORE COMELY MAN THAN THE IRISHMAN,
" NOR THAT COMETH ON MORE BRAVELY TO
" HIS CHARGE."—*Spenser's Ireland.*

These now are all noble traits in the character
of the Irish people. Fidelity—proof against every
temptation of bribery or torture; fidelity which
nothing could buy, and which nothing could in-
timidate !   " Piety and goodness whilst her people
adhered " (and they *do yet* adhere) " to the religion
of their forefathers." But above all, transcendently
stands the glorious title, " LOVERS OF JUSTICE "—
LOVERS OF EQUAL AND IMPARTIAL JUSTICE."—
Lovers of justice, *not* only when they obtain it *for*
themselves; but loving it so dearly that they are
satisfied with its execution even when *against*
themselves ! Military valour not excelled by any

nation in existence! And upon whose testimony is it, that the Irish claim the glory of these qualities? From the testimony of strangers, aliens, enemies! I challenge the world to produce an instance of such praise bestowed on any nation by persons not themselves interested in, or connected with such praise.

It may be objected that near 300 years have elapsed since these praises were bestowed; and that the Irish may have much changed since that period. But what says the truth of history? What does it exhibit in that period? The Irish have been since severely tried in the furnace of affliction; they have been assailed with treachery and persecution; and yet they have exhibited the most unalterable fidelity to the faith which they in their consciences preferred. No money could bribe—no torture could compel them to forsake the allegiance which they owed to their God. Compare their conduct in this respect with that of any other nation under the sun; and admit (for truth compels the admission) that the glory of religious fidelity supereminently belongs to the people of Ireland. You may say, perhaps, that their faith was erroneous, their creed mistaken, and their practice superstitious. Suppose it were so. Yet their fidelity was religious; it was attachment to the religion they deemed the true one; and this national trait of their character ought not to be tarnished even in the opinion of those who do not agree with them as to its object.

It will not be thus tarnished in the mind of any just or generous man.

Again, we perceived, during the late administration, the same respect paid to the attempt on the part of the Irish Government to purify the administration of justice : the same tranquillity follows, from the hope of having justice administered.

Again, behold the national movement in favour of temperance. There are more than five millions pledged to total abstinence from all intoxicating liquors. What nation upon the face of the earth can afford such an example as this ? But it may be said that this temperance movement is transitory. To those who may say so I reply, that the first trait in the Irish character is fidelity of purpose—fidelity superior to corruption, to force, and to temptation! I do therefore feel it my duty solemnly to declare, that the people of Ireland, the lovers of impartial justice, stand superior in their national characteristics to the inhabitants of any other country on the face of the globe. I am, therefore, proud of my fatherland. Nor is it the less dear to me because of the evils that have been inflicted upon it, the oppression it has endured, and the tyranny that it has nearly survived :

"More dear in thy sorrow, thy gloom, and thy showers,
Than the rest of the world in their sunniest hours."

Nor is it the less loved by me, because of the

slavery that has been treacherously imposed upon
it :

> " No ! thy chains as they rankle, thy blood as it runs,
> But make thee more painfully dear to thy sons !
> Whose hearts, like the young of the desert-bird's nest,
> Drink love in each life-drop that flows from thy breast."

It will have been observed, that the alteration
in religion, commonly, but most improperly, called
" The Reformation"—for it cannot seriously be
called a Reformation at all—occurred in the period
included in the first chapter. But I have designedly
omitted all mention of it ; having reserved it for a
separate and distinct consideration.

When Luther commenced the great schism of
the sixteenth century, all Christendom was Catholic.
Ireland, of course, was so. It has indeed been said
—for what will not religious bigotry say ?—that the
Catholic church in Ireland did not recognize the
authority of the Pope, and was severed from the
Church of Rome. This assertion was gravely
brought forward by Archbishop Usher, who was
indeed its principal fabricator. But the Right
Rev. Dr. Milner has distinctly shown that there is
the most conclusive historical evidence in the works

of Usher himself, to demonstrate the utter falsehood of his own assertion. And there is a curious incident belonging to this controversy which occurred before Milner wrote; namely, that the credit of Usher's assertion having been much impugned, a grandson of his, a Protestant Clergyman, determined to confute the impugners of his grandfather's statement; and, with that view, carefully examined the authorities upon the subject; when, to his utmost surprise, he discovered the total falsehood of that statement! Being led by this circumstance to examine the other points of difference between the Catholics and Protestants, he ended by giving up his living, resigning his gown as a Protestant clergyman, and embracing the profession of a Catholic priest.

It has been often remarked that in all the countries into which Protestantism entered, it owed its introduction to men remarkable for the badness of their character and the greatness of their vices. Protestantism was not more fortunate in Ireland than it was elsewhere. It owed its introduction into Ireland, as it did into England, to the foul passions of Henry the Eighth; but in Ireland its principal patron was *Archbishop* Browne, (as he is called; but his title to the *Arch*bishopric would not have stood canonical investigation.) The Act of Supremacy—that act which so absurdly vested in the King—and such a king—spiritual power—was

passed by a gross and glaring fraud. The proctors
of the clergy had, from the commencement of the
parliaments held in Ireland, been received as members of that body. It would have been impossible
to pass the Act of Supremacy if *they* had remained
in the house. Henry the Eighth made short work
of the matter—he expelled them! He procured then
an Act of Parliament making it high treason to *dispute* the validity of the marriage of the wretched
Ann Boleyn, or the legitimacy of her child. He
soon afterwards procured another Act of Parliament by which it was made treason to *assert* that
validity or legitimacy! That was the mode in
which Protestantism was made the law of the land!

It is curious enough that the Act of Uniformity
was passed in Ireland by another gross and ludicrous trick. The historian* informs us, that—

" It was passed by the artifice of one Mr. Stany-
    " hurst of Corduff, then Speaker of the Irish
    " Commons, who, being in the reforming
    " interest, privately got together, on a day
    " when the house was not to sit, a few such
    " members as he knew to be favourers of
    " that interest, and consequently in the ab-
    " sence of all those who he believed would
    " have opposed it. But that these absent
    " members having understood what passed

---

* Mr. Lynch, in his Cambrensis Eversus.

" at that secret convention, did soon after,
" in a full and regular meeting of the parlia-
" ment, enter their protests against it : upon
" which the Lord Lieutenant assured many
" of them in particular, with protestations
" and oaths, that the penalties of that statute
" should never be inflicted ; which they, too
" easily believing, suffered it to remain as
" it was. This, adds my author, I have often
" heard for certain truth from many ancient
" people, who lived at that time ; and I am
" the more inclined to believe it, because
" the Lord Lieutenant's promise was so far
" kept that this law was never generally
" executed during the remainder of Queen
" Elizabeth's reign ;—' that is,' observes
" Curry on the foregoing passage, ' until
" all, or most of those members were pro-
" bably dead, to whom such promise had
" been given.'
" Sir Christopher Nugent asserted publicly be-
" fore the King, the traditional report of the
" Irish, that this statute was passed in the
" fraudulent manner above mentioned."—
Analecta Sacra, p. 431.

It is right to observe that these Acts of Parliament were operative only upon a small portion of
the inhabitants of Ireland ; only ten counties being
represented, and the entire number of members of

the House of Commons did not exceed from sixty
to eighty.   It is unnecessary to say, that so far as
the English dominion extended, persecution was
vigorous. The utmost cruelty was exercised to the
extent of the power of the English Government.
Doctor Johnson says that there is no instance even
in the ten persecutions equal to the severity which
the Protestants of Ireland have exercised against
the Catholics.   This is literally true wherever the
English power extended.   The reign of Edward
the Sixth was marked by the intensity with which
the system of attempting to Protestantize Ireland
was carried on.

Take this specimen:—

" The means of conversion which the Protector
(Somerset) " designed to use in Ireland,
" were soon exemplified.   A party, issuing
" from the garrison of Athlone, attacked
" the ancient church of Clonmacnoise, de-
" stroyed its ornaments, and defiled its altars.
" Similar excesses were committed in other
" parts of the country ; and the first impres-
" sion produced by the advocates of the
" reformed religion was, that the new sys-
" tem sanctioned sacrilege and robbery."—
*Taylor's Hist. of the Civil Wars of Ire-
land,* vol. I. p. 167.

But it was in the reign of Elizabeth that the persecution of the Catholics raged with the greatest

fury; as the policy of her officers in creating their familiar instruments of famine and pestilence extended her dominion, religious persecution extended with it. Amongst the multitude of Catholic priests who were murdered in the most barbarous manner, I give two specimens in the following extracts. The first is from Curry's *Review of the Civil Wars of Ireland;* p. 9 (note) :—

"In this reign, among many other Roman
"Catholic priests and bishops, there were
"put to death for the exercise of their func-
"tion in Ireland, Glaby O'Boyle, abbot of
"Boyle of the diocese of Elphin, and Owen
"O'Mulkeren, abbot of the monastery of the
"Holy Trinity in that diocese, hanged and
"quartered by Lord Gray in 1580; John
"Stephens, priest, for that he said mass to
"Teague M'Hugh, was hanged and quar-
"tered by the Lord Burroughs in 1597;
"Thady O'Boyle, guardian of the monastery
"of Donegal, was slain by the English in his
"own monastery; six friars were slain in the
"monastery of Moynihigan; John O'Calyhor
"and Bryan O'Trevor, of the order of St.
"Bernard, were slain in their own monas-
"tery, de Santa Maria, in Ulster; as also
"Felimy O'Hara, a lay brother; so was
"Eneas Penny, parish priest of Killagh,
"slain at the altar in his parish church

"there; Cahall M'Goran, Rory O'Don-
"nellan, Peter O'Quillan, Patrick O'Kenna,
"George Power, vicar-general of the dio-
"cese of Ossory, Andrew Stretch of Lime-
"rick, Bryan O'Muirihirtagh, vicar-general
"of the diocese of Clonfert, Dorohow
"O'Molony of Thomond, John Kelly of
"Louth, Stephen Patrick of Annaly, John
"Pillis, friar, Rory M'Henlea, Tirrilagh
"M'Inisky, a lay brother. All those that
"come after Eneas Penny, together with
"Walter Farnan, priest, died in the Castle
"of Dublin, either through hard usage and
"restraint, or the violence of torture."—
Curry's Historical Review, chap. 2 (note).
My next extract is from Milner's *Letters to a
Prebendary :—*
"The penal laws were in general no less severely
"exercised against the Catholics of Ireland,
"though they constituted the body of the
"people, than they were against those of
"England. Spondanus and Pagi relate the
"horrid cruelties exercised by Sir William
"Drury on F. O'Hurle, O. S. F., the Catho-
"lic Archbishop of Cashel, who, falling into
"the hands of this sanguinary governor in
"the year 1579, was first tortured by his
"legs being immersed in jack boots filled
"with quick lime, water, &c. until they were

" burnt to the bone, in order to force him
" to take the oath of Supremacy, and then,
" with other circumstances of barbarity, exe-
" cuted on the gallows; having previously
" cited Drury to meet him at the tribunal
" of Christ within ten days, who accordingly
" died within that period, amidst the most
" excruciating pains. See in Bourke's *Hi-*
" *bernia Dominicana*, a much longer list
" and a more detailed account of Irish suf-
" ferers, especially in Elizabeth's reign, on
" the score of religion. IT WAS A USUAL
" THING TO BEAT WITH STONES THE SHORN
" HEADS OF THEIR CLERGY, TILL THEIR
" BRAINS GUSHED OUT. Others had needles
" thrust under their nails, or the nails them-
" selves were torn off. Many were stretched
" upon the rack, or pressed under weights.
" Others had their bowels torn open, which
" they were obliged to support with their
" hands, or their flesh torn with curry-
" combs."—*Milner's Letters to a Prebendary*, Letter IV. (note.)

The following anecdote I have taken from the
often quoted work of Carew :—

" Towards the end of Queen Elizabeth's reign,
" her Majesty's forces besieging the castle of
" Cloghan, and understanding that in the
" same there was a Romish priest," (to

which order of men they never gave quarter,) "having also in their hands the brother
" of the constable who had the charge of
" the castle, the commanding officer sent
" him word that if he did not presently sur-
" render the castle to him, he would hang
" his brother in their sight. But to save
" the priest, whose life they tendered, they
" persevered obstinately not to yield: where-
" upon the officer, in their sight, hanged the
" constable's brother. Nevertheless, within
" four days afterwards, the priest being
" shifted away in safety, the constable sued
" for a protection, and surrendered the
" castle."—*Pacata Hibernia,* p. 358.

The remarks of this author are quite characteristic ; he thus continues :—

" I do relate this accident, to the end that the
" reader may the more clearly see in what
" reverence and estimation these ignorant
" and superstitious Irish do hold a popish
" priest ; in regard to whose safety the con-
" stable was content to suffer his brother to
" perish."

How totally does Carew forget that the murder
of the constable's brother was the crime of the en-
lightened English officer! Whereas the "ignorant
and superstitious" Irish commander had too much
conscience to be accessory to the murder of an in-

nocent man—a man who had committed no crime
except that of being a priest! Ignorant and superstitious, indeed! I readily retort the charge with
a small variation! The English commander and
the English writer are utterly ignorant of every rule
of morality, and are alike brutal and unprincipled
in the act and in the comment.

But there is a contrast of still a higher and more
glorious nature. It is the contrast between the
virulent and murderous persecution of the English
Protestant Government, and the humane and truly
Christian demeanour of the Irish Catholics when
restored to power. The reigns of Henry the Eighth
and Edward the Sixth passed away. Queen Mary
ascended the throne. Catholicity was restored to
power in Ireland without difficulty—without any
kind of struggle. How did the Catholics—the Irish
Catholics—conduct themselves towards the Protestants, who had been persecuting them up to the
last moment? How did they—the Catholics—conduct themselves? I will take the answer from a
book, published several years ago by Mr. William
Parnell—a Protestant gentleman of high station—
the brother of a Cabinet Minister:—

> " A still more striking proof that the Irish
> " Roman Catholics, in Queen Mary's
> " reign, were very little infected with
> " religious bigotry, may be drawn from
> " their conduct towards the Protestants,

" when the Protestants were at their
" mercy.

" Were we to argue from the representations of
" the indelible character of the Catholic re-
" ligion, as pourtrayed by its adversaries,
" we should have expected that the Irish
" Catholics would exercise every kind of
" persecution which the double motives of
" zeal and retaliation could suggest:—the
" Catholic laity, in all the impunity of tri-
" umphant bigotry, hunting the wretched
" heretics from their hiding places—the
" Catholic clergy pouring out the libation
" of human blood at the shrine of the God
" of mercy, and acting before high heaven
" those scenes which make the angels weep.

" But on the contrary—though the religious
" feelings of the Irish Catholics, and their
" feelings as men, had been treated with
" very little ceremony during two prece-
" ding reigns, they made a wise and mode-
" rate use of their ascendency. THEY EN-
" TERTAINED NO RESENTMENT FOR THE PAST:
" THEY LAID NO PLANS FOR FUTURE DOMI-
" NATION.

" Even Leland allows that the only instance of
" popish zeal, was annulling grants that
" Archbishop Browne had made, to the in-
" jury of the See of Dublin; and certainly

" this step was full as agreeable to the rules
" of law and equity, as to popish zeal.
" The assertors of the Reformation during the
" preceding reigns, were every way unmo-
" lested ; or, as the Protestant historian
" chooses to term it, *were allowed to sink*
" *into obscurity and neglect.*
" Such was the general spirit of toleration, that
" MANY ENGLISH FAMILIES, FRIENDS TO THE
" REFORMATION, TOOK REFUGE IN IRELAND,
" AND THERE ENJOYED THEIR OPINIONS AND
" WORSHIP WITHOUT MOLESTATION.
" The Irish Protestants, vexed that they could not
" prove a single instance of bigotry against
" the Catholics, in this their hour of trial,
" invented a tale, as palpably false as it is
" childish, of an *intended* persecution, (but
" a persecution by the English Government,
" *not* by the Irish Catholics,) and so much
" does bigotry pervert all candour and taste,
" that even the Earl of Cork, Archbishop
" Usher, and in later times, Doctor Leland,
" were not ashamed to support the silly story
" of Dean Cole and the Knave of Clubs !
" How ought these perverse and superficial men
" to blush, who have said that the Irish Ro-
" man Catholics must be bigots and rebels
" from the very nature of their religion, and
" who have advanced this falsehood in the

" very teeth of fact, and contrary to the
" most distinct evidence of history !
" The Irish Roman Catholics bigots?   THE
" IRISH ROMAN CATHOLICS ARE THE ONLY
" SECT THAT EVER RESUMED POWER WITH-
" OUT EXERCISING VENGEANCE !
" Show a brighter instance, if you can, in the
" whole page of history.   Was this the con-
" duct of Knox or Calvin ? or of the brutal
" council of Edward VI., who signed its
" bloody warrants with tears ?   *Has this*
" *been the conduct of the Irish Protestants?*"
—*Parnell's Historical Apology*, pp. 35—37.
In the wretched history of dissension and cruelty
from the period of the Reformation to the present
moment, there is no instance in which any people,
Catholic or Protestant, have been entitled to such
a meed of approbation as the Irish Catholics.
There is no other such instance. Protestantism
can boast of nothing of the kind—nor can the
Catholics of any other state in the known world,
give such a practical proof of Christian liberality.
What a contrast between the English and the Irish
Catholics. You find the *English* Protestants flying
from *English* Catholic persecution, and receiving
refuge, shelter, and security in Ireland. Queen
Mary's persecution of Protestants leaned very heavily on Bristol. And, accordingly, the merchants
of Dublin, being Catholics, and then forming the

corporation, are known to have hired no less than seventy-four furnished houses which they filled with English Protestant refugees from Bristol and its vicinage. They lodged them,—they fed them— they maintained them, and sent them back safe and sound to England, when the death of Mary restored Protestantism to power there : and enabled the English Protestants to retaliate with sevenfold severity on their Catholic countrymen ; and— shame upon English Protestants to make use of that power—again unrelentingly to persecute the generous and liberal Catholics of Ireland !

Let me give another quotation from a modern Protestant writer of very considerable literary merit and discrimination. When this writer comes to treat of the reign of Queen Mary, he has the following passage :—

1553. " The restoration of the old religion was " effected without violence : no persecution " of the Protestants was attempted ; and SE- " VERAL OF THE ENGLISH, WHO " FLED FROM THE FURIOUS ZEAL " OF MARY'S INQUISITORS, FOUND " A SAFE RETREAT AMONG THE " CATHOLICS OF IRELAND. It is " but justice to this maligned body to add, " that on the three occasions of their obtain- " ing the upper hand, THEY NEVER " INJURED A SINGLE PERSON IN

"LIFE OR LIMB FOR PROFESSING
"A RELIGION DIFFERENT FROM
"THEIR OWN. They had suffered per-
"secution and learned mercy, as they
"showed in the reign of Mary, in the wars
"from 1641 to 1648, and during the brief
"triumph of James II."—*Taylor's History
of the Civil Wars of Ireland*, vol. I. p. 169.
I cannot better conclude my observations upon
Catholic liberality, than by giving an extract from
the historian Leland; whose prejudices and whose
interests made him necessarily most inimical to the
Catholic people and their religion. He, in fact,
confirms every thing I have said respecting the liberality exhibited by the Irish Catholics during the
melancholy reign of Queen Mary. If anything
could silence the rancorous malignity with which
the Irish people are persecuted in their character as
well as in their property, it would be this distinct
admission of their perfect tolerance to Protestants
during the reign of Queen Mary; an admission
proceeding from so powerful an adversary as Dr.
Leland. I give his words :—

"The spirit of popish zeal, which glutted all its
"vengeance in England, *was, in Ireland*
"*thus happily* CONFINED *to reversing*
"*the acts of an obnoxious prelate*," (namely,
Browne, the Protestant Archbishop of
Dublin,) "and stigmatizing his offspring

" with an opprobrious name. Those asser-
" tors of the Reformation who had not fled
" from this kingdom, were by the lenity of
" the Irish Government suffered to sink into
" obscurity and neglect. No warm adver-
" saries of popery stood forth to provoke the
" severity of persecution : the whole nation
" seemed to have relapsed into the stupid
" composure of ignorance and superstition,
" from which it had scarcely awakened.
" And as it thus escaped the effects of Mary's
" diabolical rancour, SEVERAL ENGLISH FA-
" MILIES, FRIENDS TO THE REFORMATION,
" FLED INTO IRELAND, AND THERE ENJOYED
" THEIR OPINIONS AND WORSHIP IN PRIVACY,
" WITHOUT NOTICE OR MOLESTATION."—*Leland's History of Ireland,* Book III. c. 8.

The following quotations may appear to derogate
from the merit of the Irish in resisting the spread
of that religious devastation called the Reformation.
But the facts which they record, are so characteristic of the English Protestantism of that period,
that I cannot refrain from placing them before the
public. The first of my quotations refers to the
Protestant bishops ; and the reader will, I think,
smile, at the readiness with which the author, no
less a man than the great Poet Spenser, divulges the
excuse of the Protestant prelates for appropriating
the tithes to themselves. One would imagine, that

if there were *no* clergymen fit to be recipients of the tithes, there ought not to be any tithes paid at all. If the people were not even *offered* anything in the semblance of value for the tithes, one would think the tithes should not be demanded from them. But the poetic Spenser, agreeing with the prosaic Stanley of the present day, is of a clean contrary opinion; and thinks that whether there be prayers or no prayers—religion or no religion—parsons or no parsons—still the tithes! the tithes! the tithes! ought at all events, and in every contingency, to fatten the bishops, even if there were no parsons to browse upon them :—

"Some of them" (the Protestant bishops) "whose "dioceses are in remote parts, somewhat out "of the world's eye, doe not at all bestowe "the benefices which are in their own do- "nation, upon any, *but keepe them in their* "*owne hands*, and set their own servants "and horse-boys to take up the tithes and "fruites of them; with the which, some of "them *purchase great lands, and build* "*faire castells upon the same.* Of which "abuse if any question be moved, they have "a very seemly colour and excuse, THAT "THEY HAVE NO WORTHY MINISTERS TO BE- "STOW THEM UPON !!!"—*Spenser*, 140.

It thus appearing that the talismanic word "Tithes" was mixed up with every evolution of

Protestantism, whether there were clergymen or none—good, bad, or indifferent—let us now look to the case in which there *were* actually parsons to receive the tithes ; and let us estimate their merits from Spenser's testimony.   Speaking of the Protestant clergy of Ireland, he says—

> " Whatever disorders you see in the Church of
> " England, you finde there, and many more.
> " Namely, *gross simony, greedy covetous-*
> " *ness, fleshly incontinence, carelesse sloath,*
> " and *generally all disordered life in the*
> " *common clergymen.*"—*Spenser*, 139.

Such is Spenser's character of the Protestant clergy of his day.

Let us now see what character this zealous Protestant witness gives to the Catholic clergy.   We shall find—I say it triumphantly !—that they bore the same character for zeal and piety in that day as they do at present, and occasionally extorted the praises of even their bitterest enemies.   Here is what Spenser says of them, when contrasting their conduct with that of the Protestant ministers ; one would really imagine it was some candid enemy at the present day who speaks !

> " It is greate wonder to see the oddes which is
> " betweene the zeale of popish priests, and
> " the ministers of the gospel ; for they spare
> " not to come out of Spayne, from Rome,
> " and from Remes, by long toile and dan-

" gerous travayling hither, *where they know*
"*perill of deathe awayteth them*, and no
" reward or riches is to be found, only to
" draw the people unto the Church of Rome:
" whereas some of our idle ministers, having
" a way for credit and estimation thereby
" opened unto them, and having the livings
" of the country offered to them, without
" paines and without perill, will neither for
" the same, nor any love of God, nor zeale
" for religion, or for all the good they may
" doe by winning soules to God, be drawne
" forth from their warm nests to looke out
" into God's harvest."—*Spenser*, 254.

The character given of the Protestant clergy of
that period by Carte, is as follows ; it fully accords
with the statement of Spenser :—
    " The clergy of the Established Church were
      " generally ignorant and unlearned, loose
      " and irregular in their lives and con-
      " versations, negligent of their cures, and
      " very careless of observing uniformity
      " and decency in divine worship."—*Carte*,
    I. 68.

Notwithstanding the ignorance and immorality
of the law-established clergy, they could occasionally exhibit a sufficiency of anti-Catholic zeal to
blaspheme and insult our Divine Redeemer, by
outraging the memorials of him which are held sa-

cred and venerable among the Catholics. I give a specimen :—

"One Hewson, an English minister of Swords, "fell violently on one Horish of that place, "*and took from him a crucifix, and hung* "*the same upon a gallows with these words* "*under it*, 'HELP, ALL STRANGERS, FOR "THE GOD OF THE PAPISTS IS IN DANGER.' "Upon Horish's complaining to the State, "and producing the mangled and defaced "crucifix, Sir Geoffry Fenton, Secretary, "insulted the poor man, snatched the cruci- "fix from him, and *cast it on the ground* "*under his feet;* and Horish for offering "to complain of that abuse, was thrown into "prison."—*Theatre of Catholic and Protestant Religions*, p. 117.

The memorials of our Saviour appear to have been particularly offensive to the refined piety of this Sir Geoffry Fenton :—

"The same Sir Geoffry Fenton did set a poor "fellow on the pillory in Dublin *with the* "*picture of Christ about his neck*, for "having carried the same before a dead "friend at his funeral."—*Ibid*, page 118.

A better idea may be conceived of the virulence of the persecution of the Irish Catholics during the reign of Queen Elizabeth, if we refer for one moment to her sanguinary proceedings against the

Catholics of the more favoured portion of the empire—England. Upon this subject I may refer to
the authority of a Catholic writer ; especially as,
the accuracy of his statements stood the test of the
adverse criticism of an able and virulent adversary
—Doctor Sturges. In the seventh edition of Dr.
Milner's celebrated work entitled " Letters to a
Prebendary," pp. 95, 96, there occurs the following passage :—

"I have," says Dr. Milner, " collected the names
" of 204 persons executed on that sole ac-
" count," [viz. for being Catholics,] " chiefly
" within the last 20 years of Elizabeth's
" reign. Of this number 142 were priests,
" three were gentlewomen, and the remain-
" der esquires, gentlemen, and yeomen.
" Amongst them 15 were condemned for
" denying the Queen's spiritual supremacy,
" 126 for the exercise of the priestly func-
" tions, and the rest for being reconciled to
" the Catholic faith, or for being aiding and
" abetting to priests. Besides these, I find
" a particular account, together with most
" of the names of 90 priests or Catholic lay
" persons who died in prison, in the same
" reign, and of 105 others, who were sent into
" perpetual banishment. I say nothing of
" many more who were whipped, fined, or
" stripped of their property, to the utter

" ruin of their families. In one night, 50
" Catholic gentlemen in the county of Lan-
" caster, were suddenly seized and commit-
" ted to prison on account of their non-
" attendance at church. About the same
" time, I find an equal number of Yorkshire
" gentlemen lying prisoners in York Castle
" on the same account, most of whom per-
" ished there. These were every week, for
" a twelvemonth together, dragged by main
" force to hear the established service per-
" formed in the castle chapel. An account
" was published by a contemporary writer,"
(Dr. Bridgewater,) " of 1200 Catholics, who
" had been in some sort or other victims of
" this persecution *previously to the year*
" 1588; *that is to say, during the period*
" *of its greatest lenity.*"—*Milner's Letters
to a Prebendary,* Letter IV.

To show the intensity of the persecution and the
horrible nature of the cruelties inflicted by Protestant Elizabeth and her Protestant advisers, I add
the following extract. Dr. Milner thus addresses
his antagonist, the Rev. Dr. Sturges :—

" Since, Sir, you oblige me to enter upon this
" disgusting subject, I must tell you, with
" respect to the greater part of Catholic vic-
" tims, that the sentence of the law was
" strictly and literally executed upon them.

" After being hanged up, they were cut
" down alive, dismembered, ripped up, and
" their bowels literally burned before their
" faces, after which they were beheaded and
" quartered! The time employed in this
" butchery was very considerable, and in
" one instance, lasted above half an hour.
" I must add, that a great number of these
" sufferers, as well as other Catholics, who
" did not endure capital punishment, were
" racked in the most severe and wanton
" manner, in order to extort proofs against
" themselves or their brethren."—*Ibid*,
Letter IV.

It is an object of painful curiosity to contemplate
the modes in which men tortured each other in the
sacred and holy name of Religion. The following
succinct summary, given in a note to Letter IV. of
the " Letters to a Prebendary," will afford a further
idea of the familiar instruments of Protestant persecution in the reign of Queen Elizabeth :—

" Camden, in his *Annals*, speaking of the famous
" F. Campian, says, '*that he was not so*
" *racked but that he was still capable of*
" *signing his name.*' It appears, from the
" account of one of these sufferers,* that

---

* Campian, Brian, Cottam, Sherwood, &c.

"the following tortures were in use against
"Catholics in the Tower: 1. The common
"rack, in which the limbs were stretched
"by levers. 2. The *Scavenger's Daughter*,
"so called, being like a hoop, in which the
"body was bent until the head and feet met
"together. 3. The chamber, called *Little*
"*Ease*, being a hole so small that a person
"could neither stand, sit, nor lie straight in
"it. 4. The *Iron Gauntlets.*"—*Diar. Rer.*
Gest. in Turri Lond.

"In some instances needles were thrust under
"the prisoners' nails. With what cruelty
"the Catholics were racked, we may gather
"from the following passage in a letter from
"John Nicholls to Cardinal Allen by way
"of extenuating the guilt of his apostacy
"and his perfidy in accusing his Catholic
"brethren : '*Non bona res est corpus isto*
"*cruciato longius fieri per duos ferè pedes*
"*quam natura concessit.*' Sir Owen Hop-
"ton, Lieutenant of the Tower, was com-
"monly the immediate instrument in these
"cruelties ; but sometimes Elmer, Bishop
"of London, directed them. On one occa-
"sion he caused a young lady of good birth
"to be cruelly scourged, when he could not
"prevail on her to attend the public service."
I cannot help remarking that nothing was ever

more unfounded than the notion that Protestantism
was favourable to freedom of conscience ; or that
Protestants were not persecutors. The contrary is
directly the fact. Protestants not only persecuted
Catholics, but they persecuted each other to the
death. It is worth while to read the notes on this
subject in Doctor Milner's book, appended to
" Letter IV." pp. 65, 66, of the seventh edition. I
quote the following :—

SCOTLAND.

" The Reformation may be said to have begun
" there by the assassination of Cardinal
" Beatoun, in which Knox was a party, and
" to which Fox, in his *Acts and Monuments*,
" says the murderers were instigated ' *by the*
" *Spirit of God.*' In 1560, the parliament
" at one and the same time, decreed the
" establishment of Calvinism, and the pun-
" ishment of death against the ancient re-
" ligion. ' With such indecent haste,' says
" Robertson, ' did the very persons who
" had just escaped ecclesiastical tyranny
" proceed to imitate the example.' *(Hist. of*
" *Scotland.)* See also the answer of the
" Presbytery to the King and Council in
" 1596, concerning the Catholic Earls of
" Huntly, Errol, &c., viz. that ' as they '
" (the earls) ' had been guilty of *idolatry*,

M 2

" a crime deserving of death, the civil power
" could not spare them.' "

FRANCE.

" In France, it is well known that wherever the
" Huguenots carried their victorious arms
" against their sovereign, they prohibited
" the exercise of the Catholic religion,
" slaughtered the priests and religious;
" burnt the churches and convents; dug up
" the dead to make bullets of their leaden
" coffins, &c. See *Maimbourg, Hist. Cal-*
" *vinism ; Thuanus, Hist.* L. xxxi. One
" of their own writers, Nicholas Froumen-
" teau, confesses, that *in the single pro-*
" *vince of Dauphiny they killed* 256 *priests,*
" *and* 112 *monks or friars. (Liv. de*
" *France.)* In these scenes the famous
" Baron Des Adrets signalized his barba-
" rity; forcing his Catholic prisoners to
" jump from the towers upon the pikes of
" his soldiers; *and obliging his own chil-*
" *dren to wash their hands in the blood of*
" *the Catholics.*"

THE LOW COUNTRIES.

" Dr. Sturges speaks with horror of the persecu-
" tion of the Protestants in the Low Coun-
" tries by the Duke of Alva, who, he says,

" 'boasted that he had delivered 18,000
" 'heretics' (he should have said *heretics*
" OR rebels, see Brandt) 'to the executioner.'
" I heartily join with him in condemning
" and execrating the sanguinary vengeance
" of the Spanish Governor and Government
" against their seditious subjects of the Cal-
" vinistical persuasion ; but to form an ade-
" quate judgment of this case, it is proper
" to attend to the provocations which the
" former had received from the latter. Not
" to mention the conspiracy of Carli and
" Risot to assassinate the Duke of Alva
" himself at the monastery of Groonfeldt
" near Brussels, it is certain that one class
" of the Reformers had endeavoured to erect
" the same fanatical and bloody kingdom in
" Holland, which John of Leyden actually
" established at Munster, crying out that
" *God had given up the country to them,*
" *and that vengeance awaited all who would*
" *not join them.* It was an ordinary thing
" with them to assault the clergy in the dis-
" charge of their functions ; and the air re-
" sounded with their cries of *kill the priests,*
" *kill the monks, kill the magistrates.*
" These violences became more common as
" the Reformation extended itself wider.
" Wherever Vandermerck and Sonoi, both

" of them lieutenants to the Prince of
" Orange, carried their arms, they uni-
" formly put to death in cold blood all the
" priests and religious they could lay their
" hands upon, as at Oudenarde, Ruremond,
" Dort, Middlebourg, Delft, and Shonoven.
" See *Hist. Ref. des Pays Bas*, by the
" Protestant Minister De Brandt; also
" Dr. Patinson in his *Jerusalem and Babel*,
" p. 385. A late celebrated biographer,
" Feller, *Dict. Hist. Art. Toledo*, says that
" Vandermerck slaughtered more unoffen-
" ding Catholic priests and peasants in the
" year 1572, than Alva executed Protestants
" during his whole government. He gives
" us, in the same passage, a copious extract
" from *L'Abrége de l'Histoire de la Hol-
" lande*, par Monsieur Kerroux, in which
" this Protestant writer, who professes to
" write from judicial records still extant,
" draws a most frightful picture of the in-
" fernal barbarities of Sonoi on the Catholic
" peasants of North Holland. He says that
" some of these, after undergoing the tor-
" ments of scourges and the rack, were en-
" veloped in sheets of linen that had been
" steeped in spirits of wine, which being in-
" flamed, they were miserably scorched to
" death; that others, after being tortured

" with burning sulphur and torches in the
" tenderest parts of their bodies, were made
" to die for want of sleep, executioners being
" placed on guard over them to beat and
" torment them with clubs and other weapons
" whenever exhausted nature seemed ready
" to sink into forgetfulness ; that several of
" them were fed with nothing but salt her-
" rings, without a drop of water or any
" other liquid, until they expired with thirst;
" finally, that others were stung to death by
" wasps, or devoured by rats, which were
" confined in coffins with them.   Amongst
" the cruelties there recounted, are some of
" so indecent a nature that they will not
" bear repeating ; and those which occur
" above are only mentioned, to induce Dr.
" Sturges and other writers of his class, to
" join me in burying the odious names
" of Alva and Sonoi in equal oblivion.
" Amongst the more illustrious foreign
" Protestants, *who suffered death by the*
" *violence of other Protestants*, it may be
" proper to mention the names of Servetus,
" Gentilis, Felix Mans, Rotman, Barnevelt,
" &c., not to mention Bolsec, Grotius,
" and others, who were banished, or other-
" wise persecuted for their religious opi-
" nions."

ENGLAND.

" The following is a more circumstantial account
" of the persecution which some Protestants
" have exercised upon others in this country,
" than is contained in the passage above
" quoted.   In the reign of Edward VI. in
" the year 1550, six Anabaptists were con-
" demned by Archbishop Cranmer, some
" of whom recanted and carried faggots in
" sign of their having *merited* burning; and
" one of them, a woman, Joan Knell, was
" actually burned alive.   The following year
" George Paris was condemned, and suffered
" in the same manner.   See Stow's *Annals*.
" During the reign of Elizabeth, in the year
" 1573, Peter Burchet, a gentleman of the
" Middle Temple, was examined on the
" score of heresy by Edward Sands, Bishop
" of London, but recanted his opinions.
" In 1575, twenty-seven heretics were at
" one time, eleven at another, and five at
" a third, condemned for their errors, most
" of them by the same Protestant Bishop.
" Of these, 20 were whipped and banished;
" others bore their faggots; and two of
" them, John Peterson and Henry Turwort,
" were burned to death in Smithfield.   In
" 1583, John Lewes, 'for denying the

" Godhead of Christ,' says Stow, was burned
" at Norwich ; at which place also, Francis
" Kett, M.A., suffered the same kind of
" death for similar opinions, in 1589. Two
" years afterwards, William Hackett was
" hanged for heresy in Cheapside. Five
" others suffered death in this reign for
" being Brownists, viz., Thacker, Copping,
" Greenwood, Barrow, and Penry. The
" above particulars may be seen in Stow,
" Brandt, Limborch, Collier, Neal, &c.
" Under James I., Legat and Whitman were
" executed for Arianism. In the time of
" Charles I., the Dissenters complained
" loudly of their sufferings, and particularly
" that four of their number, Leighton, Bur-
" ton, Prynne, and Bastwick, were cropped
" of their ears and set in the pillory. *Lim-*
" *borch, Hist. of Inquisition ; Neal, &c.*
" When the Presbyterians afterwards got
" the upper hand, they continued to put
" Catholics to death, and treated those of
" the former establishment with almost equal
" severity ; at the same time appointing
" days of humiliation and fasting, to beg
" God's pardon for not being more into-
" lerant. See *Neal, Hist. of Puritans;* also
" *Hist. of Churches of England and Scot-*
" *land,* vol. III. The editor of De Laune's

" *Plea for Non-Conformists,* says, that this
" writer was one of 8,000 Protestant Dis-
" senters, who ' *perished in prison in that*
" *single reign,*' (viz. of Charles II.) '*merely*
" *for dissenting from the Church.*'   Pre-
" *face,* p. 2.   He adds, ' that one of their
" people, Mr. White, had carefully collected
" a list of the sufferings of the Dissenters ;
" that the Catholics, in the reign of James
" II., offered him bribes to obtain this list;
" that he rejected the offer, to prevent the
" black record from rising up in judgment
" against the Church ; and that the dignified
" prelates sent thanks and money to Mr.
" White, in reward for his services.'   For
" the capital punishments and other suffer-
" ings of the Quakers, see *Penn's Life of*
" *George Fox,* folio."—*Milner's Letters to
a Prebendary,* Letter IV. (note.)

The subject of the change of religion and the
persecutions attending on it, have necessarily
compelled me to condense here the cruelties of
several reigns, and to range beyond the period
embraced in my first chapter, to which the present notes and illustrations should more properly
belong.

The treachery, the cruelty, the infernal injustice
of every shape and kind, whereby Elizabeth and
her followers obtained the dominion of Ulster, will

be elucidated by further extracts from Protestant
historians.

Ere I close these evidences on the subject of religious persecution, I shall give, from the Statute
Book, the following abridged record of the penal
Acts passed against the Catholics of England;
from which the reader can form his own judgment
of Protestant toleration in that country from 1548
to 1791 :—

ABSTRACT OF ACTS OF PARLIAMENT MADE IN ENG-
LAND ON THE SUBJECT OF RELIGION, FROM THE
YEAR 1548 TO THE YEAR 1791.

1548.

Any parson, vicar, or other minister, refusing
to use the Book of Common Prayer, and
other rites and ceremonies according to the
use of the Church of England, or *using
any other manner* of prayer, or speaking
against the said Book of Common Prayer,
and being afterwards thereof three times
convicted, shall suffer imprisonment during
his life.

1551.

Every person shall resort to Church where
Common Prayer shall be used, upon pain
of punishment by the censures of the

Church. And any person hearing or being present at any manner or form of Common Prayer, of administration of the Sacraments, making of ministers, or of any rites, other than those set forth in the said Book of Common Prayer, shall suffer imprisonment during his or their lives.

1558.

THE QUEEN DECLARED TO BE SUPREME HEAD OF THE CHURCH; and all persons bearing promotions and offices, ecclesiastical or temporal, refusing to take the oath of Supremacy, disabled from retaining or exercising any such offices during life. Any person asserting the jurisdiction, spiritual or ecclesiastical, of any foreign prince, prelate, &c. as heretofore used within this kingdom, shall, with his abettors, be attainted, forfeit all his estates, and suffer PAINS OF DEATH, and other penalties and forfeitures, as in cases of high treason.

1563.

Any person refusing to take the oath of the Queen's Supremacy, to incur for the first such refusal, the danger, penalties, pains, and forfeitures ordained and provided by the statute of provisions and præmunire,

made in the 16th year of King Richard II.
Refusing the oath a second time declared to
be treason.

1581.

Statute enacting it to be treason to withdraw any
person from the religion established, to the
Romish religion. Treason to be reconciled
or withdrawn to the Romish religion. All
aiders to suffer as for misprision of treason.
Any person saying or wilfully hearing mass,
shall forfeit 200 marks, and suffer 12 months'
imprisonment.
Any person over the age of 16, not going to
Church or usual place of Common Prayer,
shall forfeit £20 English per month; and
should he absent himself still, he shall give
sufficient sureties for £200 at least, 'to
their good behaviour,' and shall so continue
bound until they conform themselves and
come to Church.
Any person keeping a schoolmaster who shall
not repair to the Established Church, shall
forfeit £10 per month.
Imprisonment in default of all the above pay-
ments.

1585.

All Jesuits, seminary and other priests remaining

in England, or entering the kingdom after
40 days, shall for such offence be adjudged
a traitor, and shall *suffer, lose, and forfeit,
as in case of high treason.*

Receiving or relieving any such persons shall be
a felony ; and sending money or relief to
such persons out of England shall be punished with the penalties of præmunire ; or
in other words, with transportation and forfeiture of property.

Note.—Numerous executions of priests, &c. took
place under this Act; and so late as the 30th of
June, 1640, when England and Scotland were
in arms for *liberty of conscience,* Rushworth
mentions as an ordinary occurrence, that one
MORGAN WAS HANGED, DRAWN, AND
QUARTERED AT TYBURN FOR HAVING
RECEIVED HOLY ORDERS IN THE CA-
THOLIC CHURCH beyond seas, and having,
in defiance of this Act, come into England.—
(Rushworth, IV. 305.)

1587.

Two-thirds of the lands and other estates of every
person refusing to go to Church, shall be
taken into the Queen's possession.

1593.

All recusants (*i. e.* persons refusing to conform

to the new State creed) shall give in their
names to the curate of the parish, who will
certify the same to the justices, in order to
take proceedings against them.   Any priest
refusing to acknowledge himself as such,
shall be committed to prison.

[Quere—wherein differed this from the Spanish
Inquisition?]

Any person over the age of sixteen years, refusing to go to Church, or impugning, by
speeches, the Queen's authority ecclesiastical, or persuading others not to go to
Church, or going to any other place of religious meeting, shall be committed to prison,
there to remain without bail or mainprize,
until they conform to the Church, and hear
Divine Service as established by law.

Any person offending against this Act, and not
coming in within three months, and con-
forming to the Church, must abjure and
depart out of the realm.   Refusal to do
so is declared felony, without benefit of
clergy.

Any person keeping in his house any one
who refuses to go to Church, shall forfeit
£10 per month for every person so refusing.

The lands and goods of persons forced to depart
out of the realm by this Act, shall be for-

feited to the Head of the State Church—the Sovereign.

1605.

Churchwardens to return monthly lists of persons refusing to attend Divine Service, and of their children above nine years of age. Justices to make proclamation that all such offenders surrender their bodies to the sheriff; monthly penalty £20 each, and two-thirds of their estates to be taken for the King.

Every bishop shall examine the persons in his diocess on oath; and he who shall refuse to answer upon oath, shall be committed to prison without bail or mainprize.

[N.B.—The Inquisition again!]

Any person aged above eighteen years refusing the oath of Supremacy, shall incur the danger and penalties of præmunire. No indictments of such persons shall be reversed for want of form.

Any person reconciling another to the Church of Rome, shall have judgment, suffer, and forfeit, as in cases of high treason!

The sheriff or other officer may break open any house wherein popish recusants shall be.

1609.

Every person above the age of eighteen shall take the oath of Supremacy. Any person refusing to do so, shall be committed to prison without bail or mainprize, until the assizes ; and if he then refuse, he shall incur the danger and penalty of præmunire, except women covert, who shall be committed to prison only, there to remain without bail or mainprise till they will take the said oath and conform, or until her husband pay to the King £10 per month, or the third part of all his estate.

[Here we have perjury—foul perjury—enforced by statute, under the penalty of præmunire. We may note, that such was the rigid execution of these infernal laws, that in 1626 we find Lord Scroop accused to the King of conniving at recusancy ; inasmuch as he had convicted *only* 1670 Catholics in the East riding of Yorkshire.]

1670.

Justices of the peace, constables, &c. empowered to break open doors where any meetings of a religious nature shall be held *in any other manner than according to the Liturgy and practice of the Church of England*. Fine of £20 on preacher for the first offence—

£40 for the second.   Fine of £20 on any
one permitting such meetings in his house.

1688.

The Declaration against Popery directed to be
tendered to all Papists, who, if they refuse
the same, shall forfeit and suffer as Papist
recusant converts, under the laws already
made since 1546, or otherwise banishment
or imprisonment for life, loss of estate, and
(in some cases) loss of life.

1700.

A reward of £100 for taking a popish bishop or
priest, and prosecuting him for saying mass,
or exercising any of his functions.

1736 AND 1757.

Statutes disabling any person refusing to take
the oaths of Supremacy, &c. and the Law-
Sacrament, from suing at law or in equity ;
from being the guardian of his children ;
from being executor or administrator, or from
taking by legacy or deed of gift ; such offender to forfeit the sum of £500.

The above is a very brief and imperfect abstract
of the persecuting laws enacted in England against
Catholics, and remaining on the Statute Book until
the year 1791.

OBSERVATIONS,
PROOFS, AND ILLUSTRATIONS.

CHAPTER II.—PART II.

WE have already seen, in the shape of an Act of
Parliament passed in the reign of Queen Elizabeth,
the ludicrous " Title" she claimed from King *Gurmond*, bless the mark ! ! We now must come to
more substantial horrors.

Let us hear the Rev. Doctor Leland. He will
tell us how James set up a title derived from Henry
II., to disturb possessions of more than 400 years'
standing, since the reign of that monarch.

The following extract, in which Leland has put
this matter in the most favourable point of view he
possibly could, will serve to give my English readers
a notion of the sort of justice the Irish found at the
hands of King James :—

" In the pursuit of this favourite object," (namely,
the " Plantation" of Ulster,) "*he*" (viz.
James) " *had sometimes recourse to claims*
" *which the old natives deemed obsolete and*
" *unjust.* The seizure of those lands, whose
" possessors *had lately meditated rebellion,*

" and fled from the sentence of the law,
" produced little clamour or murmuring.
" But when he recurred to the concessions
" made to Henry II., TO INVALIDATE THE
" TITLES DERIVED FROM A POSSESSION OF
" SOME CENTURIES, the *apparent severi-*
" *ty (! ! !)* had its full effect on those who
" were not acquainted with the refinements
" of law, AND NOT PREPOSSESSED IN FAVOUR
" OF THE EQUITY OF SUCH REFINEMENTS,
" WHEN EMPLOYED TO DIVEST THEM OF THEIR
" ANCIENT PROPERTY."—*Leland,* Book IV.
chap. 8.

This is the light manner in which Leland chooses
to treat the design of spoliation, which James and
his successors not only devised, but followed out
and carried into effect. I cannot use stronger language than Leland—even Leland himself!—has
used, in describing the process of this robbery
according to law. This is the way in which he
describes what he terms " the spirit of adventure ;"
he *ought* to have called it " the spirit of robbery,"
actuating hordes of foreign robbers to plunder the
people of Ireland :—

" It was an age of project and adventure : men's
" minds were particularly possessed with a
" passion for new discoveries, and planting
" of countries. They, who were too poor,
" or too spiritless to engage in more distant

"adventures, courted fortune in Ireland."
* * * "They obtained commissions of
"inquiry into defective titles, and grants
"of concealed lands and rents belonging to
"the Crown; the great benefit of which
"was generally to accrue to the projector,
"whilst the King was contented with an
"inconsiderable proportion of the conceal-
"ment, or a small advance of rent. *Disco-*
"*verers were every where busily employed*
"*in finding out flaws in men's titles to their*
"*estates.* The old pipe-rolls were searched
"to find the original rents with which they
"had been charged; the patent rolls in the
"tower of London were ransacked for the
"ancient grants; no means of industry or
"devices of craft were left untried, to force
"the possessors to accept of new grants at
"an advanced rent. In general, men were
"either conscious of defects in their titles,
"or alarmed at the trouble and expense of
"a contest with the Crown; or fearful
"of the issue of such a contest, at a time,
"and in a country where the prerogative
"was highly strained, and strenuously sup-
"ported by the Judges." * * * "THERE
"ARE NOT WANTING PROOFS OF THE MOST
"INIQUITOUS PRACTICES, OF HARDENED CRU-
"ELTY, OF VILE PERJURY AND SCANDALOUS

" SUBORNATION, EMPLOYED TO DESPOIL THE
" FAIR AND UNOFFENDING PROPRIETOR OF
" HIS INHERITANCE."—*Leland,* Book IV.
chap. 8.

There is nothing new under the sun. In the
reigns of George IV. and William IV. somewhat of
a similar inquiry was instituted by the Department
of the Woods and Forests. A man named Weale
was employed to search for defective titles in Ireland, and a great deal of plunder was obtained by
that means; and it is principally owing to acci-
dental causes that the plunder was not much more
extensive. People were foolish enough to ascribe
this persecuting inquiry into titles, to an Orange
disposition to render property in Ireland insecure.
That was all a mistake—there is nothing new under
the sun !

In proceeding to give some specimens of the
atrocious robberies perpetrated upon the Irish under
James I., it may be both instructive and interesting
to show how the family of Parsons, now Earls of
Rosse, acquired estates in Ireland. The present
earl has given some specimens of his disposition
towards the priests and people of Ireland : a disposition that would have done no discredit to his
plundering ancestors : although the day of plunder
in the same mode is gone by. Let the reader attend to the tale of the unfortunate Byrnes ; and he
will see how much it is in human nature that the

family of Parsons should not be kindly inclined to the natives of Ireland. At all events it is perfectly safe to say, that such a specimen as we are about to afford of the most scandalous and profligate plunder, could not have been exhibited in any other country than Ireland. It is thus recorded by the intelligent historian, Dr. Taylor:—

" One case may be quoted, as a specimen of Irish
" justice in those days. Bryan and Turlogh
" Byrne were the rightful owners of a tract
" in Leinster, called the Ranelaghs. Its
" vicinity to the capital made it a desirable
" plunder : and accordingly Parsons, Lord
" Esmond, and some others, determined
" that it should be forfeited. The Byrnes,
" however, had powerful interest in England,
" and obtained a patent grant of their lands
" from the King. Parsons and Esmond
" were not to be disappointed so easily : they
" flatly refused to pass the royal grant ; *and*
" *deeming the destruction of the Byrnes*
" *necessary to their safety, they had them*
" *arrested on a charge of treason.* The
" witnesses provided to support the charge,
" were Duffe, whom Turlogh Byrne, as a
" justice of the peace, had sent to prison for
" cow-stealing ; MacArt and MacGriffin,
" two notorious thieves; and a farmer named
" Archer. This last long resisted the at-

" tempts to force him to become a perjured
" witness, AND HIS OBSTINACY WAS PUNISHED
" BY THE MOST HORRIBLE TORTURES. HE
" WAS BURNED IN THE FLESHY PARTS OF THE
" BODY WITH HOT IRONS; PLACED ON A
" GRIDIRON OVER A CHARCOAL FIRE ; AND
" FINALLY FLOGGED UNTIL NATURE COULD
" SUPPORT HIM NO LONGER, AND HE PROMISED
" TO SWEAR ANYTHING THAT THE COMMIS-
" SIONERS PLEASED. Bills of indictment
" were presented to two successive grand
" juries in the county of Carlow, and at
" once ignored, as the suborned witnesses
" were unworthy of credit, and contradicted
" themselves and each other. FOR THIS
" OPPOSITION TO THE WILL OF GOVERNMENT,
" THE JURORS WERE SUMMONED TO THE STAR-
" CHAMBER IN DUBLIN, AND HEAVILY FINED.
" The witnesses, MacArt and MacGriffin,
" being no longer useful, were given up to
" the vengeance of the law. They were
" hanged for robbery at Kilkenny; and,
" with their dying breath, declared the in-
" nocence of the Byrnes.
" The ingenuity of Parsons and his accomplices
" was not yet exhausted. The Byrnes pre-
" sented themselves before the Court of
" King's Bench in Dublin to answer any
" charge that might be brought against them.

" No prosecutor appeared; and yet the
" Lord Chief Justice refused to grant their
" discharge. During two years, repeated
" orders were transmitted from England,
" directing that the Byrnes should be freed
" from further process, and restored to their
" estates; but the faction in the castle evaded
" and disobeyed every mandate. At length,
" on learning that the Duke of Richmond,
" the generous patron of the persecuted
" Irishmen, was dead, it was determined by
" Parsons to complete the destruction of the
" victims. He had before been baffled by
" the integrity of a grand jury; on this
" occasion he took proper precautions to
" prevent a similar disappointment. The
" bills were sent before the grand jurors
" of Wicklow, *the majority of whom had*
" *obtained grants of the Byrne property*,
" and all were intimately connected with the
" prosecutors. The evidence placed before
" this impartial body was the depositions of
" four criminals *who were pardoned on con-*
" *dition of giving evidence ; but even these*
" *wretches were not brought in person be-*
" *fore the jury*. Their depositions were
" taken in Irish by one of the prosecutors,
" and translated by one of his creatures.
" These suspicious documents, however,

" PROVED SUFFICIENT, AND THE BILLS WERE
" FOUND !
" To procure additional evidence, it was neces-
" sary to use expedients still more atrocious.
" A number of persons were seized, and
" subjected to the mockery of trial by *mar-*
" *tial law, though the regular courts were*
" *sitting.* THE MOST HORRID TOR-
" TURES WERE INFLICTED ON
" THOSE WHO REFUSED TO AC-
" CUSE THE BYRNES; AND SOME
" OF THE MOST OBSTINATE WERE
" PUNISHED WITH DEATH. But
" the firmness of the victims presented ob-
" stacles which were not overcome, before
" some virtuous Englishmen represented the
" affair so strongly to the King that he was
" shamed into interference. He sent over
" commissioners from England to investigate
" the entire affair. The Byrnes were brought
" before them, and honourably acquitted ;
" BUT PARSONS HAD PREVIOUSLY CONTRIVED
" TO OBTAIN A GRANT OF THEIR ESTATES BY
" PATENT, AND WAS PERMITTED TO KEEP
" THEM UNDISTURBED."—*Taylor's Hist. of
the Civil Wars in Ireland,* vol. I. pp. 243
—246; also *Carte's Ormond,* vol. I. p. 29 ;
and *MSS. Stearne, Trin. Coll., Dublin.*

OBSERVATIONS,
PROOFS, AND ILLUSTRATIONS.

CHAPTER II.—PART III.

It may be useful, for the sake of distinctness, to give a separate consideration to the enormous iniquity perpetrated by James in the wholesale robbery of his Irish subjects, beginning with the confiscation of six entire counties in the province of Ulster. These counties were for the greater part the estates of O'Neill, Lord Tyrone; and O'Donnell, Lord Tyrconnell. The residue was principally held under them by a title which was deemed by the natives perpetual. A conspiracy was formed, falsely to accuse those lords of high treason; and so to procure the forfeiture of their estates. Attempts were made by private emissaries, to allure them into some treasonable projects, but in vain. They were upon their guard, and treated the tempters with neglect. Notwithstanding this caution on their parts, preparations were made in Dublin for their trial and execution. They had been invited to Dublin in a friendly manner; they had come thither, expecting to be treated as friends. The following passage from Doctor Anderson's " *Royal Genealogies*," p. 786, will afford the reader a graphic description of the mode wherein these unfortunate noblemen were circumvented :—

> " Artful [Secretary] Cecil, employed one St.
>   " Lawrence to entrap the Earls of Tirone
>   " and Tyrconnell, the Lord of Delvin, and
>   " other Irish Chiefs into a sham plot, which
>   " had no evidence but his.   But those chiefs
>   " being informed that witnesses were to be
>   " hired against them, foolishly fled from
>   " Dublin, and so taking guilt upon them,
>   " they were declared rebels, AND SIX EN-
>   " TIRE COUNTIES IN ULSTER WERE AT ONCE
>   " FORFEITED TO THE CROWN, *which was*
>   " *what their enemies wanted.*"

The evidence upon which the charge of high treason rests, is singularly curious. It would seem incredible that so gross a fraud should be deemed practicable ; but it is placed beyond a doubt by Protestant historians. It is thus stated by Jones, Protestant Bishop of Meath ; who, before his ordination, had held rank in Cromwell's army. His account runs thus :—

> " Anno 1607, there was a providential discovery
>   " of another rebellion in Ireland, the Lord
>   " Chichester being Deputy ; the discoverer
>   " not being willing to appear, a letter from
>   " him, *not subscribed*, was superscribed to

" Sir William Usher, Clerk of the Council,
" *and dropt in the council chamber then*
" *held in the castle of Dublin ;* in which
" was mentioned a design for sieging the
" castle and murdering the Deputy ; with a
" general revolt, and dependence on Spanish
" forces ; and this also for religion ; for
" particulars whereof," (adds the bishop,)
" I refer to that letter, dated March the
" 19th, 1607."—*Preface to Borlase's History of the Irish Rebellion.*

O'Neill and O'Donnell had the good sense not
to abide the result of the trial.   They fled to foreign
countries ; but the sordid rancour of the slobbering
monster, King James, followed them thither.   He
robbed them of their property at home.   He endeavoured to rob them of character and sympathy
abroad.   He distributed a proclamation against
the earls, which is so characteristic of the pedantic
brute that issued it, and of the spirit wherein the
English Government invariably ruled Ireland, that
I insert it here at length :—

" BY THE KING.

" A proclamation, touching the Earles of Tirone
" and Tirconnell.

" Seeing it is common and natural in all persons
" of what condition soever to speak and
" judge variably of all new and sudden acci-

" dents ; and that the flight of the Earles of
" Tirone and Tirconnell, with some others
" of their fellowes out of the north partes of
" our realme of Ireland, may haply prove
" a subject of like discourse: Wee have
" thought it not amiss to deliver some such
" matter in publique as may better cleare
" men's judgments concerning the same:
" not in respect of any worth or value in
" these men's persons, being base and rude
" in their originall, but to take away all
" such inconveniencies as may blemish the
" reputation of that friendship which ought
" to be mutually observed between Us and
" other princes.   For although it is not un-
" likely that the report of their titles and
" dignities may draw from princes and states
" some such courtesies at their first coming
" abroad as are incident to men of extraor-
" dinary rancke and qualitie ; yet, when
" Wee have taken the best means Wee can
" to lay them open in every condition, Wee
" shall then expect from our friends and
" neighbours all such just and noble pro-
" ceedings as stand with the rules of honour
" and friendship ; and from our subjects at
" home and abroad that duety and obedience
" (in their carriage toward them) which
" they owe to us by inseparable bonds and

" obligations of nature and loyaltie, whereof
" Wee intend to take streight accompt. For
" which purpose Wee doo hereby first declare
" that these persons above-mentioned *had*
" *not their creations or* POSSESSIONS *in*
" *regard of any lineall or lawfull descent*
" from ancestors of blood or virtue ; but
" were onely preferred by the late Queen
" our Sister of famous memorie, and by our-
" selves, for some reasons of State, before
" others who for their qualitie and birth (in
" those provinces where they dwell) might
" better have challenged those honours which
" were conferred upon them. Secondly,
" Wee doo professe that it is both known to
" Us and our Counsell here, and to our
" Deputy and State there, and so shall it
" appeare to the world (as cleare as the
" sunne) by evident proofes, that the onely
" ground and motive of this high contempt
" in these men's departure, hath beene the
" private knowledge and inward terror of
" their own guiltinesse : whereof, because
" Wee heare that they doe seeke to take
" away the blot and infamie, by divulging
" that they have withdrawen themselves for
" matter of religion, (a cloake that serves
" too much in these daies to cover many
" evill intentions,) adding also thereunto

" some other vaine pretexts of receiving in-
" justice when their rights and claims have
" come in question betweene them and Us,
" or any of our subjects and them, Wee
" thinke it not impertinent to say somewhat
" thereof.

" And therefore, although Wee judge it needlesse
" to seeke for many arguments to confirme
" whatsoever shall be said of these men's
" corruption and falsehood, (whose hainous
" offences remaine so freshe in memorie,
" since they declared themselves so very
" monsters in nature as they did not only
" withdraw themselves from their personall
" obedience to their sovereigne, but were
" content to sell over their native countrey
" to those that stood at that time in the
" highest termes of hostilitie with the two
" Crownes of England and Ireland,) yet, to
" make the absurditie and ingratitude of the
" allegations above-mentioned, so much the
" more cleare to all men of equall judgment,
" Wee doo hereby professe in the word of a
" Kinge, that there never was so much as
" any shadowe of molestation, nor purpose
" of proceeding in any degree against them
" for matter concerning religion. Such
" being their condition and profession, to
" thinke murder no fault, marriage of no

" use, nor any man to be esteemed valiant
" that did not glorie in rapine and oppres-
" sion ; as wee should have thought it an
" unreasonable thing to trouble them for
" any different point in religion, before any
" man could perceive by their conversation
" that they made truely conscience of any
" religion.   So doo Wee also for the second
" parte of their excuse affirme, that (not-
" withstanding all that they can claime must
" bee acknowledged to proceed from meere
" grace upon their submission, after their
" greate and unnaturall treasons) there hath
" never come any question concerning their
" rights or possessions, wherein Wee have
" not bene more inclinable to doe them fa-
" vour than to any of their competitours,
" except in those cases wherein Wee have
" plainly discerned that their onely end was
" to have made themselves by degrees more
" able than they now are to resist all lawfull
" authoritie, (when they should return to
" their vomit againe,) by usurping a power
" over other good subjects of ours that dwell
" among them, better borne than they, and
" utterlie disclaiming from any dependencie
" upon them.
" Having now delivered thus much concerning
" these men's estates and their proceedings,

" Wee will onely end with this conclusion,
" that they shal not be able to denie when-
" soever they should dare to present them-
" selves before the seate of justice that they
" have (before the running out of our king-
" dome) not onely entered into combination
" for stirring sedition and intestine rebellion,
" but have directed divers instruments, as
" well priests as others, to make offers to
" foreign states and princes (if they had bene
" as readie to receive them) of their readi-
" nesse and resolution to adhere to them
" whensoever they should seeke to invade
" that kingdome. Wherein, amongst other
" thinges, this is not to be forgotten, that
" under the condition of being made free
" from English government, they resolved
" also to comprehend the utter extirpation
" of all those subjects that are nowe remain-
" ing alive within that kingdome, formerly
" descended from the English race. In
" which practices and propositions, followed
" and fomented by priests and Jesuites, (of
" whose function in these times the practice
" and perswasion of subjects to rebell against
" their sovereigns is one speciall and essen
" tiall part and portion,) as they have found
" no such encouragement as they expected
" and have boasted of ; so Wee doe assure

" ourselves, that when this declaration shal
" bee seene and duely weighed with all due
" circumstances, it will bee of force sufficient
" to disperse and to discredit all such un-
" trueths as these contemptible creatures, so
" full of infidelity and ingratitude, shall dis-
" gorge against Us, and our just and mode-
" rate proceeding ; and shall procure unto
" them no better usage than they would wish
" should bee afforded to any such packe of
" rebells, borne their subjects, and bound
" unto them in so many and so greate obli-
" gations.

" Given at our Palace of Westminster, the fif-
" teenth day of November, in the fifth yeere
" of our raigne of Great Britaine, France,
" and Ireland.

" GOD SAVE THE KING."

It is curious that the only title that James *could*
have had to the six counties in Ulster, was the forfeiture arising from the attainder, for flight, of
Tyrone and Tyrconnell. And yet his proclamation
states that *they* had no title whatever to the possessions thus forfeited ! ! *If they had no title, their
attainder could never have transferred a title to the
King.* This was a blunder just suited to the capacity
of such a Solomon as James the First. But he was
not guilty of the practical blunder of taking his own

proclamation to be true, and admitting *in practice*
that the attainted O'Neill and O'Donnell had had
no title to their lands.

As to the attainder itself, it would have been
difficult even in those days to establish it in a court
of law upon the *only* evidence of the earls' treason
that existed—namely, an anonymous letter dropt
in the council chamber in Dublin Castle. However,
to supply the deficiency, James resolved to have
the Irish Chieftains attainted by an Act of Parliament. There had not been a parliament held in
Ireland from the year 1587, until James called
this parliament in 1613, which was packed for
the express purpose of attainting O'Neill and
O'Donnell.

Sir John Davies is quite candid in stating the
motive for which former parliaments had been
called in Ireland: namely, to attaint different persons, so as to obtain their lands. Davies even
seeks to justify the packing of the parliament of
1613, by what lawyers delight in—namely, cases
in point. These are his words :—

> "For what end was the parliament holden by
> "Lord Leonard Gray in the 28th Henry
> "VIII. but *to attaint the Giraldines*, and
> "to abolish the usurped authortiy of the
> "Pope?
> "To what purpose did Thomas, Earl of Sussex,
> "hold his first parliament in the 3rd and

"4th K. Philip and Q. Mary, *but to settle*
"*Leix and Offaley in the Crown?*
"What was the principal cause that Sir Henry
"Sydney held a parliament in the 11th year
"of Queen Elizabeth, *but to extinguish the*
"*name of O'Neill, and to entitle the Crown*
"*to the greatest part of Ulster?*
"And lastly, what was the chief motive of the
"last parliament holden by Sir John Perrot,
"but *the attainder of two great peers of*
"*this realm, the Viscount Baltinglass, and*
"*the Earl of Desmond, and for vesting*
"*their lands, and the lands of their ad-*
"*herents, in the actual possession of the*
"*Crown?"—Davies*, p. 300.

What lawyer could resist the inevitable inference?
That as former parliaments had been called and
held for the mere purposes of plunder, so James
must have a clear right to call a parliament for the
same laudable object?

There never was a crime of any kind committed
anywhere, that was not exceeded in the conduct of
the English Government towards Ireland!

The six counties sought to be forfeited, were
nearly equal in extent to Yorkshire and Lancashire;
and were the richest and best cultivated part of
Ireland. The guilt of treason, as we have seen,
was to be proved upon the authority of an anonymous letter—found with no greater difficulty as to

place and manner of discovery, than by picking it
up from the floor of the council chamber in the
Viceroy's residence! And then, in order to ef-
fectuate this gigantic robbery, whereby the inhabitants of six counties were to be despoiled of their
all, and turned adrift houseless and penniless,—
James, at one stroke of the pen, created fourteen
peers, who were to participate with other dignitaries
in the plunder; and instituted no less than forty
new boroughs, amongst the poorest villages and
hamlets in Ireland. *Close* boroughs they were, of
course; the constituency in each not exceeding
in general twelve burgesses and a returning officer.
And when complaint was made to King James by
a remonstrance signed by some of the principal
men in Ireland, his answer was this :—

" You complain of fourteen false returns. Are
" there not many more complained of in this
" parliament, yet they do not forsake the
" house for it ?.........But you complain
" of the new boroughs............What is it
" to you, whether I make many or few
" boroughs? My council may consider the
" fitness, if I require it; but what if I had
" made forty noblemen and four hundred
" boroughs? The more the merrier, the
" fewer the better cheer."

By an Irish Statute then in force—namely, an
Act of the 23rd Henry VIII., no person could re-

present a county, city, or town in Ireland unless
he were a resident therein. This act had not been
repealed, but it was in this instance trodden under
foot and disregarded. The Irish ·Lords became
alarmed. They immediately petitioned James ;
and for their sole answer, their agents, Talbot and
Luttrel, were sent—the one to the Tower, the other
to the Fleet, and kept long in custody ! Yet their
complaints were indeed reasonable, as the reader
will see from the following extract from Leland ;
who records that the Irish Lords stated the existence of—

  " A fearful suspicion that the project of
  " erecting so many corporations in places
  " which can scantly pass the rank of the
  " poorest villages in the poorest country in
  " Christendom, do tend to nought else at
  " this time, but that, by the voices of a few,
  " *selected for the purpose*, under the name
  " of burgesses, extreme penal laws should
  " be imposed upon your subjects here."—
Leland, Book IV. chap. 7.

 Again, let us learn from Leland the sort of representatives chosen for these boroughs :—

  " The recusant Lords and Commons of the Pale
  " despatched letters to the King and the
  " English Council, urging the grievance of
  " the new boroughs, incorporated with such
  " shameful partiality, *and represented by*

"*attorneys' clerks, and servants of the*
"*Lord Deputy*, AND THE VIOLENCE DONE
"TO EVERARD, CHOSEN SPEAKER BY A MA-
"JORITY OF UNDOUBTED REPRESENTATIVES;
"imploring to be heard by their agents, and
"renouncing the royal favour, should they
"fail in point of proof."—*Leland*, Book
IV. chap. 7.

The manner wherein the Speaker, Everard, was
deprived of his right to preside in the House of
Commons, is curious; and the whole scene is quite
characteristic of the times. It should be recollected
that the six counties of Ulster were the great prize
to be played for in this parliament. Leland with
all his prejudices admits that Everard was chosen
Speaker by A MAJORITY OF UNDOUBTED REPRESEN-
TATIVES. It was however too great an object to
have a Speaker devoted to the plunderers, for the
Government party to hesitate at the commission of
any fraud or violence. The following extract will
amuse as well as instruct :—

ELECTION OF SPEAKER. 1613.

"There were two elections, viz., those of the
"recusant sect had chosen Sir John Everard,
"Knight, for their Speaker, and therefore
"would in no wise accept of Sir John Davies,
"and in this division grew an uncertainty,
"who had most voices; whereupon Sir

" John Davies, with all those of the protes-
" tancy, went out to be numbered, and be-
" fore they came in again, those of the
" recusancy had shut the door, and had set
" Sir John Everard in the chair of the
" Speaker ; but when the Protestants saw
" that, they pulled Sir John Everard out of
" the chair, and held Sir John Davies there-
" in ; and thus, with great contention, the
" second and third days (of the session) were
" spent ; but the recusants prevailed not
" therein, for Sir John Davies was maintained
" in the place.   Then did the recusants of
" both houses of parliament withdraw them-
" selves, and resorted not thither any more,
" notwithstanding that they were often sent
" for by the Lord Deputy."—*Desider. Curios. Hibern.* vol. I. p. 168 ; see also *Leland,*
Book IV. chap 7.
" A band of armed soldiers, with lighted matches
" in their hands, stood at the entrance of the
" house, to embolden the Protestant party."
—*Curry,* 79.

Complaint was vain ; and although the flagrant
illegality of the returns of a number of the English
party was confessed, yet it appears from Lord
Mountmorris's instructive history of the Irish parliament, that they were all allowed to sit ; though
the defect of their title to be members was admitted

by a resolution of the house itself. I subjoin
Lord Mountmorris's evidence in proof of this
fact :—

   " November 19, 1613, it was resolved by the
   " House of Commons, That whereas some
   " persons have been unduly elected, some
   " being judges, some for not being estated
   " in their boroughs, some for being *outlawed*,
   " excommunicated, and lastly, for being re-
   " turned for places whose charters were not
   " valid ; *it was resolved not to question them*
   " *for the present*, in order to prevent stop-
   " ping public business ; but this resolution
   " was not to be drawn into precedent."—
   Mountmorris, I. 169.

   In such a parliament as this—with the real
representatives rejected, and the fictitious ones re-
tained—statutes were of course passed, giving the
entire fee simple of the six counties to the Crown ;
and this spoliation—a robbery unparalleled in the
annals of any other country—was justified in a set
speech by Sir John Davies ; a speech in which he
afforded a painful contrast between the rapacity
and iniquitous plunder of the English, with that
love of "equal and impartial justice" which he
himself acknowledged was the permanent disposition
of the Irish people. I shall cite two passages from
his discourse. The first is characteristic of the
speaker's mendacious servility—perhaps it is right

to call it lying flattery of a disgusting kind. He begins thus : He said—

"That he was glad that this occasion was offered
"of declaring and setting forth his Majesty's
"just title, as well for his Majesty's honour
"(WHO BEING THE MOST JUST PRINCE LIVING,
"WOULD NOT DISPOSSESS THE MEANEST OF
"HIS SUBJECTS WRONGFULLY, TO GAIN MANY
"SUCH KINGDOMS,) as for the satisfaction of
"the natives themselves, and of all the
"world ; for his Majesty's right, it shall
"appear," said he, "that his Majesty may
"and ought to dispose of these lands in
"such manner as he hath done, and is
"about to do, *in law, conscience, and in*
"*honour.*"

But the great object of the discourse was to justify, not so much the seizure of the lands in the actual possession of the attainted earls, or of the chief rents payable to them, *as the estates of their tenants*, which in general were perpetuities. These tenants were implicated in no treason ! were subject to no attainder ! were guilty of no crime ! Yet, upon the paltry calumnies set forth by Sir John Davies in the following extract, the inhabitants of six counties were plundered of their properties, and turned penniless beggars upon the world ! And to render this ineffable iniquity still more revolting, it is justified beneath a plea of "*conscience !*"

English "*conscience*" *! ! !*

"And as these men," says Sir John, "had no
"certain estates of inheritance, so did they
"never till now claim any such estate, nor
"conceive that their lawful heirs should
"inherit the land which they possessed :
"which is manifest by two arguments :
"1. They never esteemed lawful matrimony, to
"the end they might have lawful heirs !
"2. They never did build any houses, nor plant
"orchards or gardens, nor take any care of
"their posterities.
"If these men had no estates in law, either in
"their main chiefries or in their inferior
"tenancies, it followeth, that if his Majesty,
"who is the undoubted Lord Paramount,
"do seize and dispose of these lands, they
"can make no title against his Majesty or
"his patentees, and consequently cannot
"be admitted to traverse any office of
"those lands ! for without showing a title
"no man can be admitted to traverse an
"office.

"Thus, then, it appears, that as well by the Irish
"custom as the law of England, his Majesty
"may, at his pleasure, seize these lands and
"dispose thereof. The only scruple which
"remains, consists in this point ; whether
"the King may, in conscience or honour

" remove the ancient tenants, and bring in
" strangers among them.

" Truly his Majesty may not only take this course
" lawfully, but he is bound in conscience so
" to do.

" For, being the undoubted rightful King of this
" realm, so as the people and land are com-
" mitted by the Divine Majesty to his charge
" and government, his Majesty is bound in
" conscience to use all lawful and just courses
" to reduce his people from barbarism to
" civility ; the neglect whereof heretofore
" hath been laid as an imputation upon the
" Crown of England.   Now, civility cannot
" possibly be planted among them but by
" this mixed plantation of civil men, which
" likewise could not be without removal and
" transplantation of some of the natives, and
" settling of their possessions in a course of
" common law ; for if themselves were suf-
" fered to possess the whole country, as their
" septs have done for many hundreds of
" years past, they would never to the end of
" the world build houses, make townships or
" villages, or manure or improve the land
" as it ought to be.   Therefore it stands
" neither with Christian policy nor con-
" science, to suffer so good and fruitful a
" country to lie waste like a wilderness, when

"his Majesty may lawfully dispose it to such
"persons as will make a civil plantation
"therein."

There is a melancholy amusement in seeing the
manner in which Davies gravely acquits the King's
conscience from the robbery, by proving that the
Irish were all the better for being robbed! a mode
of reasoning which he certainly would prefer to have
practically applied to any other person than to himself.   He concludes thus :—

"Again, his Majesty may take this course in
"conscience ; because it tendeth to the good
"of the inhabitants in many ways ; for half
"their land doth now lie waste ; by reason
"whereof that which is inhabited is not im-
"proved to half the value ; but when the
"undertakers are planted among them, (there
"being place and scope enough both for
"them and the natives,) and that all the land
"shall be fully stocked and manured, 500
"acres will be of better value than 5000 are
"now!   Besides, where their estates were
"before uncertain and transitory, so as their
"heirs did never inherit, they shall now
"have certain estates of inheritance, the
"portion allotted unto them, which they
"and their children after them shall enjoy
"with security.

"Lastly, this transplantation of the natives is

" made by his Majesty, rather like a father
" than a lord or a monarch! The Romans
" transplanted whole nations out of Germany
" into France ; the Spaniards lately removed
" all the Moors out of Grenada into Barbary
" without providing them any new seats
" there: WHEN THE ENGLISH PALE WAS FIRST
" PLANTED, ALL THE NATIVES WERE CLEARLY
" EXPELLED, SO AS NOT ONE IRISH FAMILY
" HAD SO MUCH AS ONE ACRE OF FREEHOLD
" IN ALL THE FIVE COUNTIES OF THE PALE :
" and now, within these four years past, the
" Græmes were removed from the borders
" of Scotland to this kingdom, and had not
" one foot of land allotted to them here ;
" but these natives of Cavan have competent
" portions of land assigned to them, many
" of them in the same barony where they
" dwelt before ; and such as are removed,
" are planted in the same county ; *so as his*
" *Majesty doth in this imitate the skilful*
" *husbandman, who doth remove his fruit*
" *trees, not with a purpose to extirpate and*
" *destroy them, but that they may bring*
" *better and sweeter fruit after the trans-*
" *plantation.*"—*Davies*, 276.

Such were the arguments whereby a willing parliament was easily persuaded to pass a law vesting
in the Crown the entire land of six counties, the

property of the innocent tenants, and of the timid
and therefore self-banished earls.   James immediately set about distributing upwards of THREE
HUNDRED AND EIGHTY-FIVE THOU-
SAND ACRES.*   There were three divisions
made of the spoils :—

First, to English and Scotch, who were to plant
their proportions of English and Scotch tenants.

Secondly, to servitors in Ireland, that is, to persons employed under Government, who might take
English or Irish tenants at their choice.

Thirdly, to the natives of those counties who
were to be freeholders.

But persons of Irish descent who were called,
and known as, "mere Irish," were not to be permitted to reside upon the lands at all ; nor were
any Catholics to be so permitted : that is, no person
could be allowed to occupy any of the lands, who
had not taken the oath of Supremacy.

This was called the Plantation of Ulster ; and to
show the spirit in which it was made, I give the
following "Articles," extracted from the Orders
and Conditions of the Plantations of Ulster :—

   " 7. The said undertakers, their heirs and assigns,
        " shall not alien or demise their portions, or
        " any part thereof, *to the mere Irish*, or to

---

* Leland, Book IV. chap. 8.

"such persons as will not take the oath,
"which the said undertakers are bound to
"take by the former article; and to that
"end, a proviso shall be inserted in their
"letters patent.
"10. The said undertakers shall not alien their
"portions during five years next after the
"date of their letters patent, but in this
"manner, viz., one-third part in fee farm;
"another third part for forty years or under;
"reserving to themselves the other third
"part without alienation during the said five
"years. But after the said five years, they
"shall be at liberty to alien to all persons
"EXCEPT THE MERE IRISH, and such persons
"as will not take the oath which the said
"undertakers are to take as aforesaid."—
Harris's Hibernica, p. 66.

ARTICLES CONCERNING THE SERVITORS.

"They shall take the oath of Supremacy, and
"be conformable in religion as the former
"undertakers.
"9. They shall not alien their portions, or any
"part thereof, *to the mere Irish*, or to any
"such person or persons as will not take the
"like oath as the said undertakers were
"wont to take aforesaid; and to that end

" a proviso shall be inserted in their letters
" patent."—*Harris's Hibernica*, p. 65.

The documents we have thus cited give but a
faint idea of the extreme misery created by the
plunder of the six counties. It will be easily believed that the administration of the law was quite
consistent with the temper of the times ; exhibiting,
and indeed enforcing, the most glaring partiality
and injustice. Take the following testimony respecting the ecclesiastical courts from no less an
authority than Bishop Burnett :—

> " They were," says Bishop Burnett, in his Life
> of Bishop Bedell, " often managed by a
> " chancellor that bought his place, and so
> " thought he had a right to all the profits he
> " could make out of it, and their whole
> " business seemed to be nothing but oppres-
> " sion and extortion ; the solemnest, the
> " sacredest of all church censures, which
> " was excommunication, went about in so
> " sordid and base a manner, that all regard
> " to it, as it was a spiritual censure, was
> " lost, and the effect it had in law made it
> " be cried out upon as a most intolerable
> " piece of tyranny. The officers of the
> " court thought they had a sort of right to
> " oppress the natives ; and that all was well
> " got that was wrung from them."

Yet these courts proceeded to excommunicate the

Catholics for " Recusancy ;" and where they did
not extort bribes for their forbearance they punished
by imprisonment. I give a specimen, affecting
some of the more favoured of the persecuted class :—

> " It appears that at the end of this session,"
> (1615,) " eight Roman Catholics who had
> " been excommunicated by the Archbishop
> " of Dublin for recusancy, and imprisoned,
> " were released by the indulgence of parlia-
> " ment, (some said by the mediation of
> " bribes,) but their joy on that account was
> " short lived, and their release rather an
> " illusion and an aggravation of their pun-
> " ishment, for without any crime but perse-
> " verance in their religion, the same arch-
> " bishop soon after excommunicated them a
> " second time ; on which they were again
> " sent back to their long and loathsome
> " confinement."—*Analect. Sacra. Rives. in*
> *Analect.* p. 34.

The Catholic clergy were still worse treated:
here are some specimens :—

> " Cnohor O'Duana, bishop of Down and Connor,
> " was apprehended in July, 1612, and com-
> " mitted to the castle of Dublin, wherein
> " he lived in continual restraint many years;
> " but having at last escaped out of prison
> " and having afterwards been taken, he was
> " hanged, drawn, and quartered on the first

" of February."—*Theatre of Cath. and
Prot. Rel.* p. 578.

" The chaplain of this bishop, Bryan Carrulan,
" John O'Onan, Donoghoe M'Reddy, and
" John Luneas, priests, suffered also in Ire-
" land in this reign."—*Id. ib.* p. 586.

Take a few specimens also—a savour of the
quality of the criminal courts ; and of the mode in
which cases on behalf of the Crown were rendered
successful—no matter how deficient the evidence ;
no matter how strong the case of the defendant.
The ordinary modes of procuring partial jurors
were of course resorted to.   But with jurors who
had anything like a conscience, harsher measures
were pursued.   We find that they were not only
imprisoned and fined, but that some of them *had
their ears cut off.*   The fact was stated in an ad-
dress of remonstrance to the Crown, and was not,
as it could not be, contradicted.

The remonstrance of the Irish nobility and gentry at that period sets forth—

" That in the trial of criminal causes and men's
" lives, (which the law doth much favour,)
" the jurors were ordinarily threatened by
" his Majesty's counsel at law, to be brought
" into the star-chamber, insomuch that it
" was great danger for any innocent man,
" if he was accused upon malice or light
" ground of suspicion ; because the jurors,

"being terrified through *fear of imprison-*
"*ment, loss of ears, and of their goods,*
"*might condemn him.*"—*Desider. Curios.*
Hibern. p. 224.

Let it not be supposed that I exaggerate ; the
fact is admitted by the very parties themselves to
the crime. Lord Deputy Chichester confesses—

"That the justices of assize (1613) for the space
"of two or three years past, had bound over
"divers juries to the star-chamber, for their
"refusing to present recusants upon the
"testimony of the witnesses, that they come
"not to church according to the law. All
"which jurors have been punished in the
"star-chamber by fine and imprisonment."
Chichester adds—

"It is true that these jurors censured in the star-
"chamber had no counsel allowed them."—
Desid. Curios. Hibern. vol. I. p. 263.

Of course conscientious jurors *did* refuse to attend, and left the cases to the profligate partizans
of the Crown :—

"Most of the jurors did rather choose to endure
"the penalty or loss of issues, than to appear
"on juries, the course held with them was
"so strict and severe."—*Desid. Curios.*
Hibern. vol. I. p. 244.

"The star-chamber," says Chichester, "is the
"proper court to punish jurors that will not

"find for the King upon *good evidence*."—
Desid. Curios. Hib. vol. I. p. 262.

He would have been a hardy libeller indeed who
at that period should have dared to assert that the
Crown ever went to trial in any case without
"*good evidence*." But mark! there was no penalty
or punishment for finding against the best and
most conclusive evidence when tendered on behalf
of the defendant.

It is a melancholy reflection, that the Crown
prosecutor in Ireland can, whenever he pleases,
pack his jury at the present day with as great a
certainty of procuring a verdict on the "*good
evidence*" of the Crown, as his predecessor in the
reign of the First James could have done. There
is indeed *one* amelioration in our days : the ears of
the jurors can no longer be cut off.

The success of James in the spoliation of the
property of the inhabitants of the six counties of
Ulster only whetted his appetite and that of his
courtiers for more plunder. They turned their
eyes upon the province of Connaught, and determined upon a similar scheme of robbery. They
affected a great zeal for reforming abuses in particular localities. They soon extended their views
to entire provinces. The following will show with
what iniquity and what success ; I take the statement from Leland. It relates to the first proceedings under the "Commission of Defective Titles:"—

" Another device of these reformers affected the
" inhabitants of an entire province. The
" lords and gentlemen of Connaught, inclu-
" ding the county of Clare, on their com-
" position made with Sir John Perrot in the
" reign of Elizabeth, had indeed surrendered
" their estates to the Crown, but had gene-
" rally neglected to enrol their surrenders
" and to take out their letters patent. This
" defect was supplied by King James, who
" in his 13th year issued a commission to
" receive surrenders of their estates ; which
" he re-conveyed, by new patents, to them
" and their heirs, to be holden of the Crown
" by Knight's service, as of the castle of
" Athlone.   Their surrenders were made,
" their patents received the great seal, but,
" by neglect of the officers, neither was en-
" rolled in Chancery, although three thou-
" sand pounds had been disbursed for the
" enrolments. *Advantage was now taken*
" *of this involuntary omission.* THEIR
" TITLES WERE PRONOUNCED DEFECTIVE,
" AND THEIR LANDS ADJUDGED TO BE STILL
" VESTED IN THE CROWN. The project re-
" commended to the King, was nothing less
" than that of establishing an extensive
" plantation in the province of Connaught,
" similar to that of Ulster ; and in his rage

" of reformation it was most favourably re-
" ceived."—*Leland*, Book IV. chap. 8.

The alarmed proprietors sought to avert the
threatened confiscation by tendering the composition
of a heavy fine and doubling their annual rents ;
James listened to their proposition ; but the treaty
was interrupted by his Majesty's death in 1625.

The ensuing reign is the one in which the Commission of Defective Titles figured with the greatest
atrocity. For the present I shall content myself
with one extract more, descriptive of the mode in
which the commissioners exerted their authority :
it will be found that they had so far impartiality in
their conduct, that they did not confine their plun-
derings to Catholic property. Defenceless Protestants were liable in the remote countries to equal
spoliation. This is proved by Leland :—

" In other districts, the planters had not only
" neglected to perform their covenants, but
" the commissioners appointed to distribute
" the lands, scandalously abused their trusts,
" and by fraud or violence deprived the na-
" tives of those possessions which the King
" had reserved for them. Some indeed were
" suffered to enjoy a small pittance of such
" reservation ; others were totally ejected.
" In the manuscripts of Bishop Stearne we
" find, that in the small county of Longford,
" twenty-five of one sept were all deprived

" of their estates without the least compen-
" sation, or any means of subsistence as-
" signed to them. The resentment of such
" sufferers was in some cases exasperated
" by finding their lands transferred to hun-
" gry adventurers, who had no services to
" plead, and sometimes to those who had
" been rebels and traitors. Neither the
" actors nor the objects of such grievances
" were confined to one religion. The most
" zealous in the service of Government,
" and the most peaceable conformists, were
" involved in the ravages of avarice and ra-
" pine, without any distinction of principles
" or professions. The interested assiduity
" of the King's creatures in scrutinizing the
" titles to those lands which had not yet
" been found or acknowledged to belong to
" the Crown, was, if possible, still more
" detestable."—*Leland*, Book IV. chap. 8.

I conclude the collection of testimonies showing
the crimes committed on the Irish in the reign of
James, by the following short summary taken from
Leland :—

" Extortions and oppressions of the soldiers in
" various excursions from their quarters,
" for levying the King's rents, or supporting
" the civil power ; *a rigorous and tyran-*
" *nical execution of martial law in time of*

"*peace ;* a dangerous and unconstitutional
" power assumed by the privy council in de-
" ciding causes determinable by common
" law ; THEIR SEVERE TREATMENT OF WIT-
" NESSES AND JURORS IN THE CASTLE CHAM-
" BER, WHOSE EVIDENCE OR VERDICTS HAD
" BEEN DISPLEASING TO THE STATE ; *the*
" *grievous exactions of the established clergy*
" for the occasional duties of their function ;
" and the severity of the ecclesiastical
" courts."—*Leland,* Book IV. chap. 8.

OBSERVATIONS,
PROOFS, AND ILLUSTRATIONS.

CHAPTER III.—PART I.

YEARS 1625—1660.

IT is now my purpose to illustrate the reign of
Charles the First, and the dominion of the blood-
stained Cromwell. Language totally fails to describe
the crimes of this period.

The Irish had a respite on the death of James I.
It was hoped that the Commission of Defective
Titles would not be renewed. The hope was vain;
the expectation nugatory. I am not disposed to
speak unfavourably of the personal disposition of
Charles the First, but he was impelled by circumstances to act a part, which probably, or at least
possibly, was different from what he would have
been inclined to act. I do not mean however to
vindicate him. He participated too deeply in the
crimes of his agents and ministers to afford any
substantial palliation of the guilt of his criminal
reign.

It is most material to keep in mind that while the
spirit of disaffection to the reigning Monarch was

daily becoming more rife in England, and while
every means were taken to thwart his purposes and
to bring him into subjection, the Catholic people
of Ireland exhibited the most zealous and generous
loyalty. The knowledge of this fact will give added
poignancy to the base cruelty by which the spoliation of their property by the enemies of Charles—
the Cromwellians—was afterwards sanctioned and
confirmed by Charles's sons—Charles II. and
James II. I leave upon record the two following
extracts :—

" The condition of the King's affairs" (in 1626)
" was much perplexed in England ; he was
" at war with the two most powerful kings
" in Europe, and his subjects in the English
" parliament would afford him little or no
" assistance but on hard and dishonourable
" terms, though they had engaged him in the
" first war ; and seemed glad of the last, it
" being in defence of religion."—*Sir Edw.*
Walker's Historical Discourses, fol. 337.

Whilst his Majesty's affairs were thus perplexed
in England—

" The Roman Catholics of Ireland offered con-
" stantly to pay an army of five thousand
" foot, and five hundred horse, for his Ma-
" jesty's service, provided they might be
" tolerated in the exercise of their religion."
—*Id. ib.*

It however having become known, that the Irish were thus about to obtain toleration for the exercise of their religion, the bigotry of the celebrated Archbishop Usher became alarmed. He called together an assemblage of the bishops, who agreed with him in a Declaration, in which they proclaimed *toleration* to be a sin of the first magnitude. It is fit that we preserve, for the execration of the wise and the good, the Declaration of these Protestant bishops, containing their Protestant reasons for refusing to tolerate the members of the older church. They are these :

" November, 1626.

" FIRSTLY—The religion of the papists is super-
" stitious and idolatrous ; their faith and
" doctrine erroneous and heretical ; their
" church, in respect of both, apostatical.
" To give them, therefore, a toleration, or
" to consent that they may freely exercise
" their religion, and profess their faith and
" doctrine, is a grievous sin, and that in
" two respects ; for, first, it is to make our-
" selves accessary not only to their super-
" stitions, idolatries, and heresies, and, in
" a word, to all the abominations of popery ;
" but also (which is a condition of the for-
" mer) to the perdition of the seduced people
" which perish in the deluge of the Catholic
" apostacy.

" SECONDLY—To grant them a toleration, in re-
" spect of any money to be given or contri-
" bution to be made by them, is to set
" religion to sale, and with it the souls of
" the people whom Christ hath redeemed
" with his blood.   And as it is a great sin,
" so it is also a matter of most dangerous
" consequence : the consideration whereof
" we commit to the wise and judicious, be-
" seeching the God of truth to make them
" who are in authority, zealous of God's
" glory, and of the advancement of true
" religion ; zealous, resolute, and coura-
" geous, against all popery, superstition,
" and idolatry."

The Irish Catholics however persevered.   They
resolved to contribute to the extent of their power
to relieve the royal necessities ; and they agreed
to advance the enormous sum (for those times) of
£120,000 ; upon the easy terms that certain concessions of the most plain and obvious justice should
be made by the Crown.   These " graces " were
granted under the King's own hand.   The following
is the abstract of these " graces," as accurately
specified by Lingard :—

" By these graces, in addition to the removal of
" many minor grievances, it was provided
" that the recusants should be allowed to
" practice in the courts of law, and to sue

" the livery of their lands out of the Court
" of Wards, on taking an oath of civil alle-
" giance in lieu of the oath of Supremacy;
" that the undertakers in the several planta-
" tions should have time allowed them to
" fulfil the conditions of their leases; that
" the claims of the Crown should be confined
" to the last sixty years; that the inhabitants
" of Connaught should be permitted to make
" a new enrolment of their estates; and
" that a parliament should be holden to con-
" firm these graces, and to establish every
" man in the undisturbed possession of his
" lands."—*Lingard's England, Reign of
Charles I.* chap. 1.

It will be important to keep in recollection this
composition or purchase money, especially in relation to the proceedings under the Commission for
Defective Titles. Because, if there really had
been any substantial defect in the title of the inhabitants, particularly of Connaught, it lay within the
prerogative of the Crown—and in point of justice
the Crown was bound—gratuitously to release
defects, whether caused by the negligence of its
public officers, or which might have accidentally
occurred. But it was still a stronger case when
the Crown *agreed* to release these defects, and to
confirm the titles, on obtaining the payment of so
large a sum of money. It was unjust to seek to

disturb those titles at all. But, as the injustice
of British Government towards Ireland constantly
reduplicates, it was doubly, and most iniquitously
unjust, to seek to disturb those titles *after the payment* of so large a sum of money for a perpetual
release.

It is said that one-third of the money was paid
by Protestants, and that the Catholics paid only
two-thirds. Even if the fact were so, it makes no
difference : because the estates of the Protestants
who contributed were liable to the same nominal
" defect" with those of the Catholics.

The base iniquity of receiving the money for the
" graces," and of afterwards violating the promise
to concede those graces, is still farther enhanced by
the proceedings of Strafford, with relation to an
Irish parliament called shortly after. He opened
that parliament with a speech from the throne, in
which he deliberately stated the falsehood so often
avowed in his correspondence ; namely, that if a
free and unconditional grant of supplies were made
to the King, the "graces" (including *security of
title* to their estates) would certainly be conceded.
He treated all doubt upon that subject as debasing.
He closed with this phrase :—

" Surely so great a meanness cannot enter your
    " hearts, as once to suspect his Majesty's
    " gracious regards of you and performance
    " with you ; where you affie yourselves upon

" his grace."—*Strafford's State Letters,*
vol. I. p. 223.

The supplies were accordingly moved for on the
following day ; and six entire subsidies were
unanimously voted to his Majesty, payable in four
years : and these subsidies far exceeded his expectation.   Strafford says himself—

" Each of these subsidies amounted to £50,000 ;
" and I never propounded more to the King
" than £30,000.   So that the subsidies
" raised in this first, were more than I pro-
" posed to be had in both sessions ; and
" were freely given and without any contra-
" diction."—*Ibidem,* 273.

Thus the Irish—and especially the Catholic
Irish—in order to obtain the confirmation of their
titles to their estates against an objection in its own
nature frivolous and unjust—had, in 1628, agreed
to pay, and actually paid £120,000 : and in 1634
the parliament I have spoken of, granted (on the
faith of the Lord Deputy's most emphatic promise
that the graces should be immediately conceded)
supplies nearly doubling in amount the most sanguine expectations of the griping Lord Deputy.

Is it credible that all this time, this very Lord
Deputy had determined that the graces should *not*
be granted ? that the act of justice which ought to
have been done gratuitously, should not be done at
all ? that the people's money should be obtained

under a false pretence, and no value given? that
the plighted honour—the honour of Protestant
England—should be pledged to Catholic Ireland,
and should be pledged, only to exhibit another instance of shameless knavery? another most dis-
graceful breach of public faith?

Why, in its own nature it *is* incredible. Yet, it
is literally true. And it is proved by no less evidence than the letter of that Lord Deputy himself.
The letter is dated the 16th August, 1634, and is
addressed to Secretary Coke at London.

The House of Commons had, in pursuance of the
compact, voted the supplies; and then pressed for
the graces: and particularly for a statute to limit
the claims of the Crown to 60 years. This is the
passage out of the above-mentioned letter to which
I implore the attention of every reader :—

  " Both houses have, during this sitting, likewise
    " extreamly pressed for the graces ; espe-
    " cially the law in England for threescore
    " years' possession, to conclude the rights of
    " the Crown ; and in the lower house none
    " so earnest as Fingal and Ranelagh, urging
    " his Majesty's promise at every turn.
  " The Commons' House have named a committee
    " to attend the Chancellor ; the Chief Jus-
    " tice of the Common Pleas, the Chief Baron,
    " Master of the Rolls, and Sir George Rad-
    " cliffe, appointed by me to make ready all

" good and fit laws to be transmitted against
" our next meeting, which is, by God's
" grace, to be the 4th of November, which
" they do incessantly, calling for the graces,
" and in especially that law of threescore
" years.

" So as considering that many of these graces are
" by no means to pass into laws ; and not
" foreseeing what inconvenience might fall
" upon his Majesty if these pressures were
" suffered to go on too far, I consulted these
" two judges, and Sir George Radcliffe,
" how we might incline the board to give
" them the negative answer, and take it
" off the King, which on Thursday last I
" effected, being, in good faith, very excel-
" lently assisted at the table by them all
" three ; so as now we are resolved, not only
" privately to transmit our humble advices
" upon every article of the graces, but on
" Tuesday next to call this committee of the
" Commons before us, and plainly tell them
" that we may not with our faith to our
" master give way to the transmitting of this
" law of threescore years, or any other of
" the graces prejudicial to the Crown ; nay,
" must humbly beseech his Majesty they
" may not be introduced to the prejudice of
" his royal rights, and clearly represent

" unto the King THAT HE IS NOT BOUND,
" EITHER IN JUSTICE, HONOUR, OR CON-
" SCIENCE TO GRANT THEM. And so putting
" in ourselves mean betwixt them and his
" Majesty's pretended ingagements, take
" the hard part wholly from his Majesty and
" bear it ourselves as well as we may."—
Strafford, I. 279—80.

It may be supposed that Charles was no party to
this villanous duplicity. Alas, alas! for poor human
nature! And alas, for royal nature, too! Pause,
and read his reply. He thus writes to Strafford:—
" Wentworth,

    " Before I answer any of your particular
    " letters to me, I must tell you that your
    " last public despatch has given me a great
    " deal of contentment; and especially for
    " keeping off the envy" (odium) " of a
    " necessary negative from me of those un-
    " reasonable graces that people expected
    " from me."—*Strafford's State Letters*, vol.
    I. 331.

Both these men lost their heads upon the scaffold.
Strafford was a consummate political villain. Charles
was spoiled by his education and his advisers. But
Ireland suffered without any compensation, from
the deliberate villany of the one, and the regal
treachery of the other.

Wentworth, having by this villanous treachery

plundered the Irish people of more *money* than he
had expected to get, immediately commenced his
plan of confiscation.   It was a magnificent wholesale plan, to confiscate the property of the inhabi
tants of the three remaining provinces.   We have
seen how James effected the plunder of Ulster.
Wentworth began with Connaught.   Leland describes his project in the following words :—

"HIS PROJECT WAS NOTHING LESS
"THAN TO SUBVERT THE TITLE
"TO ÆVERY ESTATE IN EVERY
"PART OF CONNAUGHT, and to
"establish a new plantation through this
"whole province ; a project which, when
"first proposed in the late reign, was re-
"ceived with horror and amazement; but
"which suited the undismayed and enter-
"prising genius of Lord Wentworth.   For
"this he had opposed the confirmation of
"the royal graces, and taken to himself the
"odium of so flagrant a violation of the
"royal promise.   The parliament was at
"an end, and the Deputy at leisure to exe-
"cute a scheme, which, as it was offensive
"and alarming, required a cautious and
"deliberate procedure.   Old records of
"state, and the memorials of ancient mo-
"nasteries, were ransacked to ascertain the
"King's original title to Connaught.   It

" was soon discovered, that in the grant of
" Henry III. to Richard De Burgo, *five*
" *cantreds were reserved to the Crown* ad-
"jacent to the castle of Athlone ; that
" THIS GRANT INCLUDED THE
" WHOLE REMAINDER OF THE
" PROVINCE, which was now alleged to
" have been forfeited by Aedh O'Connor,
" the Irish provincial chieftain ; that the
" lands and lordship of De Burgo descended
" lineally to Edward the Fourth, and were
" confirmed to the Crown by a statute of
" Henry the Seventh. The ingenuity of
" court lawyers was employed to invalidate
" all patents granted to the possessors of
" these lands, from the reign of Queen
" Elizabeth."—*Leland,* Book IV. chap. 1.
Strafford commenced with the county of Roscommon. It will be recollected that the practice
of fining jurors for finding a verdict unpleasing to
the Crown, was fully established in Ireland. This
will make the next extract perfectly intelligible. It
is an extract from a despatch addressed by Strafford
to the English Secretary, and relates to the county
of Roscommon, with which Strafford had begun :—
    " Before my coming from Dublin I had given
    " order that the gentlemen of the best estates
    " and understandings should be returned,
    " which was done accordingly, as you will

" find by their names. My reason was, that
" this being a leading case for the whole pro-
" vince, it would set a great value in their
" estimation upon the goodness of the King's
" title, BEING FOUND BY PERSONS OF THEIR
" QUALITIES, and as much concerned in their
" own particulars as any other. Again, find-
" ing the evidence so strong, as unless they
" went against it they must pass for the King,
" *I resolved to have persons of such means*
" *as might* ANSWER THE KING A ROUND FINE
" in the castle chamber in case they should
" prevaricate, who, in all seeming, even
" out of that reason, would be more fearful
" to tread shamefully and impudently aside
" from the truth, than such as had less, or
" nothing to lose."—*Strafford*, I. 442.

I extract the next passages, as especially exhibiting the subsequent conduct of Strafford towards
the counsel employed upon this occasion :—

" Having thus prepared the matter........I sent
" for half a dozen of the principal gentlemen
" among them, and in the presence of the
" commissioners desired them that they
" would acquaint the rest of the country that
" the end of our coming was the next day to
" execute his Majesty's commission for find-
" ing a clear and undoubted title in the
" Crown to the province of Connaught, pur-

" posing to begin first with the county of
" Roscommon.   Wherein nevertheless to
" manifest his Majesty's justice and honour,
" I thought fit to let them know, it was his
" Majesty's gracious pleasure, any man's
" counsel should be fully and willingly
" heard in the defence of their respective
" rights, BEING A FAVOUR NEVER BEFORE
" AFFORDED TO ANY UPON TAKING OF THESE
" KIND OF INQUISITIONS."—*Ibid*.

The trial proceeded; and as if to make it a complete mockery of justice, it concluded with a speech
from Strafford of which I shall give the commencement and conclusion.   The scene is unparalleled
in the history of any other country :—

" So presently," says Strafford, " we went to the
" place appointed, read the Commission,
" called and swore the jury, and so on with
" our work............The counsel on both
" sides having said all they would, I told
" the jury the first movers of his Majesty to
" look into this his undoubted title, were
" the princely desires he hath to effect them
" a civil and rich people; which cannot by
" any so sure and ready means be attained
" as by a plantation, which therefore in his
" great wisdom he had resolved.".........

Strafford gives us the conclusion of his speech as
follows.   He tells the jury that—

" If they would be inclined to truth, and do best
" for themselves, they were undoubtedly to
" find the title for the King. If they were
" passionately resolved to go over all bounds
" to their own will, and without respects at
" all to their own good, to do that which
" were simply best for his Majesty, then I
" should advise them, roughly and pertina-
" ciously to deny to find any title at all.
" And there I left them to chant together
" (as they call it) over their evidence.
" The next day they found the King's title with-
" out scruple or hesitation."—*Strafford*, I.
442, 443.

And the jurors were wise who did so. For
Strafford exceeded his predecessor Chichester in
cruelty to nonconforming jurors. His custom in
that particular is thus authenticated by the records
of the House of Commons. They tell us—

" That jurors who gave their verdict according
" to their consciences, were censured in the
" castle chamber in great fines; SOME-
" TIMES PILLORED WITH LOSS OF
" EARS, AND BORED THROUGH
" THE TONGUE, AND SOMETIMES
" MARKED IN THE FOREHEAD
" WITH A HOT IRON, AND OTHER
" INFAMOUS PUNISHMENTS."—
Commons Journals, vol. I. p. 307.

From the same despatch of the 14th of July,
1635, I take the following extract :—

" In all this business I have been very well
" assisted by Sir Gerard Lowther, Chief
" Justice of the Common Pleas, so as I crave
" leave to recommend him to his Majesty
" and my Lords as a passing able and well-
" affected servant of the Crown ; Mr. Ser-
" jeant Catelin hath performed his part also
" very excellently well. Nor must I forget
" Sir Lucas Dillon, THE FOREMAN OF THE
" JURY, who hath behaved himself with so
" much discretion, and expressed all along
" so good affections, as I cannot choose but
" here to mention him, and hereafter to be-
" seech his Majesty he may be remembered,
" when, *upon the dividing of the lands*, his
" own particular come in question. In truth
" he deserves to be extraordinarily well
" dealt withal, and so he shall, if it please
" his Majesty to leave it to me. I confess
" I delight to do well for such as I see
" frame to serve my master the right and
" cheerful way, albeit it be no more than we
" are all of us bound to do, and churlish
" enough I can be to such as do otherwise."
—I. 444.

What a gross and barefaced demand, that the
chief justice who presided at the trial and the fore-

man of the jury should be richly rewarded ! that is,
that their bribes should be abundantly paid.   It is,
perhaps, the most frank avowal of bribery upon
record.   What the amount of the bribe given to
the chief justice might have been is not publicly
known.   Judges are a discreet class, and can
transact business privately.   But it has been said
that Dillon, the foreman of the jury, got for *his*
share, lands to the value of ten thousand pounds
a-year.   He certainly got a large and valuable
estate.

These were the means by which Strafford succeeded in getting a verdict confiscating the entire
of the county of Roscommon.   He succeeded by
similar means in Mayo and Sligo.   And yet he
himself admits that so far as the case of the Crown
had any appearance of substance, it was a pure
fabrication.   To demonstrate this, I give three
passages from his letters ; by which it will mani-
festly appear that the whole thing was fraud and
fabrication :—

"*How* to make his Majesty's title to these plan-
"tations of Connaught and Ormond, (which,
"considering they have been already at-
"tempted and foiled, is of all the rest the
"greatest difficulty,) I have not hitherto
"received the least instruction from your
"Lordship, or any other minister of that
"side."—*Strafford*, I. p. 339.

Again, he writes as follows :—

" But I trust, singly (with your Majesty's coun-
" tenance to support me) to work through
" all these difficulties."—*Idem*, 342.

Again :—

" I will redeem the time as much as can be; treat
" with such as may give furtherance in find-
" ing of the title, which, as I said, is the
" principal ; and ENQUIRE OUT FIT
" MEN TO SERVE UPON JURIES."—
Strafford, I. 339.

Indeed this scandalous avowal is perhaps more
distinctly contained in another passage, which I
subjoin from a subsequent despatch of Strafford's.
It shows not only the consciousness of the utter
want of any title which could be reasonably established in a court of justice ; but it also confirms
that most vital fact in the history of Irish misgovernment, viz., that Protestantism was ever made the
pretext and instrument of every tyranny and oppression upon the native Irish. The passage is
this :—

" This house is very well composed, so as the
" Protestants are the major part, clearly and
" thoroughly with the King." * * * " And
" considering, in truth, that the popish party
" only have appeared to be averse to all re-
" formation or order in the Government, it
" will be a good rod to hold over them when

" they shall see it is in the King's power to
" pass upon them by a plurality of voices all
" the laws of England concerning religion,
" which, howbeit, I do not now dispute
" whether it be fit or not fit ; yet to have
" the power with the King is not amiss, and
" may be otherwise used with great advan-
" tage for his Majesty's service. It may
" serve of great use to confirm and settle his
" Majesty's title to the plantations of Con-
" naught and Ormond. *For this you may*
" *be sure,* ALL THE PROTESTANTS ARE FOR
" PLANTATIONS; *all the others against them;*
" so as those being the greater number, you
" can want no help they may give you
" therein.   NAY, IN CASE THERE
" BE NO TITLE TO BE MADE GOOD TO
" THESE COUNTRIES FOR THE CROWN, YET
" SHOULD I NOT DESPAIR FORTH
" OF REASON OF STATE, AND FOR THE
" STRENGTH AND SECURITY OF THE KING-
" DOM, TO HAVE THEM PASSED TO
" THE KING BY IMMEDIATE ACT
" OF PARLIAMENT."—-*Strafford*, I.
p. 353.

Notwithstanding the total deficiency of the King's
title as against the possessors—a title, against
which it was admitted that there was an adverse
possession of nearly three centuries—yet Strafford

determined to work out the iniquity to its full consummation.   Elated with the success that had
attended him in Roscommon, Mayo, and Sligo, he
proceeded to consummate similar robbery on the
inhabitants of the wealthier and more populous
county of Galway.   But here he was foiled for a
time.   In spite of all his artifices, the jury found
a verdict in favour of the defendants; as they were
bound to do, if they had any regard to the evidence,
or to their oaths.   Let every reasonable and just
man listen to the consequences.   These are Strafford's own words :—

   " We then bethought us of a course to vindicate
        " his Majesty's honour and justice, not only
        " against the persons of the jurors, but also
        " against the sheriff for returning so insuffi-
        " cient, indeed, as we conceived, a packed
        " jury, to pass upon a business of so great
        " weight and consequence; and *therefore*
        " *we fined the sheriff in a thousand pounds*
        " *to his Majesty, and bound over the jury to*
        " *appear in the castle chamber, where, we*
        " *conceive, it is fit that their pertinacious*
        " *carriage be followed with all just seve-*
        " *rity."—Strafford*, I. p. 451.

We shall see what the "*just severity*" towards
the jury was :—

   " They were fined four thousand pounds each;
        " their estates were seized, and themselves

"imprisoned, till the fines were paid."—
Carte's Ormond.

Leland adds :—

" The jurors of Galway were to remain in pri-
" son till each of them paid his fine of
" £4,000, and acknowledged his offence in
" court upon his knees."—*Leland,* Book V.
chap 1.

In the same despatch in which Strafford an-
nounced his having committed the outrage of fining
the sheriff and imprisoning the jurors, he proposed
to cut the work short in the following summary
manner :—

" We therefore have resolved, that I, the De-
" puty, shall forthwith give order to the
" King's learned counsel to put the King's
" title into a legal proceeding, (if his Ma-
" jesty in his wisdom shall not find reason to
" direct the contrary,) which we conceive
" may be in a fair and orderly way by an
" Exchequer proceeding TO SEIZE FOR HIS
" MAJESTY THE LANDS OF THE JURORS, and
" of all that shall not lay hold on his Ma-
" jesty's grace offered them by the procla-
" mation."—*Strafford,* I. 453.

He, however, advised other precautions.   He
advised—

" That his Majesty would be pleased to give
" warrant to me, his Deputy, to add two

" hundred to the number of the horse troops
" already listed here, yet without any new
" addition of charge to his Majesty in respect
" of captains or other officers ; but that by
" them the old troops may be reinforced by
" a distribution among them of these new
" supplies, as I, his Majesty's Deputy, shall
" think fit, or as I shall be better directed
" by his Majesty. This increase of horse
" we should indeed advise at any time;
" much rather *now, till the intended plan-*
" *tation be settled.* For it will be necessary
" that some strength of horse may stand and
" *look on,* as an excellent assistant to coun-
" tenance the plantation."—*Strafford,* I.
453, 454.

It will be recollected that Strafford at the commencement of these inquisitions, when he had
secured the jury for the county of Roscommon,
made a parade of the great liberality with which
the Crown had permitted counsel to defend the
rights of the people against itself. That this declaration was intended merely as a trap, will appear
from the following extract from the same despatch,
dated 25th August, 1635 :—

" For those counsellors of the law, who so
" laboured against the King's title, we con-
" ceive it is fit, that such of them as we shall
" find reason so to proceed withal, be put to

" take the oath of Supremacy, which if they
" refuse, that then they be silenced, and not
" admitted to practice as now they do ; it
" being unfit that they should take benefit
" by his Majesty's graces, that take the
" boldness after such a manner to oppose
" his service."—*Strafford*, I. 454.

It is manifest therefore, that the permission to
use counsel, must have been given in the expectation that such counsel would neglect their duty to
their clients, and betray their own consciences, to
please the Lord Deputy. The counsel disappointed
this unholy expectation. They were accordingly
driven from the practice of their profession; for
they would not and could not take the oath of
Supremacy.

I cannot refrain from here stating a fact which
has occurred in my own time. There was an individual at the Irish Bar who practised exclusively in
the criminal courts; and who for nearly twenty
years contrived to be appointed counsel for all the
persons prosecuted by the Crown. Yet that man
had, for the last eighteen years of his life, a *private
pension* of £300 per annum from the Crown. This
was not discovered by the public until after his
death. *What was this pension given for ?*

To return to Wentworth, and the methods
whereby he procured verdicts—here is a spe
cimen :—

" Your Majesty was graciously pleased, upon my
" humble advice, TO BESTOW FOUR SHILLINGS
" IN THE POUND UPON YOUR LORD CHIEF
" JUSTICE AND LORD CHIEF BARON IN THIS
" KINGDOM, *forth of the first yearly rent*
" *raised upon the Commission of Defective*
" *Titles*. Which, upon observation, I find
" to be the best given that ever was ; FOR
" NOW THEY DO INTEND IT WITH A CARE AND
" DILIGENCE SUCH AS IT WERE THEIR OWN
" PRIVATE; AND MOST CERTAIN, THE GAINING
" TO THEMSELVES EVERY FOUR SHILLINGS
" ONCE PAID, SHALL BETTER YOUR REVENUE
" FOR EVER AFTER AT LEAST FIVE POUNDS."
Strafford, II. p. 41.

The unhappy Galway jurors remained for years
in prison. They sent agents to London to obtain
mercy from the King—but in vain! On the contrary, Strafford had the audacity to demand that
these agents should be punished !—punished merely
for going to sue for mercy. There is this passage
in his despatch of the 14th December, 1635 :—

" I find that nothing would give these commis-
" sioners so much satisfaction, and even in
" my own judgment so much enable us, and
" dispose all to a speedy and happy conclu-
" sion, as to remit these agents of *Gallway*
" in the condition of *prisoners*, and their
" propositions intirely to *our* consideration

"and legal proceeding on this side."—
Strafford, I. 493.

And, accordingly, the agents were transmitted
as prisoners, to abide the tender mercies of Strafford.

It has been said that the unhappy Charles was
ignorant of these enormities, and would have condemned them. Alas! the fact is otherwise. Strafford, in the year 1636, went over to England;
reported to the King in council his proceedings in
the Galway case : the King replied—

"That it was *no severity;* and wished him to go
"on in that way; for that if he served him
"otherwise, he would not serve him as he
"expected. So," adds Wentworth, "I
"kneeled down, kissed his Majesty's hand,
"and the council rose."—*Carte's Ormond,*
vol. III. p. 11.

If any one will reflect upon the multitude of
crimes of which the King thus expressed his ap-
proval, he will not be surprised at the ultimate fate
of the unfortunate monarch. Assuredly the forms
of law were never before used to inflict such a
complication of iniquities as were perpetrated by
Strafford, and approved of by the King.

The palliation, or rather justification, which
obtrudes itself in all Strafford's despatches, is, that
all these things were done, not only to augment the
King's revenue, but first, and especially, for the

advancement of Protestantism, and the good of
Protestants.

Oh, Protestantism ! what horrors have been
committed in your name in Ireland !

I pass hastily over another grievance of the
utmost magnitude sustained by the Irish. It was
the institution of the Court of Wards.

> " This was a new court, never known in Ireland
> " till the 14th of James I. It had no war-
> " rant from any law or statute, whereas that
> " of England was erected by an Act of
> " Parliament."—*Carte's Ormond*, vol. I. p.
> 517.

The object of this court was to vest in persons
appointed by the Crown the custody of the estates
of minors. It is easy to see how it worked in Ireland ; especially during the rule of Strafford.

> " Sir William Parsons, by whom it was first pro-
> " jected, was appointed master of it ; a man
> " justly and universally hated by the Irish.
> " And such were the illegal and arbitrary
> " proceedings of that court, that ' the heirs
> " ' of Catholic noblemen and other Catholics
> " ' were destroyed in their estates, bred in
> " ' dissolution and ignorance ; their parents'
> " ' debts unsatisfied, their sisters and younger
> " ' brothers left wholly unprovided for ; the
> " ' ancient appearing tenures of mesne lords
> " ' disregarded ; estates valid in law, and

" ' made for valuable considerations, avoided
" ' against law ; and the whole land filled
" ' with frequent swarms of escheators,
" ' feudatories, pursuivants, and others, by
" ' authority of that court.' "—*Remonstrance from Trim* (apud *Curry*, p. 125).

Another court was instituted still more recently,
and if possible with less authority. It was Lord
Strafford who proposed to erect this other court, in
the year 1633. It inflicted on the Catholics—

" An incapacity for all offices and employments ;
" a disability to sue out livery of their estates
" without taking the oath of Supremacy ;
" severe penalties of various kinds inflicted
" by that court on all those of the Catholic
" religion ; although the Catholics were an
" hundred to one more than those of any
" other religion."—*Remonstrance from
Trim* (ut supra).

The proceedings in this court were of a nature
so cruelly oppressive, and so utterly indefensible,
that even Leland speaks of them in the following
terms :—

" These regulations in the ecclesiastical system
" were followed by an establishment too
" odious, and therefore too dangerous to be
" attempted during the sessions of parlia-
" ment, that of an *High Commission Court,*
" which was erected in Dublin after the

" English model, with the same formality,
" and the same tremendous powers."—
Leland's Ireland, Book V. chap. 1.

I cannot proceed without giving the following
exquisite *morçeau*. It is part of Lord Strafford's
defence of himself, in which he, with great *naïveté*,
relies upon *cases in point*, of cruelty. Let it speak
for itself :—

" I dare appeal to those that know the country,
" whether in former times many men have
" not been committed and executed by the
" deputies' warrant, that were not thieves
" and rebels, but such as went up and down
" the country. *If they could not give a*
" *good account of themselves*, the provost-
" marshal, by direction of the deputies,
" using in such cases to hang them up. I
" dare say THERE ARE HUNDREDS
" OF EXAMPLES IN THIS KIND."—
Rushworth's Collectanea, VIII. p. 649.

I may here, also, by way of parenthesis, bring
before the reader other significant passages from
Protestant historians, which show that the virulence
wherewith Catholicity was persecuted was not confined to the ecclesiastical courts.

" In this year (1629) the Roman clergy began
" to rant it, and to exercise their fancies
" called religion so publicly, as if they had
" gained a toleration. For whilst the Lords

" Justices were at Christ Church in Dublin
" on St. Stephen's day, they were celebrating
" mass in Cook-street ; which their lord-
" ships taking notice of, they sent the arch-
" bishop of Dublin, the mayor, sheriffs, and
" recorder of the city, with a file of mus-
" keteers, to apprehend them ; which they
" did, taking away the crucifixes and para-
" ments of the altar; the soldiers hewing
" down the image of St. Francis ; the priests
" and friars were delivered into the hands
" of the pursuivants, at whom the people
" threw stones, and rescued them. The
" Lords Justices being informed of this, sent
" a guard and delivered them, and clapped
" eight popish aldermen by the heels for not
" assisting their mayor. On this account,
" fifteen houses, [viz. chapels,] by direction
" of the Lords of the Council in England,
" were seized to the King's use, and the
" priests and friars were so persecuted,
" THAT TWO OF THEM HANGED THEMSELVES
" IN THEIR OWN DEFENCE."—*Hammon
L'Estrange*, quoted in *Harris's Fiction
Unmasked.*

It will be easily believed that the priests and
friars were saved the trouble of hanging themselves.

All these proceedings were approved of by the
unhappy Charles.

" His Majesty, in person, was pleased openly,
" and in the most gracious manner, to ap-
" prove and commend their ability and good
" service; whereby they might be sufficiently
" encouraged to go on, with the like resolu-
" tion and MODERATION, till the work
" was fully done, as well in the city as in
" other places of the kingdom, leaving to
" their discretion when and where to carry
" a soft or harder hand."—*Scrinia Sacra.*

It is just worth while to pause for one moment,
and to see what was doing in England about the
same time ; or, as the modern phrase is, " was *being
done.*"

" Besides Richard Herst, Edmund Arrowsmith,
" and others, put to death in 1628, merely
" for exercising the functions of Roman Ca-
" tholic priests ; Thomas Bullaker, Thomas
" Holland, Paul Heath, Francis Bell, Rho-
" dolphus Colman, (condemned, but re-
" prieved,) Henry Morse, —— Morgan,
" Philip Powel, and Martin Woodcock, to-
" gether with Reading and Whitaker, were
" executed in England for the same causes,
" between the years 1641 and 1646..........
" The condition of a missionary at the be-
" ginning of this reign was different from
" what it was at the latter end of it ; when
" religious zeal against popery was heigh-

" tened and inflamed with all the rage of
" faction. If a Turkish dervise had then
" preached Mahomet in England, he would
" have met much better treatment than a
" popish priest."—*Grainger's Biographical
Hist. of England*, II. pp. 206, 7, 8.

It will be remembered that nothing more tended
to foment the great rebellion in England against
Charles the First, than the oppressions practised
by the Court of Wards and the High Commission
Court. Ireland felt more than double the severity
inflicted upon England by these institutions.

The reason why I have dwelt in these notes upon
the enormities committed in the administration of
what was called "justice" in Ireland, is, that by
the most singular perversion of the facts of history,
not only Temple, but Clarendon, and, after *him*,
Hume, and a multitude of other calumniators of
Ireland, have gravely stated the astounding falsehood that Ireland was *well governed* in the reigns
of James the First and of Charles the First!

Well governed! when the ecclesiastical courts
hunted the Catholics like wild beasts, and crowded
them, when caught, into loathsome prisons! when
the Court of Wards spoliated the properties of all
Catholic minors, and perverted their religion! when
the High Commission Court punished with more
than Star-chamber severity, every supposed slight
or insult to any person in power ; punished every

resistance (however necessary and justifiable) to the will or caprice of men in authority ! when the sheriffs were intimidated, and punished if the verdicts of the juries did not satisfy the ruling tyrants! when the chief justice and other judges were bribed by the highest authority in the land ; bribed with a stipulated proportion of the property in dispute, for procuring judgment against the unhappy possessors of that property ! when the jurors who obeyed the impulses of conscience were thrown to rot in prison ; were ruined by fines so enormous as to amount to a confiscation of their property ; were pilloried—had their ears cut off—their tongues bored through ; were————But I will not pursue this subject.   What need I ?

Well governed !   This is what English writers of the highest class call good government.

OBSERVATIONS,
PROOFS, AND ILLUSTRATIONS.

CHAPTER III.—PART II.

I AM not writing the history in detail of the civil
war. I am merely justifying my statement in
the text. No person can deny that the cause of the
King had now become identified with that of
the Irish Catholics.

Now for the cruelties perpetrated by the English
Protestant parliamentarians and Cromwellians.

My first extract is from a Protestant clergyman—
the historian Leland. He shows the design with
which these cruelties were committed.

" The *favourite* object of the Irish Governors,
" and the English parliament, was the
" utter EXTERMINATION OF ALL
" THE CATHOLIC INHABITANTS
" OF IRELAND. *Their estates were*
" *already marked out and allotted to their*
" *conquerors ;* so that they and their poste-
" rity were consigned to inevitable ruin."—
Leland, Book V. chap. 4.

My second quotation establishing the same fact

is from another Protestant clergyman named Rev.
Dr. Warner.

> " It is evident from their" [the Lords Justices]
> " last letter to the Lieutenant, that they
> " hoped for an EXTIRPATION, not of
> " mere Irish only, but of all the old English
> " families that were Roman Catholics."—
> *Warner's History of the Rebellion and
> Civil War in Ireland,* p. 176.

Upon this subject—namely, the design of UT-
TER EXTIRPATION—my next quotation is
from the equally undeniable authority of Lord
Clarendon.

> " The parliament party......had grounded their
> " own authority and strength upon such
> " foundations as were inconsistent with any
> " toleration of the Roman Catholic religion,
> " and even with any humanity to the Irish
> " nation, and more especially to those of the
> " old native extraction, THE WHOLE RACE
> " WHEREOF THEY HAD UPON THE MATTER
> " SWORN TO EXTIRPATE."—*Lord
> Clarendon,* I. p. 215.

This hideous determination of massacre was
occasionally somewhat relaxed when the fortunes
of the parliamentarians waned; it was relaxed,
however, only to be renewed with redoubled ala-
crity when their fortunes prospered again. The
following is from Carte's *Ormond :*—

" Mr. Brent lately landed here, and hath brought
" with him such letters as have somewhat
" changed the face of this Government from
" what it was, when the parliament pamphlets
" were received as oracles, their commands
" obeyed as laws, and EXTIRPATION
" PREACHED FOR GOSPEL."–*Carte's
Ormond*, III. 170.

There were *two* objects to be gratified by the
English Protestant rulers of the day. The first
was the increase of plunder to themselves in the
confiscation of the estates of the Catholics. The
second was the indiscriminate slaughter of those
Catholics, without any distinction of age, sex, rank,
or condition. The following accusation—fully
borne out by the facts—is quoted from the same
English Protestant historian, Carte :—

" There is too much reason to think, that as the
" Lord's Justices really wished the rebellion
" to spread, and more gentlemen of estates
" to be involved in it, THAT THE FORFEI-
" TURES MIGHT BE THE GREATER, AND A
" GENERAL PLANTATION BE CARRIED ON BY
" A NEW SET OF ENGLISH PROTESTANTS ALL
" OVER THE KINGDOM, TO THE RUIN AND
" EXPULSION OF ALL THE OLD ENGLISH
" AND NATIVES THAT WERE ROMAN CATHO-
" LICS ; so, to promote what they wished,
" they gave out such a design, and that in

" a short time *there would not be a Roman*
" *Catholic left in the kingdom.* It is no
" small confirmation of this notion, that the
" Earl of Ormond, in his letters of January
" 27th, and February 25th, 1641–2, to Sir
" W. St. Leger, *imputes the general revolt*
" *of the nation, then far advanced, to the*
" *publishing of such a design :* and when a
" person of his great modesty and temper,
" the most averse in his nature to speak his
" sentiments of what he could not but con-
" demn in others, and who, when obliged
" to do so, does it always in the gentlest
" expressions, is drawn to express such an
" opinion, *the case must be very notorious.*
" I do not find that the copies of those
" letters are preserved ; but the original of
" Sir William St. Leger's, in answer to
" them, sufficiently shows it to be his Lord-
" ship's opinion ; for after acknowledging
" the receipt of these two letters, he useth
" these words : ' The undue promulgation
" ' of that severe DETERMINATION TO EX-
" ' TIRPATE THE IRISH AND PAPACY
" ' OUT OF THIS KINGDOM, YOUR LORDSHIP
" ' RIGHTLY APPREHENDS TO BE TOO UNSEA-
" ' SONABLY PUBLISHED.' "—*Carte's Orm.*
I. 263.
This St. Leger was himself one of the chief

extirpators: and I pray the reader to observe that he does not at all condemn the system of massacring the Irish to the last man. The only thing that he finds fault with is the *unseasonable* publication of the purpose to do so. It will, however, be more clearly understood what his real dispositions were, from a letter written by Lord Upper Ossory, quoted by Carte, in which the writer says,—

" That Sir William St. Leger" (who was Lord
    President of Munster) "was so cruel and
    " merciless, that he caused men and women
    " to be most execrably executed; *and that*
    " he ordered, among others, a woman great
    " with child to be ripped up, from whose
    " womb three babes were taken out; through
    " every of whose little bodies his soldiers
    " thrust their weapons; which act" (adds
    Lord Upper Ossory) "put many into a sort
    " of desperation."—*Carte's Ormond*, vol.
    III. p. 51.

I only implore Englishmen and Protestants to read these extracts from Protestant historians, and to reflect how much of disrepute they fling upon Protestantism in general, and the English nation in particular. If they had such a case to make in *point of fact* against the Catholics, we should never hear the end of it !

But as the cruelties of individuals will bring the fact more pointedly before the mind, and cause its more easy retention in the recollection, I will select some specimens of the *sçavoir faire* of that Sir Charles Coote whom I have mentioned in the text. To work out the purposes of the English Government, power of life and death was given to him. Mark the following description of him and his cruelties :—

"It was certainly a miserable spectacle to see "every day NUMBERS OF PEOPLE EXECUTED "BY MARTIAL LAW, AT THE DISCRETION, OR "RATHER CAPRICE OF SIR CHARLES COOTE, "AN HOT-HEADED AND BLOODY MAN, AND AS "SUCH ACCOUNTED EVEN BY THE ENGLISH "PROTESTANTS. Yet, this was the man "whom the Lords Justices picked out to "entrust with a commission of martial law "to put to death rebels or traitors—*that is,* "*all such as he should deem to be so ;* "WHICH HE PERFORMED WITH DELIGHT AND "A WANTON KIND OF CRUELTY. And yet "all this while the justices sat in council, "and the judges at the usual seasons sat in "their respective courts, SPECTATORS OF, "AND COUNTENANCING so extravagant a tri- "bunal as Sir Charles Coote's, and so illegal "an execution of justice."—*Lord Castle- haven,* quoted in *Carte's Orm.* vol. I. pp. 279, 280.

Another specimen of the services upon which

Sir Charles Coote was employed, we have on the authority of Borlase, as well as of Carte. The public faith had been pledged to protect a Mr. King, one of the gentlemen assembled at Swords. The Lords Justices observed their plighted faith by sending a party of horse and foot, on the 15th December, 1641, to Clontarf, the property of Mr. King, with orders to fall upon and cut off the inhabitants, and burn the village.

" These orders," says Borlase, " were excellently " well executed."—*Hist. Reb.* p. 62.

Carte adds :—

" Sir Charles Coote, who, by the Lords Justices' " special designation, was appointed to go " on this expedition, *as the fittest person to* " *execute their orders, and one who best* " *knew their minds,* at this time pillaged " and burned houses, corn, and other goods " belonging to Mr. King, to the value of " four thousand pounds."—*Carte's Ormond,* I. 249.

The next extract I shall give is of some length ; but it is exceedingly significant. It relates to the murder of Father Higgins, the parish priest of Naas ; a man of innocent life, of humanity, and of piety ; a man whose character was never tar- nished. Yet his innocence, his active humanity, and his piety, could not—in the midst of Dublin, and in the presence of the Government—avail him

aught! Every part of this extract is pregnant
with meaning : the object to discourage submissions,
lest they should diminish confiscations, was well
worthy of our pious Protestant English governors.
Here is the story of his assassination :—

" The cruelties of the martial law under Sir C.
   " Coote have been already mentioned ; but
   " about this time, when it was thought politic
   " to discourage the submissions which were
   " growing frequent, Father Higgins, a very
   " quiet, pious, inoffensive man, who had put
   " himself under the protection of Lord Or-
   " mond, and whom his lordship had brought
   " with him to Dublin, was one morning
   " seized ; and without any trial or delay, or
   " giving his lordship any notice of the inten-
   " tion, *by Sir C. Coote's order, hanged.*
   " Father Higgins officiated as a priest at
   " Naas, and in that neighbourhood ; HAD
   " DISTINGUISHED HIMSELF GREATLY BY SAV-
   " ING THE ENGLISH IN THOSE PARTS FROM
   " SPOIL AND SLAUGHTER ; and had relieved
   " several whom he found to have been
   " stripped and plundered, so far was he
   " from engaging in the rebellion, or giving
   " any encouragement to it.   Lord Ormond
   " had therefore taken him under his protec-
   " tion ; and when he heard of the execution
   " of this innocent man, for no other reason

" than his being a priest, his lordship was
" very warm in his expostulations with the
" Justices upon it at the council board.
" They pretended to be surprised; and ex-
" cused themselves from having had *any*
" *other hand in the affair than giving Sir*
" *C. Coote a general authority to order such*
" *executions without consulting them.* Lord
" Ormond insisted that Coote should be tried
" for what he had done, as having hanged
" an innocent, nay, a deserving subject,
" WITHOUT EXAMINATION, WITHOUT TRIAL,
" AND WITHOUT A PARTICULAR WARRANT TO
" AUTHORISE HIM IN IT. The Justices, who
" had either directed him to do it, or were
" determined to support their favourite in a
" proceeding which was agreeable to them,
" would not give him up. Their hanging
" a man of character at all, deserving in
" many respects, and exceptionable in none
" but his religion, inclines one to think that
" THEY INTENDED THIS WAR
" SHOULD BE UNDERSTOOD TO
" BE A WAR OF RELIGION. But
" their hanging him in such a manner, by
" martial law, by Sir C. Coote's authority
" only, against justice and humanity, when
" brought thither and protected by Lord
" Ormond, could only be meant to prevent

" all submissions, or to offer such an indig-
" nity to his lordship as should provoke him
" to resign his commission, and to oppose
" them no longer in council."—*Warner*,
p. 182.

I now give Clarendon's version of the same
transaction; because it shows the brutality of even
the soldiers who were under the command of Ormond, while he was serving the English party.   It,
however, does not appear that these soldiers knew
he was a priest.   They were ready to murder him
merely for being a Papist.

" The Marquis of Ormond, having intelligence
" that a party of the rebels intended to be
" at such a time at the Naas, he drew some
" troops with the hope of surprising them;
" and, marching all night, came early in the
" morning into the town, from which the
" rebels, upon notice, were newly fled.   In
" the town some of the soldiers found the
" Rev. Mr. Higgins, who might, 'tis true,
" have as easily fled, if he had apprehended
" any danger in the stay.   When he was
" brought before the Marquis, he voluntarily
" acknowledged that he was a Papist, and
" that his residence was in the town, from
" whence he refused to fly away with those
" who were guilty; because he not only
" knew himself very innocent, but believed

" that he could not be without ample evi-
" dence of it, having by his sole charity and
" power preserved very many of the English
" Protestants from the rage and fury of the
" Irish : and therefore, he only besought
" the Marquis to preserve him from the
" violence of the soldiers, and to put him
" securely into Dublin, to be tried for any
" crime : which the Marquis promised to
" do, and performed it, though with so much
" hazard, that when it was spread abroad
" among the soldiers that he was a Papist,
" the officer into whose custody he was
" entrusted was assaulted by them ; and it
" was as much as the Marquis could do to
" relieve him, and compose the mutiny.
" When he came to Dublin he informed the
" Lords Justices of the prisoner he had
" brought with him ; of the good testimony
" he had received of his peaceable carriage;
" and of the pains he had taken to restrain
" those with whom he had credit, from en-
" tering into rebellion ; and of many chari-
" table offices he had performed, of which
" there wanted not evidence enough, there
" being many then in Dublin who owed
" their lives, and whatever of their fortunes
" was left, purely to him : so that he doubted
" not that he would be worthy of protection.

" Within a few days after, when the Marquis
" did not suspect the poor man's being in
" danger, he heard that *Sir Charles Coote,*
" *who was Provost-marshal General, had*
" *taken him out of prison, and caused him*
" *to be put to death in the morning, before,*
" *or as soon as it was light :* of which bar-
" barity the Marquis complained to the
" Lords Justices ; but was so far from bring-
" ing the other to be questioned, that he
" found himself to be upon some disadvan-
" tage, for thinking the proceeding to be
" other than it ought to have been."—
Clarendon's Hist. Irish Reb.

I wish to specify in particular the cruelties of
Sir Charles Coote in the county of Wicklow. *Let
it be recollected that Coote's crimes are NOT the
crimes of an individual only.* The Government
who selected and employed him is of course respon-
sible for those crimes. Here is the short and pithy
account given by Leland of an expedition of his
into the county of Wicklow :—

" Sir Charles Coote," says Leland, " in revenge
" of the depredations of the Irish, committed
" SUCH UNPROVOKED, SUCH RUTHLESS, AND
" INDISCRIMINATE CARNAGE in the town of
" Wicklow, as rivalled the utmost extrava-
" gancies of the northerns."—*Leland's Hist.
Ireland,* Book V. chap. 4.

Fortified by this corroboration, I do not hesitate to give the following account of the English cruelties in the county of Wicklow, from a pamphlet published in London in the year 1662, although it was written by an Irish Catholic. But as the writer appeals confidently to then living Protestant witnesses,* and indeed is corroborated in the most important of his statements by Leland and Warner, both Protestant clergymen, it is manifest that his details can with perfect safety be relied on.

"COUNTY OF WICKLOW.

"October, 1641. Three women, whereof one "gentlewoman was big with child, and a "boy, were hanged on the bridge of Neuragh "by command of Sir Charles Coote, in his "first march to that county; and he caused "his guide to blow into his pistol, and so "shot him dead. He also hanged a poor "butcher on the same march, called Thomas "Mac William. Mr. Dan. Conyam, of "Glanely, aged, and unable to bear arms, "was *roasted to death* by Captain Gee, of "Colonel Crafford's regiment: and in the

* Among the Protestants of note then living, to whom the writer of the work now quoted appeals for the truth of his statement, are Sir Audley Mervyn, Sir Robert Hannah, (the father of Lady Mountrath,) and several general and other officers.

"marches of 1641, 1642, and 1643, the
"English army killed all they met in this
"country, *though no murders are charged*
"*in the said county to be committed on*
" *Protestants by the Abstract.* In the Usur-
"per's time, Captain Barrington, garrisoned
"at Arklow, MURDERED DONAGH O'DOYLE
"OF KILLECARROW, AND ABOVE FIVE HUN-
"DRED MORE PROTECTED BY HIMSELF ; *and*
"*it is well known that most of the com-*
"*monalty were murdered.*"
Here is another passage from the same writer,
confirmed by Carte and Warner in like manner.
It is given in abstract by those Protestant historians, but in fuller detail in the following quotation :—

          "COUNTY OF DUBLIN.
"1641. About the *beginning* of November, five
"poor men (whereof two were Protestants)
"coming from the market of Dublin, and
"lying that night at Santry, three miles
"from thence, were murdered in their beds
"by one Captain Smith and a party of the
"garrison of Dublin, and their heads brought
"next day in triumph into the city ; which
"occasioned Luke Netterville and George
"King, and others of the neighbours, to
"write to the Lords Justices to know the
"cause of the said murder : whereupon their

"lordships issued forth a proclamation that
"within five days the gentry should come
"to Dublin to receive satisfaction, and in
"the mean while (before the five days were
"expired) old Sir Charles Coote came out
"with a party, plundered and burned the
"town of Clontarf, distant two miles from
"Dublin, belonging to the said George
"King, nominated in the proclamation; and
"killed 16 of the townsmen and women,
"and three sucking infants. Which unex-
"pected breach of the proclamation (having
"deterred the gentlemen from waiting on
"the Lords Justices) forced many of them
"to betake themselves to their defence, and
"abandon their houses."

The character of Sir Charles Coote requires no
further elucidation. He was the man to whom the
English Government gave unlimited power of life
and death over the Irish. "He was," as Carte
says, "*the fittest person to execute their orders,
and one who best knew their minds.*" It is not
surprising therefore, that a Protestant clergyman
should give of him the following mitigated character :—

"He" (Sir Charles Coote) "was a stranger to
"mercy, and committed many acts of cru-
"elty without distinction."—*Warner's Hist.
Irish Reb.* p. 135.

This Sir Charles Coote was of inestimable value to his employers. The object of the English party, headed by the Lords Justices, was, as we have seen, to drive the Catholics into rebellion; and they began by falsely accusing them of treasonable practices. For that purpose they spared no methods however infamous, to *fabricate* evidence against the Catholic nobility and gentry. The rack and torture were familiar instruments of this villainy. This fact is admitted by all contemporary historians. Speaking of some of the principal Catholic gentry, Leland says—

> "They" (the Chief Governors) "resolved to
> "supply the want of legal evidence by put-
> "ting some prisoners to the *rack*. They
> "began with Hugh M'Mahon, who had
> "been seized on the information of O'Con-
> "noly, and from whom they expected some
> "important discoveries. But torture could
> "force nothing from him essential to their
> "great purpose."—*Leland*, Book V. chap. 4.

Even in this cruelty there is a very characteristic trait. The Irish gentry, unwilling to be driven into armed resistance, entrusted Sir John Read with a petition to the King. Parsons (whom we have already named—the ancestor of the present Earl of Rosse) obtained the confidence of Sir John Read, and of course betrayed him. Let Warner tell the story :—

" Sir John Read, by the same stretch of arbitrary
" power, WAS BROUGHT TO THE RACK. This
" gentleman was of the privy chamber to the
" King, a lieutenant-colonel in the late dis-
" banded army, and engaged by the Lords
" of the Pale to carry over their petitions to
" the King and Queen. He intended to
" make no secret of his journey, and there-
" fore sent a letter by a servant of his own
" to Parsons, to desire a pass; who, in an-
" swer, *required him to repair to Dublin,*
" *that the council might confer with him.*"
—*Warner,* p. 177.

He was tortured. But no evidence could be extorted from him—because he had no evidence to
give against the Catholic gentry whom it was sought
to convict, save that which he had avowed and
considered no crime; namely, their having petitioned the Sovereign for protection. He was however made to feel that if the fact of petitioning were
not a crime, it was at least punishable as such. Let
the English reader pause upon the consequences :—

" Sir J. Read was *sent a prisoner* to England ;
" and whilst absent, and in those circum-
" stances, *was indicted and outlawed for*
" *high treason ; his lady and goods were*
" *seized upon, and she and his children*
" *turned out of doors ;* and when she peti-
" tioned to these worthy Justices to assign

" her some part of her effects to maintain
" her family, they absolutely refused to
" allow her any."—*Warner*, 178.

Aye—his wife and children turned out to starve!
There is a specimen of English humanity and justice for you! While the wife and children were
famishing, the Government proceeded in their reck-
less career :—

" The racking M'Mahon and Sir John Read did
" not content this merciless administration ;
" AND SO MR. BARNEWAL OF KILBREW WAS
" PUT TO THE SAME TORTURE. He was one
" of the most considerable gentlemen of the
" Pale ; *a venerable old man of sixty-six*
" *years of age, delighting in husbandry, a*
" *lover of quiet, and highly respected in his*
" *country.* He had sent intelligence to the
" Government of the motion of the Ulster
" rebels in the month of November ; and
" the only thing that could be said against
" him was, that he had obeyed the sheriff's
" summons for the meeting at the hill of
" Crofty, when Lord Gormanston declared
" an union with them. It does not appear
" that he approved the union, or that he
" actually had joined them upon any occa-
" sion ; and so little did the ministers get
" by putting him to the torture, that *it only*
" *served to make his innocence, and their*

" own inhumanity, the more conspicuous."
—*Warner*, p. 179.

The object was avowed—to force the Catholics
of property into rebellion. They were allowed no
means of defending their houses against the insurgents who had already been driven to take up arms.
They thronged into Dublin, where they would have
been under the immediate inspection of the Government, and would have joined in resisting the
insurgents. But the object of the English Protestant party was to *force* these Catholics of wealth to
join those whom they called rebels. It required
no less than three proclamations to force them out
of Dublin. But I will give the original authority :—

" The gentlemen of the Pale, banished Dublin
" by three successive proclamations, and on
" pain of death ordered to repair to their
" own houses, unable to make resistance,
" and seeing not any, even the least prospect
" of relief or succour, opened their defence-
" less habitations to the enemy ; which gave
" the Lords Justices occasion to complain
" 'that the rebels were harboured and lodged
" in gentlemen's houses of that county, as
" fully as if they were good subjects.' This
" correspondence, however necessitated it
" was at first, involving them in the guilt of
" rebellion, according to the rigour of the
" law, which they had no reason to think

" would be relaxed, on account of their
" unhappy situation, by any favour or ten-
" derness they might hope from the then
" Government, *made the gentlemen in ge-*
" *neral, and the high sheriff in particular,*
" *to join the rebels, and put the fate of their*
" *persons and fortunes upon the issue of the*
" *rebellion."—Carte's Ormond,* I. 238.

Thus, they were to be punished with death if
they remained in Dublin. Driven to their own
houses, they must submit to the insurgents, and
thus incur the penalties of treason. What were
they then to do ? Several of these unhappy gentlemen fled back from the insurgents, aud surrendered themselves to the mercy of the Justices.
This was the proceeding taken against them :—

" All the gentlemen that surrendered themselves
" were, without being admitted to the pre-
" sence of the Justices, committed prisoners
" to the castle. Preparations were made
" for their trial, and it was publicly said
" they should be prosecuted with the utmost
" severity. *But as they had never appeared*
" *in the field, nor been engaged in any*
" *warlike action,* PROPER FACTS WERE WANT-
" ING TO SUPPORT A CHARGE AGAINST THEM.
" To supply this defect, the Lords Justices
" had recourse to the RACK, though against
" the law, *in order to extort such confessions*

" *as these miscreants had a mind to put into*
" *the mouths of the unhappy men who were*
" *to undergo it.*"—*Warner*, p. 176.

The premeditation with which the Lords Justices
arranged their plans for driving the Irish into rebellion, is well illustrated by the following extract;
which shows that no devices were omitted to drive
the Catholic Irish to despair, and to force them to
defend themselves with the sword :—

" Some time before the rebellion broke out,"
says Carte, " it was confidently reported
" that Sir John Clotworthy, who well knew
" the designs of the faction that governed
" the House of Commons in England, had
" declared there in a speech THAT THE CON-
" VERSION OF THE PAPISTS IN IRELAND WAS
" ONLY TO BE EFFECTED BY THE BIBLE IN
" ONE HAND AND THE SWORD IN THE OTHER;
" AND MR. PYM GAVE OUT THAT THEY WOULD
" NOT LEAVE A PRIEST IN IRELAND. To the
" like effect Sir William Parsons, out of a
" strange weakness, or detestable policy,
" positively asserted before so many wit-
" nesses, at a public entertainment, that
" WITHIN A TWELVEMONTH NO CATHOLIC
" SHOULD BE SEEN IN IRELAND. He had
" sense enough to know the consequences
" that would naturally arise from such a
" declaration; which, however it might con-

" tribute to his own selfish views, he would
" hardly have ventured to make so openly
" and without disguise, if it had not been
" agreeable to the politics and measures
" of the English faction, whose party he
" espoused, and whose directions were the
" general rule of his conduct."—*Carte's
Ormond,* vol. I. p. 235.

" It is evident," says Dr. Warner, (a Protestant
clergyman,) "from the Lord Justices' letter
" to the Earl of Leicester, then Lord Lieu-
" tenant, that THEY HOPED FOR AN EXTIR-
" PATION, NOT OF THE MERE IRISH ONLY,
" BUT OF ALL THE OLD ENGLISH FAMILIES
" ALSO WHO WERE ROMAN CATHOLICS."—
Warner's Hist. of the Irish Rebel.

Coming back for one moment to Sir Charles
Coote, the catalogue of whose horrors we have
already described, I will revive the recollection of
them by the following passage from Clarendon :—

" Sir Charles, besides plundering and burning
" this town" [Clontarf] " at that time, did
" massacre 16 of the townspeople, men and
" women, besides three sucking infants ; and
" in the very same week 56 men, women,
" and children, of the village of Bulloge, being
" frightened at what was done at Clontarf,
" took boats, and went to sea to shun the
" fury of a party of soldiers that were come

" out of Dublin under the command of
" Colonel Crafford ; but being pursued by
" the soldiers in other boats, they were
" overtaken and thrown overboard."—*Appendix to Clarendon's Hist. Irish Reb., Wilford, London*, 1720.

Was Coote punished for his sanguinary conduct, not exceeded in atrocity by that of the modern Robespierre ?   You shall learn :—

" Sir Charles Coote, immediately after his inhu-
" man executions and promiscuous murders
" of the people in Wicklow, *was made*
" *Governor of Dublin*."—*Carte's Ormond*,
I. 259.

The hideous monster Coote, indeed was, as I have already said, of inestimable value to his employers.   To him was given the part of the archfiend.   It was death and destruction to place the least confidence in him.   The Lords Justices proposed a treaty with the Lords of the Pale ; who were most anxious to accept any terms.   But they would not put themselves into the power of Sir Charles Coote, who they knew would have murdered every one of them.

" The Lords Justices, as soon as they were satis-
" fied that the Lords of the Pale would not
" trust themselves in the city in the hands
" of Sir Charles Coote, *though they were*
" *ready to treat with commissioners sent*

"*from thence to any place out of his power,*
"TOOK MEASURES IN ORDER TO CONVICT
"THEM OF TREASON, AND FORFEIT
"THEIR ESTATES."—*Carte's Orm.*
I. 276.

For the present—so much for Sir Charles Coote!
I go on with my extracts.

The next is, the orders given in February,
1641—2, by the Lords Justices to the Earl of Ormond; communicated to him in the shape of a resolution, as follows:—

"It is resolved, That it is fit that his lordship do
    "endeavour with his Majesty's forces to
    "*wound, kill, slay, and destroy,* by all the
    "ways and means he may, all the said
    "rebels, their adherents, and *relievers;* and
    "*burn, spoil, waste, consume, destroy, and*
    "*demolish,* ALL THE PLACES, TOWNS, AND
    "HOUSES, WHERE THE SAID REBELS ARE, OR
    "HAVE BEEN, RELIEVED AND HARBOURED;
    "and all the hay and corn there; AND KILL
    "AND DESTROY ALL THE MEN THERE INHA-
    "BITING CAPABLE TO BEAR ARMS. Given at
    "his Majesty's Castle of Dublin, 23rd Feb-
    "ruary, 1641—2.
        "R. DILLON,   F. WILLOUGHBY,
        "THO. ROTHERHAM, J. TEMPLE,
        "AB. LOFTUS,   ROBERT MEREDITH."
—*Carte,* III. 61.

With what fiendish pleasure this tribunal of blood gloated over every word that could signify destruction or massacre ! The French Revolutionists were but poor copyists of English cruelty in Ireland ! The orders were of course carried into effect, beyond the letter, but according to the spirit.   Here is what Leland says :—

> " In the execution of these orders, the Justices
> " declare, that the soldiers slew all persons
> ' promiscuously, NOT SPARING THE WOMEN,
> " AND SOMETIMES NOT THE CHILDREN."—
> *Leland,* Book V.

It will be remarked that the original orders were of the most cruel injustice : because they not only sanctioned the slaughter of those who were called " rebels, and their aiders and abettors," but also of all male adults who happened to reside in any of the quarters where the so-called rebels had been received; although such persons might be perfectly innocent of the " *crime*" of having given them any assistance.   But villainous and blood-thirsty as were the instructions, yet the cruelty of the execution went beyond them.   That indeed was almost a matter of course, when one considers the sanguinary spirit that prevailed against the Irish.

That these massacres were committed, not by the over zeal of the meaner sort, but were deliberately planned and ordained by the persons in the highest authority, can be established by the most

abundant proofs. We have seen the diabolical
orders issued by the Lords Justices. Read now
the following extract from Lord Ormond :—

> " Sir William Parsons hath by late letters advised
> " the Governor to the burning of corn,
> " and to PUT MAN, WOMAN, AND
> " CHILD TO THE SWORD ; and Sir
> " Adam Loftus hath written in THE
> " SAME STRAIN."—*Ormond's Letters*,
> II. 350.

Here is a specimen of a massacre of prisoners in
the streets of Dublin, who were taken at the battle
of Rathmines ; it is Lord Ormond who speaks :—

> " The army, I am sure," says his lordship, " was
> " not *eight thousand* effective men ; and of
> " them it is certain that there were not
> " above *six hundred* killed ; and the most
> " of them that were killed *were butchered*
> " *after they had laid down their arms,*
> " *and had been almost an hour prisoners,*
> " *and divers of them murdered after they*
> " *were brought within the works of Dub-*
> " *lin.*"—*Ormond*, II. 396.

Those who (according to the practice of the day)
were massacred as prisoners were not all Irish :—

> " Some Walloons, whom the soldiers took for
> " Irishmen, were put to the sword."—
> *Whitelock's Memorials of English Affairs.*
Unlucky Walloons !

As I have referred to Whitelock, I may as well give two other short extracts from that writer, significant of the practice of the time :—

" *Their friars and priests were knocked on* " *the head,* promiscuously with the others, " who were in arms."—*Whitelock,* page 412.

Again :—

" Sir Theophilus Jones had taken a castle, put " some men to the sword, *and thirteen* " *priests.*"—*Whitelock,* p. 527.

I will give the following instances of the conduct of General Monroe, who was employed by the Government in the northern expedition :—

" Monroe put sixty men, eighteen women, and " two priests to death at Newry."—*Leland,* III. 203.

The second is this :—

" He," [Monroe,] " at Lord Conway's instance, " who attended him in the expedition, ad- " vanced with 3,600 foot, three troops of " horse, and four field pieces. He did no " other service than taking a view of the " place on the 16th July, 1642, and saw " some parties of the enemy who had no " powder to fire ; he did not attack them ; " but making a prey of cattle, *and killing* " *seven hundred country people, men, wo-* " *men, and children,* who were driving away

"the cattle, he returned to Newry."——
Carte, vol. I. p. 311.

One trait more of Monroe :—

[Other] "forces joining Monroe, he made up the
"strongest army that had been seen in Ire-
"land during the war; it amounting to at
"least 10,000 foot, and 1,000 horse. It
"was unfit, however, for any great under-
"taking, not being furnished with above
"three weeks' victual. Monroe advanced
"with it into the county of Cavan, from
"whence he sent parties into Westmeath
"and Longford, which burnt the country,
"*and put to the sword all the country peo-*
"*ple that they met.*"—*Carte's Ormond,*
I. 495.

The following massacre took place upon the hill
above Rathcoole. It was one of the few instances
which savoured of retaliation ; but it was so horrible, that I cannot refrain from giving the particulars as stated by Colonel Mervyn Touchet to his
brother Lord Castlehaven. Sir Arthur Loftus,
Governor of Naas, marched out with a party of
horse, which was joined by another party sent from
Dublin by the Marquis of Ormond, and killed such
of the Irish as they met.

"But the most considerable slaughter was in a
"great straight of furze, seated on a hill,
"where the people of several villages taking

"the alarm had sheltered themselves. Now,
"Sir Arthur having invested the hill, set
"the furze on fire on all sides, where the
"people, being in considerable number,
"were all burned or killed, men, women,
"and children. I saw the bodies and furze
"still burning."—*Castlehaven's Memoirs.*

It is manifest that this was not a solitary instance
of such cruelty. Clarendon treats it as the usual
practice :—

"In the year 1641—2, many thousands of the
"poor innocent people of the county of
"Dublin, shunning the fury of the English
"soldiers, fled into thickets and furze, which
"the soldiers did usually fire, killing as many
"as endeavoured to escape, or forced them
"back again to be burned, and the rest of
"the inhabitants for the most part died of
"famine."—*Appendix of Clarendon's Hist.
of the Irish Reb., Wilford, London,* 1720.

This horrible roasting alive of the inhabitants of
several villages serves only to relieve by its variety
the sanguinary slaughter of the sword.

Let us now turn to another scene. Two quotations more from Carte will show, *how* the insurrection in Munster was, according to the technical
phrase, "*made to explode.*" That is, how the people were COMPELLED to take arms in their own
defence. They will also show the active humanity

of the Catholic clergy, and of many of the Catholic
laity at that disastrous period, when—I say it with
bitter regret—no such instances were shown upon
the part of the Protestant clergy or laity :—

It was the middle of December before any one
" gentleman in the province of Munster ap-
" peared to favour the rebellion. *Many*
" *had shown themselves zealous to oppose it,*
" and had tendered their services for that
" end.   Lord Muskerry, who had married
" a sister of the Earl of Ormond's, offered
" to raise a thousand men at his own charge ;
" and if the State could not supply them with
" arms, *he was ready to raise money by a*
" *mortgage of his estate to buy them*.........
" Nor did any signs of uneasiness or disaf-
" fection appear among the gentry, till Sir
" W. St. Leger came to Clonmell, which was
" on the first of that month, three days be-
" fore the action I have just now related."
[viz., at a place called Mohill.] " There had
" been a few days before, some robberies (of
" cattle) committed in the county Tipperary.
" ....Sir W. St. Leger, upon notice
" thereof, came in two or three days after
" with two troops of horse in great fury to
" Ballyowen ; and being informed the cattle
" were driven into Eliogarty, he marched
" that way.   As he set forth, HE KILLED

" THREE PERSONS AT BALLYOWEN, who were
" said to have taken up some mares of Mr.
" Kingsmill's ; and not far off, at Grange,
" HE KILLED OR HANGED FOUR INNOCENT
" LABOURERS ; AT BALLY-O'MURRIN, SIX ;
" AND AT BALLYGARBURT, EIGHT, AND BURNT
" SEVERAL HOUSES. Nor was it without
" great importunity and intercession that he
" spared the life of Mr. Morris Magrath,
" (grandson to Milerus, Archbishop of
" Cashel in Queen Elizabeth's time,) a civil,
" well-bred gentleman, it being plainly
" proved that he had no hand in the prey,
" notwithstanding which proof he still kept
" that gentleman in prison. From thence
" Captain Peisley marching to Armaile,
" KILLED THERE SEVEN OR EIGHT POOR MEN
" AND WOMEN WHOM HE FOUND STANDING
" ABROAD IN THE STREETS NEAR THEIR OWN
" DOORS INOFFENSIVELY. AND PASSING OVER
" THE RIVER EWYER EARLY IN THE MORNING,
" MARCHED TO CLONOULTA, WHERE MEETING
" PHILIP RYAN, THE CHIEF FARMER OF THE
" PLACE, A VERY HONEST AND ABLE MAN, NOT
" AT ALL CONCERNED IN ANY OF THE ROB-
" BERIES, GOING WITH HIS PLOUGH-IRON IN
" A PEACEABLE MANNER TO THE FORGE, HE,
" WITHOUT ANY INQUIRY, EITHER GAVE OR-
" DERS FOR, OR CONNIVED AT HIS BEING

" KILLED, AS APPEARED BY HIS CHERISHING
" THE MURDERER. FROM THENCE HE WENT TO
" GOELLYN BRIDGE, WHERE HE KILLED AND
" HANGED SEVEN OR EIGHT OF DR. GERALD
" FENNELL'S TENANTS, HONEST INHABITANTS
" OF THE PLACE, AND BURNED SEVERAL
" HOUSES IN THE TOWN."—*Carte's Ormond,*
I. 265.

The Catholic nobility and gentry of Munster remonstrated with St. Leger. This was his answer :—

" He, in a hasty, furious manner, answered them,
" that they were all rebels, and he would
" not trust one soul of them ; but thought it
" more prudent to hang the best of them."
—*Carte,* I. 266.

The murders of the Irish went on ; some of the meaner sort occasionally, as was inevitable. One is not surprised to hear that some of the kinsmen of the murdered Philip Ryan, in reprisal for this and other murders, slew thirteen of the English. But this crime served to bring out the virtues of the Catholic Irish ; thus they conducted themselves on that occasion :—

" *All the rest of the English were saved by the*
" *inhabitants of that place in their houses,*
" *and had the goods which they confided to*
" *them safely restored. Dr. Samuel Pullen,*
" [Protestant] *Chancellor of Cashel and*

" *Dean of Clonfert, with his wife and chil-*
" *dren, was preserved by Father James*
" *Saul, a Jesuit. Several other Romish*
" *priests distinguished themselves on this*
" *occasion by their endeavours to save the*
" *English; particularly F. Joseph Everard*
" *and Redmond English, both Franciscan*
" *friars, who hid some of them in their*
" *chapel, and even under their altar.........*
" *The English who were thus preserved,*
" *were, according to their desire, safely*
" *conveyed into the county of Cork, by a*
" *guard of the Irish inhabitants of Cashel.*"
—*Carte's Ormond*, vol. I. p. 267.

I will now revert to the proofs given by the English parliament of their malignant enmity towards the unhappy natives of Ireland. The following extract is taken by Rushworth from the Journals of the English House of Commons :—

" October 24, 1644.

" An ordinance of the Lords and Commons as-
" sembled in parliament, commanding that
" no officer or soldier, either by sea or land,
" shall give any quarter to an Irishman, or
" to any Papist born in Ireland, which shall
" be taken in arms against the parliament
" of England :

" The Lords and Commons assembled in the
" parliament of England do declare, *that*

" *no quarter shall be given to any Irishman,*
" *or to any Papist born in Ireland,* which
" shall be taken in hostility against the par-
" liament, either upon sea, or within this
" kingdom, or dominion of Wales: and
" therefore do order and ordain that the
" Lord General, Lord Admiral, and all
" other officers and commanders both by
" sea and land, *shall except all Irishmen,*
" *and all Papists born in Ireland, out of all*
" *capitulations, agreements, and composi-*
" *tions hereafter to be made with the enemy;*
" *and shall, upon the taking of every such*
" *Irishman and Papist born in Ireland as*
" *aforesaid,* FORTHWITH PUT EVERY SUCH
" PERSON TO DEATH.

" And it is further ordered and ordained, that
" the Lord General, Lord Admiral, and
" the Committees of the several counties,
" do give speedy notice hereof to all subor-
" dinate officers and commanders by sea and
" land respectively; who are hereby required
" to use their utmost care and circumspection
" *that this ordinance be duly executed;* and
" lastly, the Lords and Commons do declare,
" that every officer and commander by sea
" or land, *that shall be remiss or negligent*
" *in observing the tenor of this ordinance,*
" *shall be reputed a favourer of the bloody*

"*rebellion of Ireland,* and shall be liable to
"such condign punishment as the justice of
"both houses of parliament shall inflict
"upon him."—*Rushworth,* vol. V. p. 783.
The following specimen of the readiness with
which this cruelty was anticipated by national antipathy, and carried into effect against Ireland, is
full of horror :—

"The Earl of Warwick, and the officers under
"him at sea, had, as often as he met with
"any Irish frigates, or such freebooters as
"sailed under their commission, taken all
"the seamen who became prisoners to them
"of that nation (Ireland), *and bound them*
"*back to back, and thrown them overboard*
"*into the sea, without distinction of their*
"*condition, if they were Irish.* In this
"cruel manner very many poor men per-
"ished daily ; of which the King said
"nothing, because.........his Majesty could
"not complain of it without being concerned
"in the behalf, and in favour of the rebels
"of Ireland."—*Clarendon,* II. 478.

Clarendon is of course anxious to excuse or palliate the conduct of Charles—but how does his
excuse aggravate the demoniacal disposition of the
English aristocracy and gentry, as well as of the
people in general, towards the Irish? Let any
reasonable man but reflect for one moment on these

deliberate cruelties—cruelties not committed in the rage of fight, or in the heat of blood.

Here were Protestant Christians—ENGLISH Protestant Christians—coolly and calmly going through the slow process of tying back to back, and then deliberately drowning a number of their fellow creatures—merely because they had them in their power, and because they were Irish !

There is nothing new under the sun! The drownings of the loyalists in France, the "*noyades,*" as they were called, by the revolutionary monster Carrier, and his colleagues, had their precedent in the conduct of Englishmen to Irishmen. But what a difference between the cases ! Carrier was a low-born vulgar monster—an avowed Atheist. He affected no conscientious scruples—he was a godless wretch. But the English who perpetrated these cruelties were "noblemen" and "gentlemen"— men (in *their* way) of fervent piety! with the Bible—the Word of God—in their hands; with prayer upon their lips ; proclaiming themselves the disciples of the God of mercy and of charity. Yes, they were " English Protestant Christians"— they, who, even in the name of that God, committed these barbarous cruelties !

Indignation and execration are vain. What country ever inflicted on another such ineffable cruelties as England has inflicted on Ireland ? Let me give another instance in which the bloody orders

of the English Commons were anticipated. In the
month of May, A.D. 1644—

"The Marquis of Ormond had sent Captain
"Anthony Willoughby with 150 men, which
"had formerly served in the fort of Galway,
"from thence to Bristol. The ship which
"carried them was taken by Swanley, WHO
"WAS SO INHUMAN AS TO THROW SEVENTY
"OF THE SOLDIERS OVERBOARD, under the
"pretence *that they were Irish;* THOUGH
"THEY HAD FAITHFULLY SERVED HIS MA-
"JESTY against the rebels during all the
"time of the war."—*Carte,* I. 481.

Some may possibly be so absurd as to suppose
that Captain Swanley was punished for these brutalities. He had barbarously assassinated faithful
soldiers, serving their King and their country. He
had basely assassinated them, for no other reason
than that they were Irish. How did the representatives of the English people treat him? Recollect
that these representatives were the chosen spirits of
the age—the master minds of England—the advocates of Liberty—and the zealous promoters of
(what *they* called) Religion. Listen, Englishmen;
attend, Protestants; my authority is no less than
the Journals of your House of Commons. Here
is the fact :—

"June, 1644," (the next month after his murderous outrage,) "Captain Swanley was

" called into the [English] House of Com-
" mons, and had THANKS GIVEN HIM
" FOR HIS GOOD SERVICE ; AND
" A CHAIN OF GOLD OF TWO
" HUNDRED POUNDS VALUE ; and
" Captain Smith, his vice-admiral, had ano-
" ther chain of £100 value."—*Journals*,
III. 517.

It will be borne in mind that I am making
selections—not giving *all* the instances of cruelty ;
no, nor probably the one-thousandth part of them.
It is on that account alone that I quit the navy, and
give another specimen of the English land-service.
Just mark, I pray you, the mode of procuring the
esteem of parliament :—

" Sir Richard Grenville.........was very much
" *esteemed* by the Earl of Leicester, and
" more by the parliament, *for the signal*
" *acts of cruelty he did every day commit*
" *upon the Irish*.........*hanging old men*
" *who were bedrid*, because they would not
" discover where their money was that he
" believed they had ; *and old women*, some
" of quality, after he had plundered them,
" and found less than he expected."—*Clarendon*, II. p. 414.

We must ever bear carefully in mind, that a large
portion of the astounding horrors and diabolical
crimes committed against Ireland by England, were

confessedly perpetrated for the support, and on the behalf of the " Protestant religion."

In 1643, a cessation of hostilities had been proclaimed in Ireland, which was equally desirable to the wretched King, and to the Irish people. The reader will remember, that, in the reign of Elizabeth, Spenser had recommended the destruction of provisions, in order that the Irish might be driven by famine " to devour each other." Spenser's diabolical policy (which had been acted upon at the time) was now revived, and patronised by the Protestant parliament of England. That parliament deemed it conducive to the interests of the Protestant religion, that the Irish Catholics should be compelled by famine "*to eat one another*." Accordingly, the cessation of hostilities—

" Was no sooner known in England, but the two
" houses declared against it, with all the
" sharp glosses upon it to his Majesty's dis-
" honour that can be imagined ; *persuading*
" *the people that the rebels were now brought*
" *to their last gasp, and* REDUCED TO
" SO TERRIBLE A FAMINE, THAT,
" LIKE CANNIBALS, THEY EAT
" ONE ANOTHER ; and must have been
" destroyed immediately, and utterly rooted
" out, if, by the popish counsels at court, the
" King had not been persuaded to consent
" to this cessation."—*Clarendon*, II. 323.

That the persecuting bigotry of Protestantism deliberately purposed to prolong the horrible famine thus described, as a means of strengthening and propagating the Protestant religion, is a fact of which the record stands upon the Journals of the English parliament :—

"Sept. 20, 1643. It was resolved, upon the "question, that this house doth hold that a "present *cessation of arms with the rebels* "*in Ireland is destructive to the Protestant* "*religion.*"—*Journals*, III. 248.

Rushworth's testimony adds the fullest confirmation (if any were wanted) to the fact, that these horrors were quite congenial with the Protestant bigotry of the English Legislature. Here are his words :—

"The Lords and Commons have reason to de-"clare against this plot and design of a "*cessation* of arms, as being treated and "carried on without their advice ; so *also* "*because of the great prejudice which will* "*thereby redound to the Protestant religion,* "and the encouragement and advancement "which it will give to the practice of po-"pery, when these rebellious Papists shall, "by this agreement, continue and set up "with more freedom their idolatrous wor-"ship, their popish superstitions, and Romish "abominations, in all the places of their

" command, to the dishonouring of God, *the*
" *grieving of all true Protestant hearts*, the
" dissolving of the laws of the Crown of
" England, and to *the provoking the wrath*
" *of a jealous God!* as if both kingdoms
" had not smarted enough already for this
" sin of too much conniving at, and tolera-
" ting of antichristian idolatry, under pre-
" text of civil contracts and politic agree-
" ments."—*Rushworth*, V. 557.

Oh, Protestantism! what unspeakable horrors
and miseries—what demoniac persecutions—have
been inflicted in your name upon the Catholic people of Ireland!

Let us now come back to Sir Charles Coote the
elder. Here is an additional accusation brought
against him. There is no doubt stated as to the
fact of the monstrous cruelty; the only question is,
as to his mode of expression. There is no doubt
that he did not *prevent* the cruelty; and indepen-
dently of the authority, it is difficult to doubt the
expression. At all events the poor babe in question
was brutally massacred. This act of English friendship was perpetrated :—

" Tuesday, December 7, a party of foot being
" sent out into the neighbourhood of Dublin
" in quest of some robbers that had plun-
" dered an house at Buskin, came to the
" village of Santry, and *murdered some in-*

" *nocent husbandmen,* (whose heads they
" brought into the city in triumph, and
" among which were one or two Protestants,)
" under pretence that they had harboured
" and relieved the rebels who had made
" inroads and committed depredations in
" those parts. Hard was the case of the
" country people at this time, when not
" being able to hinder parties of robbers and
" rebels breaking into their houses and
" taking refreshments there, this should be
" deemed a treasonable act, AND SUFFI-
" CIENT TO AUTHORIZE A MAS-
" SACRE. This following so soon after
" the executions, which Sir Charles Coote
" ....had ordered in the county of Wick-
" low, among which, when A SOLDIER
" WAS CARRYING ABOUT A POOR
" BABE ON THE END OF HIS PIKE,
" he" [namely, Coote] " was charged with
" saying THAT HE LIKED SUCH
" FROLICS, made it presently be imagined
" that it was determined to proceed against
" all suspected persons in the same undis-
" tinguishing way of cruelty ; and it served
" either for an occasion or pretence to some
" Roman Catholic gentlemen of the county
" of Dublin (among which were Luke Net-
" tervile, George Blackney, and George

" King) to assemble together at Swords, six
" miles from Dublin, and put themselves with
" their followers in a posture of defence."—
Carte's Ormond, I. 244—5.

Let me give another specimen of the merits of
one of Coote's coadjutors; his efforts were directed
to produce that hideous famine which the English
parliament deemed of such utility to the Protestant
religion :—

> " Among the several acts of public service per-
> " formed by a regiment of Sir William Cole,
> " consisting of 500 foot and a troop of horse,
> " we find the following hideous article re-
> " corded by the historian Borlase, *with*
> " *particular satisfaction and triumph :*—
> " ' STARVED AND FAMISHED OF THE
> " ' VULGAR SORT, WHOSE GOODS
> " ' WERE SEIZED ON BY THIS RE-
> " ' GIMENT, SEVEN THOUSAND.' "
> —*Leland*, Book V. chap. 5 *(note)*.

To come back for the last time to Coote himself
—I take the following extract from a pamphlet
entitled " A Collection of some of the Massacres
and Murders committed on the Irish in Ireland,
since the 23rd of October, 1641 :"—

" COUNTY OF MEATH—1642.

" Mr. Barnewall, of Tobertinian, and Mr. John
" Hussey, innocent persons, were hanged

"at Trim by old Sir Charles Coote's party.
" Gerald Lynch of Donower, aged 80 years,
" was killed by troopers of Trim, being in
" protection. Mr. Thomas Talbot, of Craw-
" ly's Town, about 80 years old, being pro-
" tected, and a known servitor to the Crown,
" was killed at his own door by some of
" Captain Morroe's troop. About the month
" of April the soldiers under the said Gren-
" ville's command, killed in and about the
" Navan 80 men, women, and children,
" who lived under protection. Captain
" Wentworth and his company, garrisoned
" at Duno, killed no less than 200 pro-
" tected persons in the parish of Donamora
" Slane, and barony of Margellion and
" Ovemorein, the town of Ardmulchan,
" Kingstown, and Harristown, all protected
" persons."

My next quotation will be rather long. It gives
so many particulars of murders committed by the
soldiers of the garrisons in Meath, that I am tempted
to give it at length. It is in the same book. I
confess I cannot resist inserting it ; even if it were
from the circumstance alone that it was in that
county—Meath—that the hellish miscreant Sir
Charles Coote met his death ; it is supposed from
one of his own party.

" In April, (1642,) Mrs. Ellinor Taaffe, of Tul-

" laghanoge, sixty years old, and six women
" more, were murdered by the soldiers of
" the garrison of Trim ; and a *blind woman,*
" *aged eighty years, was encompassed with*
" *straw by them, to which they set fire and*
" *burned her.* The same day they hanged
" two women in Kilbride, and two old de-
" crepit men that begged alms of them. In
" the same year, Mr. Walter Dulin, an old
" man, unable to stir abroad many years
" before the war, was killed in his own
" house by Lieut. Col. Broughton's troopers,
" notwithstanding the said Broughton's pro-
" tection, which the old man produced.
" Mr. Walter Evers, a justice of the peace
" and quorum, an aged man, and bedrid of
" the palsy long before the rebellion, was
" carried in a cart to Trim, and there
" hanged by the Governor's orders. Many
" ploughmen were killed at Philberstowne.
" Forty men, women, and children in pro-
" tection, reaping their harvest in Bones-
" town, were killed by a troop of the said
" garrison ; who, on the same day, killed
" Mrs. Alison Read at Dunsaughlin, being
" 80 years old ; and forty persons more,
" most of them women and children, shun-
" ning the fury of the said troop, were
" overtaken and slaughtered. About 70

" men, women, and children, tenants to Mr.
" Francis M'Ovoy, and under protection,
" were killed by Grenville's soldiers, and
" 160 more in the parish of Rathcoare,
" whereof there was one aged couple blind
" about 15 years before. Captain Sandford
" and his troop murdered in and about
" Mulhussey upwards of 100 men, women,
" and children under protection, and caused
" one Connor Breslan to be stuck with a
" knife into the throat, and so bled to death.
" *And one Eleanor Cusack,* 100 *years old,*
" *was tied about with lighted matches, and*
" *so tortured to death,* in Clonmoghon.
" James Dowlan, about 100 years old, Do-
" nagh Comyn, Darby Denis, Roger Bolan,
" and several other labourers and women to
" the number of *one hundred and sixty,*
" making their harvest, were slaughtered by
" the garrison of Trim."

One instance more in Meath ; it is an atrocity
committed by the men under command of Sir
Richard Grenville, whom I have already mentioned :—

    " Sir Richard Grenville's troop killed 42 men,
       " women, and children, and *eighteen infants,*
       " at Doramstown. *A woman under pro-*
       " *tection was, by Captain Morroe's soldiers,*
       " *put into the stock of a tuckmill, and so*

" *tucked to death.*"—*(From a pamphlet published in London, in* 1662, *entitled* " *A Collection of the Massacres and Murders committed on the Irish.*")

Let me now place before the reader the account of the death and funeral of Sir Charles Coote. It is exceedingly characteristic. Here it is :—

" In April, 1642, pursuing the rebels at Trim,
" he was unfortunately shot in the body, as
" it was thought, by one of his own troopers,
" whether by design or accident was never
" known. And this end had this gallant
" gentleman, who began to be so terrible to
" the enemy, as his very name was formid-
" able to them. His body was brought to
" Dublin, and there interred with great
" solemnity, *floods of English tears accom-*
" *panying him to his grave.* By his death
" the fate of the English interest in Ireland
" seemed eclipsed, if not buried."—*Borlase's Hist. of the Irish Reb.* p. 104.

Floods of English tears ! *Floods of English tears !*

This one fact at least is certain—that a more hideous, a more horrible villain never existed. The French Revolution—fertile in sanguinary monsters—produced nothing like him, who spared neither man, woman, nor child ; neither priest nor layman. Yet this most superlative of diabolic miscreants

was embalmed with "English tears!"—"*English
tears!*" How heartily they wept for the man who
was perfect in one talent—that of shedding Irish
blood! A dry eye at *his* funeral would indeed
have been, according to the modern phrase, "un-
English."

We now approach more nearly to the period of
Cromwell's arrival in Ireland, and we may as well
prepare for the extracts exhibiting his atrocities, by
showing what the intentions of the Irish Government were. Nothing was so offensive to *them* as
the submission of the Irish; their object being the
confiscation of the property and the extermination
of the persons of the natives. In this they were in
general faithfully aided by their subordinates.

" The Chief Governors......severely condemned
" the protection granted to Galway. Their
" orders were express and peremptory that
" the Earl of Ormond should receive no
" more submissions: every commander of
" every garrison was ordered not to presume
" to hold any correspondence with the Irish,
" or Papists; TO GIVE NO PROTECTION, BUT
" TO PERSECUTE ALL REBELS AND THEIR
" HARBOURERS WITH FIRE AND SWORD. IN
" THE EXECUTION OF THESE ORDERS THE
" JUSTICES DECLARE, THAT THE SOLDIERS
" SLEW ALL PERSONS PROMIS-
" CUOUSLY, NOT SPARING THE

"WOMEN, AND SOMETIMES NOT
"THE CHILDREN."—*Leland*, Book V.
chap. 5.

From Galway let us now go to Donegal. The
following are specimens of English humanity in
that county :—

"COUNTY OF DONEGALL.

"About the same time," (viz. November, 1641,)
   "Captain Fleming, and other officers of the
   "said regiment commanding a party, smo-
   "thered to death 220 women and children
   "in two caves. And about the same time
   "also, Captain Cunningham murdered about
   "63 women and children in the isles of
   "Ross.

"The Governor of Letterkenny gathered toge-
   "ther *on a Sunday morning* 53 poor peo-
   "ple, most of them women and children,
   "and caused them to be thrown off the
   "bridge into the river, and drowned them
   "all.

"In November, one Reading murdered the wife
   "and three children of Shane O'Morghy, in
   "a place called Letterkenny of Ramaltan ;
   "and after her death cut off her breasts
   "with his sword.

"1641—2. About two thousand poor labourers,
   "women, and children, of the barony of

" Tirbue, were massacred by the garrisons
" of Ballyshany and Donegall; and Lieute-
" nant Thomas Poe, an officer among them,
" coming under colour of friendship to visit
" a neighbour that lay sick in his bed, *and*
" *to whom he owed money*, carried a dagger
" under his cloak, which, whilst he seemed
" to bow towards the sick man in a friendly
" manner, asking how he did, he thrust it
" into his body, *and told his wife her hus-*
" *band should be no longer sick.*"

I will next introduce the head of the O'Brien
family, Lord Inchiquin; I believe the direct ancestor of the present Marquis of Thomond. He
was renowned for his acts of cruelty. He had
sought to be made President of Munster under the
King : but having been refused that office, to which
another was appointed, he, from the paltry motive
of selfish resentment, joined the English rebels, and
committed the most horrible cruelties upon the
Irish. He is celebrated in the recollection of the
people, even till the present day, for his massacres
in the cathedral of Cashel. There is something
very characteristic in the following traits of his
cruelty :—

" Inchiquin commits great destruction as far as
" he dares venture, about Dublin and Tredah
" [Drogheda], by burning and driving away
" their cattle, *hangs all he can meet with,*

"*going to the Lord Lieutenant.*"—*White-lock.*

" The Lord Inchiquin took Pilborne castle by
" storm, *and put all in it but eight to the*
" *sword.*"—*Whitelock.*

The next fact has " damned him to everlasting
fame :"—

" Inchiquin marched into the county of Tippe-
" rary, and hearing that many priests and
" gentry about Cashel had retired with their
" goods into the church, he stormed it, and
" being entered, put three thousand of them
" to the sword, *taking the priests even from*
" *under the altar.*"—*Ludlow's Memoirs,*
vol. I. p. 106.

The massacre not only of men and women, but
even of little children, by the Cromwellian army,
is familiar in the traditions of our peasantry at the
present day.   The common phrase in which these
ruffians justified the slaughter of unoffending infants,
is original in its disgusting phraseology.   We have
the odious fact authenticated by the Rev. Dr. Nalson ; and he, too, was a Protestant clergyman.
Here are his words :—

" I have heard a relation of my own, who was
" captain in that service, relate, that no
" manner of compassion or discrimination
" was showed either to age or sex ; but that
" the little children were promiscuously suf-

" ferers with the guilty ; and that if any
" who had some grains of compassion repre-
" hended the soldiers for this unchristian
" inhumanity, they would scoffingly reply,
" ' WHY ?   NITS WILL BE LICE !'
" AND   SO   WOULD   DESPATCH
" THEM."—*Nalson*, vol. II. (Introduction)
p. vii.

To come back to Dublin county.   The author
of the " *Collection*," speaking of the first week in
November, 1641, says,—

" In the same week, 56 men, women, and chil-
" dren, of the village of Bulloge, (being
" frightened at what was done at Clontarf,)
" took boats and went to sea, to shun the
" fury of a party of soldiers come out of
" Dublin under the command of Colonel
" Crafford ; but being pursued by soldiers
" in other boats, were overtaken, and thrown
" over board.   One Russell, a baker in Dub-
" lin, coming out of the country in company
" with Mr. Archbold of Clogram, (who went
" to take hold of the proclamation of the
" Lords Justices,) were both hanged and
" quartered.   In March, a party of horse,
" of the garrison of Donshaghlin, murdered
" seven or eight poor people in protection,
" tenants of Mr. Dillon of Huntstowne,
" having quartered in their houses the night

" before, and receiving such entertainment
" as the poor people could afford. About
" the same time, a party of the English
" quartered at Malahyde, hanged a servant
" of Mr. Robert Boyne's at the plough, *and*
"*forced a poor labourer to hang his own*
"*brother:* and soon after they hanged 15
" of the inhabitants of Swords who never
" bore arms, in the orchard of Malahyde;
" they likewise hanged a woman bemoaning
" her husband hanged among them."

There is an incident of some interest given by
the same author, immediately following my last
extract. It relates to the cause why a Colonel
Washington resigned his command and quitted the
service. Its date is the same year—1641 :—

" In the same year, after quarter given by
" Lieutenant Colonel Gibson to those of the
" castle of Carrigmain, they were all put to
" the sword, being about 350, *most of them*
"*women and children ;* and Colonel Wash-
" ington, endeavouring to save a pretty
" child of seven years old, carried him un-
" der his cloak, *but the child against his*
"*will was killed in his arms,* which was a
" principal motive of his quitting that
" service."

Several of the extracts already quoted, relate to
periods subsequent to Cromwell's arrival in Ireland.

The following extract refers to a period long before
that arrival :—

> " Sir Henry Tichbourne, who had the chief
> " command in that driving of O'Nial from
> " Dundalk, performed that service, and
> " afterwards pursued it with such an ama-
> " zing slaughter of the Irish in those parts,
> " that he boasts himself that for some weeks
> " after there was neither man nor beast to be
> " found in sixteen miles, between the two
> " towns of Drogheda and Dundalk ; nor on
> " the other side of Dundalk in the county of
> " Monaghan, nearer than Carrickmacross,
> " a strong pile twelve miles distant."—
> *Carte's Ormond.*

I shall add to my catalogue the following, which
I take from Borlase, than whom a more hostile
witness could not be cited. I shall only mention
one in Connaught, and two or three in Munster:—

> " Sir Frederick Hamilton," says Borlase, " en-
> " tering Sligo about the first of July, 1642,
> " burnt the town, and slew in the streets
> " three hundred of the Irish."—*Borlase*, p.
> 112.

Here are the instances referring to Munster :—

> " Lord Dungarvan and Lord Broghill summon-
> " ing the castle of Ardmore in the county
> " of Waterford, 21st of August, 1642, it
> " was yielded *upon mercy*. Nevertheless,

" *one hundred and forty men were put to*
" *the sword.*"—*Borlase,* p. 111.

We cannot therefore wonder that this Lord
Broghill on another occasion declared—
" That he knew not what quarter meant."—
Borlase, p. 110.

Before I proceed further, I wish to give one
extract from the relation of the many massacres
committed in Munster. The county of Cork has
claims upon me, and perhaps it is therefore that I
cannot avoid multiplying my instances with the
following quotation :—

" COUNTY CORK.

" 1642. At Cloghnekilty about 238 men, wo-
" men, and children were murdered, of
" which number 17 *children were taken by*
" *the legs by soldiers who knocked out their*
" *brains against the walls.* This was done
" by Phorbis's men, and the garrison of
" Bandon Bridge."

" The English party of this county burned
" O'Sullivan Beare's houses in Bantry, and
" in all the rest of that country, killing
" man, woman, and child, *turning many*
" *into their houses then on fire to be burned*
" *therein :* and among others Thomas De
" Bucke, a cooper, about 80 years old,
" and his wife being little less ; and all this

"was done without provocation, the said
" O'Sullivan *being a known reliever of the*
" *English* in that country. Observe that
" this county is not charged in the late Ab-
" stract with any murders."

In honour of Bandon, I insert the following
short extract :—

    " 1641. At Bandon Bridge, the garrison there
    " tied 88 Irishmen of the said town, back to
    " back, and threw them off the bridge into
    " the river, where they were all drowned."—
    Coll. p. 5.

We will now go back a little. The first great
slaughter that occurred in the civil war after the
Irish were driven into insurrection—(and never
were such pains taken to compel an unwilling
people to rise against a government as were taken
by the Administration in Ireland to *force* the Irish
to resist their tyranny !)—is the incident I am now
going to describe. It is taken from the " *Col-
lēction*," and requires no preface to excite attention. It was the fruitful source of many a crime.
The following is the *Irish* account :—

    " 1641. About the beginning of November, the
    " English and Scotch forces at Knockfergus
    " murdered in one night all the inhabitants
    " of the territory of the Island Magee, to
    " the number of about 3,000 men, women,
    " and children, all innocent persons, at a

" time when none of the Catholics of that
" country were in arms or rebellion.—Note,
" that this was the first massacre committed
" in Ireland of either side."

Now, I will place in juxtaposition with the above,
the English Protestant account of the same transaction :—

" In one fatal night they" [the garrison of Car-
rickfergus] " issued from Carrickfergus into
" an adjacent district called Island Magee,
" where a number of the poorer Irish resided,
" unoffending, and untainted by the rebel-
" lion. If we may believe one of the leaders
" of this party, thirty families were assailed
" by them in their beds, and massacred with
" calm and deliberate cruelty."—*Leland,*
Book V. chap. 3.

There is no substantial difference between these
two accounts. The difference in the *number* of the
slain is easily accounted for by recollecting that upon
that point the Irish would naturally be the better
informed. Both agree in the circumstances of this
most unprovoked and diabolical massacre. The
inhabitants of the district of Island Magee, innocent,
unoffending—unarmed ; without a shadow of crime,
or the least suspicion of guilt, were attacked at
night in their beds, by English and Scotch soldiers,
commanded and led on by their officers ; and put
to death with calm and deliberate cruelty. Talk

of the barbarity of uneducated savages in any part of the globe! you cannot find it exceeding this deliberate slaughter, committed by English and Scotch Protestant soldiers on unarmed beings, who admittedly were guilty of no other crime than that of being Irish Catholics!

One or two facts more, touching the manner in which those English and Scotch soldiers conducted themselves in that country. I take it from the same " *Collection*" I have quoted already :—

> " Mr. M'Naghten having built a small fortress
> " in the said county (Antrim) to preserve
> " himself and his followers from outrages,
> " until he understood what the cause of the
> " then rebellion was ; as soon as Colonel
> " Campbell came near with part of the army,
> " he sent to let him know that he would
> " come to him with his party, which he did;
> " and they were next day murdered to the
> " number of 80, by Sir John Clotworthy,
> " now Lord Massareen's, soldiers."

> " About the same time, 100 poor women and
> " children were murdered in one night, at
> " a place called Balliaghuin, by direction of
> " the English and Scotch officers command-
> " ing in that country."

I now come to the master-demon ; he who steeped his hands in the blood of his Sovereign, and came to Ireland reeking from that crime ; in order, by horrible cruelties committed on the Irish, to acquire popularity in England. And he did so acquire it, until it was sufficient to confer upon him regal power, and to enable him to place his hand upon that throne which he had not moral courage to occupy. I begin with an extract descriptive of the taking of Wexford; although, in point of time, this was the second town in which he displayed his barbarity. The following is the short and pithy account of this transaction by the Protestant clergyman, Doctor Warner :—

"As soon as Cromwell had ordered his batteries
   "to play on a distant quarter of the town,
   "on his summons being rejected, Stafford"
   (the commander of the garrison) "admitted
   "his men into the castle, from whence
   "issuing suddenly, and attacking the wall
   "and gate adjoining, they were admitted,
   "either through the treachery of the towns-
   "men or the cowardice of the soldiers, or
   "perhaps both; *and the slaughter was
   "almost as great as at Drogheda.*"—*Warner*, 476.

The more recent historian, Dr. Lingard, has added from the original authorities, the following most striking and melancholy circumstance :—

"No distinction was made between the defence-
   "less inhabitant and the armed soldier; *nor
   "could the shrieks and prayers of* 300 *fe-*

" *males, who had gathered round the great*
" *cross, preserve them from the swords of*
" *those ruthless barbarians.* By Cromwell
" himself the number of the slain is re-
" duced to two, by some writers it has been
" swelled to five, thousand."—*Lingard,*
A.D. 1649.

Three hundred women screaming for pity, round
the emblem of salvation—the cross. Three hundred Irish women slaughtered in one mass—by
English Protestant " Christians"—men of great
zeal and profound piety!

I now come back to Drogheda. And as the
slaughter there is a subject to be dwelt upon, I will
give three different versions of it; I do so, because
each contains some circumstances not specified in
the others. Here are the accounts of Carte and
Leland:—

" The assault was given, and his" (Cromwell's)
" men twice repulsed; but in this third at-
" tack, Colonel Wall being unhappily killed
" at the head of his regiment, his men were
" so dismayed thereby, as to listen, before
" they had any need, to the enemy *offering*
" *them quarter*, admitting them" (viz. Cromwell's army) " upon those terms, and thereby
" betraying themselves and their fellow sol-
" diers to the slaughter. *All the officers*
" *and soldiers of Cromwell's army promised*

" *quarter to such as would lay down their*
" *arms*, and performed it as long as the
" place held out ; which encouraged others
" to yield.   But when they had once all in
" their power and feared no hurt that could
" be done them, Cromwell, being told by
" Jones, that he had now all the flower of
" the Irish army in his hands, *gave orders*
" *that no quarter should be given !* So that
" his soldiers were forced, many of them
" against their will, to kill their prisoners !
" The brave governor Sir A. Aston, Sir
" Edward Verney, the Colonels Warren,
" Fleming, and Byrne, WERE KILLED IN
" COLD BLOOD : AND INDEED ALL THE
" OFFICERS, except some few of least consi-
" deration, that escaped by miracle.   The
" Marquis of Ormond, in his letters to the
" King and Lord Byron, says, ' THAT ON
" ' THIS OCCASION CROMWELL EXCEEDED
" ' HIMSELF, AND ANYTHING HE HAD EVER
" ' HEARD OF, IN BREACH OF FAITH AND
" ' BLOODY INHUMANITY ; AND THAT THE
" ' CRUELTIES EXERCISED THERE FOR FIVE
" ' DAYS AFTER THE TOWN WAS TAKEN,
" ' WOULD MAKE AS MANY SEVERAL PICTURES
" ' OF INHUMANITY AS THE BOOK OF MAR-
" ' TYRS OR THE RELATION OF AMBOYNA.' "
—*Carte*, II. 84.

OBSERVATIONS,

Leland adds—

"A number of ecclesiastics were found within
"the walls; and Cromwell, as if imme-
"diately commissioned to execute divine
"vengeance on these ministers of idolatry,
"ordered his soldiers to plunge their wea-
"pons into the *helpless wretches*."—*Leland*,
Book VI. chap. 4.

I next shall give the account of Lord Clarendon.
Here it is:—

"Before the Marquis of Ormond could draw his
"army together, Cromwell had besieged
"Tredah" [Drogheda]: "and though the
"garrison was so strong in point of number,
"and that number of so choice men that
"they could wish for nothing more than
"that the enemy would attempt to take them
"by storm, the very next day after he came
"before the town, he gave a general assault,
"and was beaten off with considerable loss.
"But after a day more, he assaulted it again
"in two places, with so much courage that
"he entered in both; and though the go-
"vernor and some of the chief officers
"retired in disorder into a fort where they
"hoped to have made conditions, a panic
"fear so possessed the soldiers that they
"threw down their arms upon a general
"offer of quarter: so that the enemy entered

" the works without resistance, and put
" every man, governor, officer, and soldier,
" to the sword : and the whole army being
" entered the town, they executed all manner
" of cruelty, and put every man that related
" to the garrison, and all the citizens who
" were Irish, *man, woman, and child*, to
" the sword ; and there being three or four
" officers of name, and of good families, who
" had found some way, by the humanity of
" some soldiers of the enemy, to conceal
" themselves for four or five days, being
" afterwards discovered, they were butchered
" in cold blood."—*Lord Clarendon's History*, vol. VI. 395.

Let the reader again peruse the above account.
It is worth any Englishman's while to read it thrice
over.   For an Irishman once would be enough.

I shall now give the statement from Lingard :—
" Aware that the royalists could assemble no army
    " in the field, he marched to the siege of
    " Drogheda.   The defences of the place
    " were contemptible ; but the garrison con-
    " sisted of two thousand five hundred chosen
    " men, and the governor, Sir Arthur Aston,
    " had earned in the civil war the reputation
    " of a brave and experienced officer.   In two
    " days a breach was made ; but Aston ordered
    " trenches to be dug within the wall, and

" the assailants on their first attempt were
" quickly repulsed. In the second, more
" than a thousand men penetrated through
" the breach ; but they suffered severely for
" their temerity, and were driven back with
" considerable loss. Cromwell now placed
" himself at the head of the reserve, and led
" them to the assault, animating them with
" his voice and example. In the heat of the
" conflict, it chanced that the officer who
" defended one of the trenches fell ; his men
" wavered : quarter was offered and accep-
" ted ; and the enemy, surmounting the
" breastwork, obtained possession of the
" bridge, entered the town, and successively
" overcame all opposition. *The pledge*
" *which had been given was now violated ;*
" and, as soon as resistance ceased, a gene-
" ral massacre was ordered or tolerated by
" Cromwell. *During five days the streets*
" *of Drogheda ran with blood;* revenge
" and fanaticism stimulated the passions
" of the soldiers : from the garrison
" THEY TURNED THEIR SWORDS
" AGAINST THE INHABITANTS,
" AND ONE THOUSAND UNRE-
" SISTING VICTIMS WERE IMMO-
" LATED TOGETHER WITHIN
" THE WALLS OF THE GREAT

"CHURCH, WHITHER THEY HAD
"FLED FOR PROTECTION."—*Lin-gard's England*, A.D. 1649.

I believe there is not in the history of Christen-dom a more horrible instance of quiet, deliberate cruelty, systematic and cold-blooded. First, the garrison who were promised quarter, and who, on the faith of that promise, had ceased to resist, were slaughtered deliberately and in detail. And next, the unoffending inhabitants were for five days de-liberately picked out and put to death—the men, the women, and even the little children. And this was done, not by New Zealand savages, but by Christian Englishmen—the choice spirits of the age—men of the most intense piety and Protestant sanctity—every man of them with his Bible in one hand and his sword in the other! Men overflowing with scripture quotations—men fond of preaching, or listening to, long sermons—praying long prayers —full of all that there is of ascetism in their Eng-lish Christianity!

Would not these English "Christians" spare the unarmed citizens? Surely they could fear no dan-ger from the hapless females? Would they not at least spare the children—the infants?

Oh, England! England! in what letters of blood have you not written your cruel domination in Ire-land! It is true that the *garrison* deserved their fate. They put faith in an English promise made to

Irishmen—Sir Arthur Aston, Sir Edward Verney, Colonel Byrne, and the rest of them. Fie upon them—oh, fie! They *did* indeed deserve their fate!

What a trumpet-tongued lesson to Irishmen! But such times can never come again.

There is in this fiendish transaction one colouring yet wanted, to make the monsters who committed it more hideous than the devils in hell. It is the colouring of hypocrisy. Let the reader, if he can, calmly peruse Cromwell's own despatch; and then admit with me, that human language is utterly inadequate to describe the ineffable horror of the English crime. Here are extracts from Cromwell's despatch to the Speaker of the House of Commons:—

" Sir,

" It has PLEASED GOD to bless our " endeavours at Drogheda."............

One shudders at such an introduction of the name of the adorable Creator—the God of mercy and of charity! I begin again:—

" Sir,

" It has pleased God to bless our endeavours " at Drogheda. After battering we stormed " it. The enemy were about 3,000 strong " in the town."

Cromwell then goes on to describe shortly the circumstances of the attack and of the slaughter; and coolly says,—

" I believe *we put to the sword the whole number*
" of the defendants. I do not think thirty
" of the whole number escaped with their
" lives ; and those that did, are in safe
" custody for the Barbadoes."
He then goes on as follows :—
" THIS HATH BEEN A MARVELLOUS
" GREAT MERCY. The enemy being
" not willing to put an issue upon a field of
" battle, had put into this garrison almost
" all their prime soldiers, being about 3,000
" horse and foot, under the command of
" their best officers, Sir Arthur Aston being
" made governor. There were some seven
" or eight regiments, Ormond's being one,
" under the command of Sir Edward Verney.
" I do not believe, neither do I hear, that
" *any officer escaped with his life, save only*
" *one lieutenant.*"
Could any one imagine that human nature could
be so destitute of all that belongs to humanity, or to
religion, as to be capable of calling such cruelty
" *a marvellous great mercy ?*" Oh, it was truly an
English mercy ! But there is more ; for this is
the conclusion of Cromwell's despatch :—
" I WISH THAT ALL HONEST HEARTS
" MAY GIVE THE GLORY OF THIS
" TO GOD ALONE, TO WHOM IN-
" DEED THE PRAISE OF THIS

"MERCY BELONGS. For instruments
"they were very inconsiderable to the work
"throughout.

"O. CROMWELL."

The flesh creeps—the heart sinks, at the unparalleled atrocity, profanity, and blasphemy of such a despatch. But exclamations weaken the horrors by which we are thus surrounded.

Perhaps some persons may be found so absurdly credulous as to believe that the English parliament revolted at the cruelty perpetrated by Cromwell; and that they inflicted upon his sanguinary barbarity, if not punishment, at least censure. No such thing. *The victims were Irish Catholics;* and it is manifest that the English parliament had not only no sympathy but no humanity for the unhappy natives of Ireland. To cap the climax of English atrocity, let the following extract from the Journals of the House of Commons be read:—

"1649—October 2nd. This day the House re-
"ceived despatches from the Lord Lieute-
"nant Cromwell, dated Dublin, September
"17th, giving an account of the taking of
"Drogheda. For this important success of
"the parliament's forces in Ireland, the
"House appointed A THANKSGIVING
"DAY to be held on the 1st of November
"ensuing throughout the nation. They
"likewise ordered that a Declaration should

" be prepared and sent into the several
" counties, signifying the grounds for setting
" apart that day of public thanksgiving.
" A letter of thanks was also voted to be
" sent to the Lord Lieutenant of Ireland ;
" and to be communicated to the officers
" there ; in which notice was to be taken,
" THAT THE HOUSE DID AP-
" PROVE OF THE EXECUTION
" DONE AT DROGHEDA, as an act
" both of *justice* to them, and *mercy* to
" others who may be warned by it."—*Parliamentary Hist.* vol. III. p. 1334.

I am sickened and disgusted with the hideous
catalogue of English crimes. I could multiply the
instances tenfold ; but I have given enough, and
infinitely more than enough, to satisfy every
human being that no country on the face of the
earth ever suffered so much from another as Ireland has suffered from England : nor is any
country on the face of the earth so stained with
diabolic cruelty as England in her conduct towards
Ireland!

Religious bigotry inflamed and augmented the
national hostility of England to Irishmen. To
show how distinctly the purpose of *exterminating
the Catholic people of Ireland for the good of the
Protestant religion* was avowed by the first authorities in the State, let me here quote the following

testimony from page 55 of a book of Cromwell's
acts, entitled " *Cromwelliana :*"—

" April 12, 1649. Those who were appointed
" to go to the Common Council about the
" furnishing £120,000, came unto Guildhall.
" The first that spoke was Mr. Lisle : after
" him Mr. Whitlock, who very notably
" urged the accommodation of the parlia-
" ment with the sum appointed for the
" service of Ireland : after whom the Lord
" Chief Baron Wild did press the same with
" many arguments, and among others *he*
" *rightly distinguished the state of the war*
" *in that kingdom as not being between*
" *Protestant and Protestant, or Indepen-*
" *dent and Presbyterian, but* PAPIST AND
" PROTESTANT ; and that was the interest
" there ; PAPACY OR POPERY BEING NOT TO
" BE ENDURED IN THAT KINGDOM ; which
" notably agreed with that maxim of King
" James, when first King of the three king-
" doms : ' Plant Ireland with Puritans, and
" ROOT OUT PAPISTS—and then se-
" cure it.' "

Cromwell gorged himself with human blood.
He committed the most hideous slaughters ; deliberate, cold-blooded, persevering. He stained the
annals of the English people with guilt of a blacker
dye than has stained any other nation on earth.

And—after all—for what? *What* did he gain
by it?   Some four or five years of unsettled and
precarious power !   And if his hideous corpse was
interred in a royal grave, it was so, only to have
his bones thence transferred to a gibbet !

Was it for *this* that he deliberately slaughtered
thousands of men, women, and children?   Female
loveliness, and the innocent and beautiful boy—aged
but seven years—of Colonel Washington?

It has often been said that it was not the people,
but the Government of England, who were guilty
of the attempts to exterminate the Irish nation.
The observation is absurd.   The Government had
at all times in their slaughter of the Irish the approbation of the English people.   Even the present
administration is popular in England in the precise
proportion of the hatred they exhibit to the Irish
people ; and *this* is a proposition of historic and
perpetual truth.   But to the Cromwellian wars, the
distinction between the people and the Government
could never apply.   These were the wars, emphatically, of the English people.   They were
emphatically the most cruel and murderous wars
the Irish ever sustained.

The natural result of the promiscuous slaughter
of the unarmed peasantry wherever the English
soldiers could lay hold on them, was, as a matter
of course, an appalling famine.   The ploughman
was killed in the half-ploughed field.   The labourer

met his death at the spade. The haymaker was
himself mowed down. A universal famine, and its
necessary concomitant—pestilence, covered the
land. An eye-witness—himself employed in hunting to death the Irish—has left the description
which follows : and although the victims *were* Irish,
yet possibly in the present day their miseries may
draw a tear from English eyes. Thus was consummated English Protestant power :—

" About the year 1652 and 1653, the plague and
" famine had so swept away whole countries,
" that a man might travel twenty or thirty
" miles and not see a living creature, either
" man, beast, or bird ; they being either all
" dead, or had quit those desolate places ;
" our soldiers would tell stories of the place
" where they saw a smoak ; it was so rare
" to see either smoak by day or fire or
" candle by night. And when we did meet
" with two or three poor cabins, none but
" very aged men, with women and children,
" and those, like the prophet, might have
" complained, ' We are become as a bottle
" in the smoak, our skin is black like an
" oven because of the terrible famine.'—*I*
" *have seen those miserable creatures pluck-*
" *ing stinking carrion out of a ditch, black*
" *and rotten*, and been credibly informed
" that *they digged corpse out of the grave*

" *to eat :* but the most tragical story I ever
" heard was from an officer commanding a
" party of horse, who, HUNTING FOR TORIES
" IN A DARK NIGHT, discovered a light,
" which they supposed to be a fire, which
" the tories usually made in those waste
" countries to dress their provisions and
" warm themselves ; but drawing near, they
" found it a ruined cabin, and besetting it
" round, some did alight, and peeping at
" the window, where they saw a great fire
" of wood, and a company of miserable old
" women and children sitting round about it,
" and betwixt them and the fire, a dead corpse
" lay broiling, which, as the fire roasted,
" they cut off collops, and eat."—*Colonel
Laurence's Interest of Ireland,* part 2, pp.
86, 87.

Such, I repeat, were the demoniacal means by
which Protestantism and English power achieved
and consummated their ascendency in Ireland.

OBSERVATIONS,
PROOFS, AND ILLUSTRATIONS.

CHAPTER III.—PART III.

I HAVE said in the text, that however aggravated
and atrocious the actual cruelties perpetrated by
England on the Irish were, there was a greater
cruelty still; namely, in the slander and calumnies
affixed upon the character and conduct of the Irish
people. Alas! the spirit of calumny lives to the
present day. Indeed I do not know any spirit of
hostility to Ireland which was ever displayed, which
is not still alive and vigorous. The mode of
exhibiting that spirit is different. Its virulence
is turned into another channel. But its existence
and vitality are not the less marked by unequivocal
characters.

It was not sufficient for the English party to commit those most horrible atrocities of which I have
collected a small proportion of instances. They
carried their malignity farther; and they accused
the Irish of those very crimes which they themselves
committed upon that unhappy people. It is scarcely

credible—it would not be credible of any other people except the Irish—that when they were massacred in tens of thousands, they should be accused of the very crime that was committed against themselves.   Yet it is literally true.

What Clarendon and Temple originally asserted, has been of course taken up by that infidel falsifier of history, Hume : and the Catholics of Ireland for more than a century were persecuted to the loss of their lives and properties; and (what was still more grievous and afflicting) by the loss of their reputation for that conduct, which, while it really merited the applause of all good men, was converted into the imputation of foul and horrible slaughter.

The charge was brought against the Irish by Clarendon in these words :—

" On the 23rd of October, 1641, a rebellion broke
   " out in all parts of Ireland except Dublin,
   " where the design of it was miraculously
   " discovered the night before it was to be
   " executed............But that, in the other
   " parts of the kingdom, they observed the
   " time appointed, not hearing of the misfor-
   " tune of their friends in Dublin.........That
   " a general insurrection of the Irish *spread*
   " *itself over the whole country* in such an
   " inhuman and barbarous manner, that there
   " were *forty or fifty thousand Protestants*
   " *murdered* before they suspected themselves

" in any danger, or could provide for their
" defence, by drawing together into towns
" or strong houses."—*Hist. Reb.*

Temple aggravates the crime. This is *his* statement :—

" *One hundred and fifty thousand Protestants*
" *were massacred* in cold blood, in the first
" two months of the rebellion."—*Sir John
Temple, Hist. Irish Reb.*

Milton, in the second edition of his *Iconoclastes*,
has the following passage :—

" The rebellion and horrid massacre of the Eng-
" lish Protestants in Ireland, to the amount
" of 154,000 *in the province of Ulster only,*
" by their own computation ; which, added
" to the other three, *makes up the total sum*
" *of that slaughter, in all likelihood, four*
" *times as great.*"

It is true this passage has been softened in subsequent editions ; but the enemies of Ireland had
the full benefit of Milton's falsehood at the very
time that it was most important for them to have it.

One may throw in here by way of parenthesis,
that it has been demonstrated by Sir William Petty
and others that there could have scarcely been at
that period more than 200,000 Protestants in all
Ireland.

It will of course be recollected that the parliamentary party had forced the insurrection to explode,

and had made it purely a religious war. Now, let the reader look back, at Clarendon, Temple, and Milton: and then let him look at this extract from another Protestant historian; a clergyman of the established Protestant church, whom I have quoted more than once already :—

"The number of people killed, upon positive
"evidence collected in two years after the
"insurrection broke out, adding them all
"together, *amounts only to two thousand*
"*one hundred and nine*; on the reports
"of other Protestants, *one thousand six*
"*hundred and nineteen more;* and on the
"report of some of the rebels themselves a
"further number of three hundred; THE
"WHOLE MAKING FOUR THOU-
"SAND AND TWENTY-EIGHT."—
Warner, p. 297.

Thus—upon positive evidence, and upon evidence of mere report, which latter is the thing in the world the most exaggerating; and after all the provocation which the Irish had sustained—is it not marvellous, that *in* and *out of* battle, there should have been returned as killed, (and that too, by adding to authentic fact the evidence of rumour,) a number of Protestants altogether amounting to only twenty-eight more than four thousand in two full years of civil war? And this fact vouched— *not* by a Catholic or an Irishman; but by an Eng lish Protestant clergyman ; a Fellow, by the bye, of the Protestant University of Dublin!

Notwithstanding all this, for considerably more than a century after the Restoration, the Catholics of Ireland were set down as wholesale murderers, and were charged with murdering 50,000 Protestants on the 23rd of October, 1641. And this atrociously false calumny was reiterated in books and pamphlets, in speeches and sermons and acts of parliament! The arch liar, Hume, the man who of all historians is least to be relied on—for throughout his history scarcely one fact is stated accurately—has given great circulation to this enormous falsehood ; and *he* is the more criminal, inasmuch as shortly after the appearance of the volume of his history containing the reign of Charles the First, documents were furnished to him demonstrating the utter falsehood of his account of the alleged massacre. But all in vain. The immoral infidel adhered to his falsehood, as it gave a greater interest to his fictitious history.

At the present day, however, no writer of character would venture to repeat the calumny. The horrible charge fulfilled the purpose for which it was intended. And the odious practice of falsely imputing crime to Catholics has partially ceased among the better class of English—and altogether in the better class of American writers.

Doctor Lingard, whose work is the only one that

deserves the name of a history of England, has, in
his text, very properly omitted all mention of what
is called " the Irish massacre." He has thrown
into his notes the reason for this omission. It is
impossible for any one to read that reason, without
the most thorough conviction of the utter falsehood
of the story told by Clarendon and Temple. It
will be recollected that Clarendon places the "great
massacre" as having occurred suddenly on the 23rd
of October. It is only requisite to read the following extracts from Lingard's Notes, borne out
by the authorities which he so distinctly quotes, to
be fully convinced that the alleged massacre of the
23rd of October is purely a fiction :—

> " We have the despatches [of the Lords Justices]
> " of October the 25th; with the accom-
> " panying documents *(Lords' Journals,* iv.
> " 412 ; *Nalson,* ii. 514—523): BUT IN
> " THESE THERE IS NO MENTION
> " OF ANY ONE MURDER. After
> " detailing the rising, and plundering by
> " the insurgents, they add, ' *This, though*
> " ' *too much, is ALL that we yet hear is*
> " ' *done by them.'*—*(Journals, ibid ; Nalson,*
> " ii. 516.)"—*Lingard,* X. 464, note (A).

The next, perhaps, is more convincing still.
For it shows that the Lords Justices carefully record
the murder of *ten* of the garrison of the Lord
Moore's house at Mellifont :—

" In the fourth [despatch] of November 25, they
" describe the progress of the rebellion.
" 'In both counties, as well Wickloe as
" Wexford, all the castles and houses of the
" English, with all their substance, are
" come into the hands of the rebels ; and
" the English, with their wives and children
" stript naked, are banished thence by their
" fury and rage.   The rebels in the county
" Longford do still increase also, as well in
" their numbers as in their violence.   The
" Ulster rebels are grown so strong, as they
" have sufficient men to leave behind them
" in the places they have gotten northward,
" and to lay siege to some not yet taken......
" They have already taken Mellifont, the
" Lord Moore's house, though with a loss of
" about 120 men of theirs, and there (in
" cold blood) they murdered TEN of those
" that manfully defended that place.........
" In the county of Meath also, the rebels
" rob and spoil the English Protestants till
" within six miles of Dublin.'—(*Ibid*. p.
" 900.)"—*Lingard*, X. 466, note (A).

The next extract, if possible, more fully cor-
roborates the fact that no general massacre could
possibly have taken place.   It contains, to be sure,
an accusation of great inhumanity on the part of
the Irish.   But let it be remarked that an accusation

is not *proof* of the fact alleged ; whereas this species
of accusation demonstrates that another, and a
worse accusation, was not withheld : it proves the
readiness to accuse the Irish, whether truly or
falsely, of all that could possibly be brought against
them ; but it does *not* accuse them of the slaughter
by the sword of a single Protestant.

It is also observable, that during all this time
these Lords Justices themselves were, by means of
Sir Charles Coote and their other minions, putting
to death in cold blood all the Irish Catholics—
armed and unarmed—men, women, and children,
that came within their reach.   These villains had
therefore the deepest interest in falsely accusing
the Irish of cruelty.   It is manifest that nothing
could gratify them more than being able to sub-
stantiate against the Irish the charges of massacre
or murder.   The absence of any such charge is
indeed a trumpet-tongued acquittal :—

" We have a fifth despatch of November 27th,—

  " ' The disturbances are now grown so
  " ' general, that in most places, and even
  " ' round about this city within four miles of
  " ' us, not only the open rebels of mere Irish,
  " ' but the natives, men, women, and chil-
  " ' dren, joyn together and fall on the
  " ' neighbours that are English and Protes-
  " ' tants, and rob and spoil them of all they
  " ' have, nor can we help it.'—(*Nalson*, 902.)

" I shall add a sixth, of December 14th,—
" ' They continue their rage and malignity
" ' against the English and Protestants, who,
" ' if they leave their goods or cattel for more
" ' safety with any Papists, those are called
" ' out by the rebels, and the Papists' goods
" ' or cattel left behind ; and now upon some
" ' new councils taken by them, they have
" ' added to their former, a farther degree
" ' of cruelty, even of the highest nature,
" ' which is to proclaim, that if any Irish
" ' shall harbour or relieve any English,
" ' that be suffered to escape them with his
" ' life, that it shall be penal even to death
" ' to such Irish ; and so they will be sure
" ' though they put not those English actu-
" ' ally to the sword, yet they do as certainly
" ' and with more cruelty cut them off that
" ' way, than if they had done it by the
" ' sword ; and they profess they will never
" ' give over till they leave not any seed of
" ' an Englishman in Ireland.'—*(Ibid.* p.
" 911.)"—*Lingard*, X. 467, note (A).

There remains another proof afforded by the
Lords Justices, of the utter falsehood of Clarendon's
and Temple's narrative.   Here it is :—

" On the 23rd of December the same Lords Jus-
" tices granted a commission to Henry Jones,
" Dean of Kilmore, and seven other clergy-

" men, in these words : ' Know ye that we
" ' do hereby give unto you.........full power
" ' and authority.........to call before you,
" ' and examine upon the holy Evangelists
" ' .... .as well all such persons as have
" ' been robbed and spoyled, as all the wit-
" ' nessess that can give testimony therein,
" ' what robberies and spoils have been com-
" ' mitted on them since the 22nd of October
" ' last, or shall hereafter be committed on
" ' them or any of them: what the particulars
" ' were, or are, whereof they were or shall
" ' be so robbed or spoiled ; to what value,
" ' by whom, what their names were, or
" ' where they now or last dwelt that com-
" ' mitted these robberies.   On what day or
" ' night the said robberies or spoils commit-
" ' ted or to be committed, were done ; what
" ' traitorous or disloyal words, speeches, or
" ' actions were then or at any other time
" ' uttered or committed by those robbers or
" ' any of them, and how often ; and all
" ' other circumstances concerning the said
" ' particulars, and every of them.   And
" ' you, our said commissioners, are to re-
" ' duce to writing all the examinations, and
" ' the same to return to our Justices and
" ' Council of this our realm of Ireland.' "—
Temple, Irish Reb. 137.

It is utterly incredible that if there had been ANY massacre of Protestants by the Irish, an inquiry into that most important subject should have been totally omitted in such a commission as the above. Indeed it would have necessarily been the leading feature in an inquisition of that description. Yet—such a commission *did* issue to inquire into matters, comparatively of trivial importance, without so much as *one single word* respecting the alleged massacre! This is indeed "the part of Hamlet left out by special desire."

Multiplied proofs would but weaken the demonstration arising from those we have given.

It may be some relief to give specimens of the kind of evidence adduced to prove the reality of the alleged massacre. The first I shall give is the following extract from Sir John Temple's "*History of the Irish Rebellion :*"—

"Hundreds of the ghosts of Protestants," says Temple, "that were drowned by the rebels "at Portadown Bridge, were seen in the "river bolt upright, and were heard to cry "out for revenge on these rebels. One of "these ghosts was seen with hands lifted up; "and standing in that posture from the 29th "of December to the latter end of the following Lent."

My next specimen is taken from the testimony of no less a person than a Protestant bishop. And when a Protestant bishop outrages all that is probable in order to blacken the Irish Catholics, it would amuse one to conjecture what the minor inventors of fables may not do :—

Dr. Maxwell, Protestant bishop of Kilmore, " who," says Borlase, " was a person whose " integrity and candour none ever dared " to question," has described, in his own prolix examination, the different postures and gestures of these apparitions—(the ghosts of Protestants)—" as having some- " times been seen, by day and night, walk- " ing upon the river at Portadown; some- " times brandishing their naked swords; " sometimes singing psalms; and at other " times shrieking in a most fearful and " hideous manner." This bishop adds, " that he never heard any man so much as " doubt the truth thereof ; but that he " obliged no man's faith in regard he saw " them not with his own eyes; otherwise he " had as much certainty as could morally " be required of such matters."—*Borlase's Hist. of the Irish Rebellion, Appendix,* page 392.

I close with an emphatic quotation from Warner, giving the true character of the original Protestant historians of this disastrous period :—

" IT IS EASY ENOUGH," SAYS THIS

PROTESTANT CLERGYMAN, "TO "DEMONSTRATE THE FALSE-"HOOD OF THE RELATION OF "EVERY PROTESTANT HISTO-"RIAN OF THIS REBELLION."— *Warner,* p. 296.

OBSERVATIONS,
PROOFS, AND ILLUSTRATIONS.

CHAPTER III.—PART IV.

THE subject of this fourth part of my illustrations and proofs, is to bring forth into contrast with the acts of the English and Protestant party, the conduct of the Irish Catholics. And here—after having selected so many instances, to which I might have added hundreds more, of most horrible cruelties perpetrated by the English Protestant party— I am bound to say, and I *do* say it with the deepest regret, that I do not find these horrors mitigated by any acts of general or individual humanity or mercy. It is all murder on murder—slaughter upon slaughter—massacre after massacre—men, women, and children. No staying of the hand— no stopping of the sword! Nobody interfering to preserve the victims from assassination; or if there *be* rare instances, like that of Colonel Washington, who tried to save the child of seven years, the attempt becomes vain, and the victim is sacrificed.

But with what proud and glowing gratulation do I turn to the conduct of the Irish Catholics during the civil war. I collect from Protestant historians—for on this subject I shall scarcely use one other—multitudinous facts of lenity, forbearance, and mercy ; of protection and kindness, of benevolence and charity ! The horrors of war mitigated by the multiplied exercise of the tenderest humanity. O ! what a contrast ! What a glorious contrast !

This contrast is rendered still more striking, when we bear in mind that during the time that these virtues were exhibited by the Irish Catholics, the Protestants were committing the horrible cruelties of which I have cited so many.

On the one side was the demon spirit, animating the Protestant party to slaughter and death : on the other was the angelic benevolence of the Catholic Irish, protecting and rescuing from the sword as many as possible, of all those whom the actual fight had spared.

I begin with general testimony borne by Protestant writers to the humane intentions of the Irish. It was in Ulster that the insurrection was first made to explode. In that province, almost all the Protestants were Scotch. Yet we find preserved by Carte the following fact. At the commencement of the insurrection,—

> " *The Irish made proclamation, on pain of*
> " *death, that no Scotsman should be mo-*
> " *lested in body, goods, or lands.*"—*Carte's*
> *Ormond*, I. 178.

How well these Scots merited so humane and proper a determination on the part of the Irish, will be appreciated by those who recollect that it was the garrison of Carrickfergus (chiefly Scotch) that began the work of massacre, by slaughtering unarmed in their beds three thousand inhabitants or refugees in Island Magee!

The next admission is from the profligate Temple : an admission so inconsistent with the principal object of his history! He, too, speaking of the commencement of the insurrection, has this passage :—

> " It was resolved" [by the Irish party] "*not to*
> " *kill any*, but where, of necessity, they
> " should be forced thereunto by opposi-
> " tion."—*Temple*, p. 65.

Even Leland himself—the anti-Irish, the anti-Catholic Leland—has, in other words, the same admission :—

> " In the beginning of the insurrection it was
> " determined" [by the Irish] " that the
> " enterprise should be conducted in every
> " quarter with as little bloodshed as pos-
> " sible."—*Leland*, Book V. chap. 3.

The reader will remember that I have cited many Protestant authorities to show, what indeed no man acquainted with the history of the times will dream of denying, that the object of the English party—of the Lords Justices themselves—was to exterminate the Catholics of Ireland, whether of native Irish, or of English descent. To remind the reader the more forcibly of this, I will here just insert one passage from Carte :—

> " The Lords Justices had set their heart on the
> " EXTIRPATION, not only of the mere
> " Irish, but likewise of all the old English
> " families that were Roman Catholics, *and*
> " *the making of a new plantation all over*
> " *the kingdom, in which they could not fail*
> " *to have a principal share.*"—*Carte*, I.
> 330.

Yet, it is admitted that the Irish—driven to defend themselves from EXTIRPATION—*resolved, as the very first rule of their conduct, to shed as little blood as possible!*

I have given so many instances of the cruelties perpetrated by Sir Charles Coote and his son, (who was afterwards created Lord Mountrath for his own and his father's services,) that I wish to begin my collection of facts illustrating the humanity of the Irish, with an incident in which his family were concerned. It is this :—

> " Lady Mountrath, and Sir Robert Hannah, her
> " father, with many others, being retreated
> " to Belleek for security, were all conveyed
> " safe to Mannor Hamilton ; and it is obser-
> " vable, that the said lady, and the rest,
> " came to Mr. Owen O'Rorke's, *who kept*

"*a garrison at Drumaheir* for the Irish,
"before they came to Mannor Hamilton,
"whose brother was prisoner with Sir
"Frederick Hamilton ; and the said Mr.
"O'Rorke, having so many persons of qua-
"lity in his hands, sent to Sir Frederick to
"enlarge his brother, and that he would
"convey them all safe to him : but Sir
"Frederick, instead of enlarging his brother,
"HANGED HIM THE NEXT DAY,
"which might have well provoked the
"gentleman to revenge, if he had not more
"humanity than could well be expected
"upon such an occasion and in times of so
"great confusion ; YET HE SENT
"THEM ALL SAFE WHERE THEY
"DESIRED."—*Collection*, p. 97.

I doubt much whether there be anything finer
than this, in ancient or modern story. It would
seem as if Sir Frederick Hamilton had been conscious of O'Rorke's humanity, when he committed
the outrage of executing O'Rorke's brother, whilst
that chief had so many English persons of condition
in his hands. But Sir Frederick was quite safe.
O'Rorke was an Irish Catholic ; and although he
endured the murder of his brother, yet he could
not endure to stain his own soul with the blood of
a prisoner.

The next specimen I shall give, is that of the

conduct of a Catholic baronet in Munster. I must say, that in order to appreciate fully the value of such acts of humanity, it should be constantly recollected that the English Protestant party were massacring the unfortunate Catholics in every direction around them where they had the power to do so :—

> " Sir Richard Everett, baronet, in the beginning
> " of the rebellion, sent the richest of the
> " English planters in his country, with
> " their stock and goods, into the English
> " quarters. *The poorer English, consisting*
> " *of eighty-eight persons, he kept and main-*
> " *tained at his own charge till the middle*
> " *of June,* 1642, then conveyed them to
> " Mitchelstown; and when that place was
> " afterwards taken by the Irish, *he sent for*
> " *some of those families that were very poor,*
> " *and maintained them for a long time.*
> " As soon as the cessation was made, some
> " of the poor tenants came back to him, and
> " he settled, and protected them on his
> " lands, till Cromwell came into the coun-
> " try."—*Carte's Ormond,* vol. I.

The next act illustrative of Irish humanity I shall bring before the reader, is one that occurred in the county of Cavan, where the civil war raged, and of course some Protestants lost their lives, which Carte calls " being murdered." Let it be so. I am not disposed to mitigate the shedding of blood, even by the use of a word :—

> " By the humanity of Mr. Philip O'Reilly, one
> " of the most considerable chiefs of the
> " rebels, scarce any murders were commit-
> " ted in the county of Cavan. *Such of the*
> " *Protestants as put themselves under his*
> " *protection, were safely conveyed into the*
> " *English quarters ; and those that were*
> " *stript and in necessity, he fed and clothed*
> " *till they were sent away.* Among these
> " was Mr. Henry Jones, a nephew of Pri-
> " mate Usher, and Dean of Kilmore, who,
> " although he afterwards turned a noted
> " partizan of Cromwell's, was promoted to
> " the see of Clogher, and thence, after the
> " Restoration, to the see of Meath."—*Carte's*
> *Ormond,* vol. I.

I have already, in page 281, in stating the atrocious cruelties perpetrated in the county Tipperary by the English Protestant party, mentioned the murder in cold blood, and unprovoked, of Mr. Philip Ryan and several others. I have also mentioned that the inhabitants retaliated by murdering thirteen of the English party. The following paragraph made part of my quotation, but is so very suitable to my present subject, that I think it a duty to repeat it here :—

" All the rest of the English were saved by the

" inhabitants of that place in their houses,
" and had the goods which they confided to
" them safely restored. Dr. Samuel Pullen,
" Chancellor of Cashel and Dean of Clonfert,
" with his wife and children, was preserved
" by Father James Saul, a Jesuit. Several
" other Romish priests distinguished them-
" selves on this occasion by their endeavours
" to save the English; particularly F. Jo-
" seph Everard and Redmond English, both
" Franciscan friars, who hid some of them
" in their chapel, and even under the altar
" ....The English who were thus pre-
" served, were, according to their desire,
" safely conveyed into the county of Cork,
" by a guard of the Irish inhabitants of
" Cashel."—*Carte's Ormond*, vol. I. p. 267.
In making my selection of instances of the humanity shown by the Catholic party, I think the
following has an interest about it, which gives it a
title to particular notice :—

" Doctor Maxwell, afterwards Bishop of Kilmore,
" deposeth that Mrs. Catharine Hovenden,
" widow, and mother to Sir Phelim O'Nial,
" preserved four and twenty English and
" Scotch in her own house, and fed them
" there for seven and thirty weeks, out of
" her own store ; and that, when her chil-
" dren took her away, upon the approach of

"our army, she left both them, and the
"deponent, at liberty. That Captain Alex-
"ander Hovenden, her son, conducted five
"and thirty English out of Armagh to
"Drogheda, whereof some were of good
"quality; when it was thought he had secret
"directions to murder them. Twenty more
"he sent safe to Newry, and he would trust
"no other convoy but himself."—*Carte;*
and *Appendix to Borl. Hist. Irish Reb.*

Again, it must not be forgotten, that all this
charity and humanity was exhibited and practiced
by the Catholics during the atrocious cruelties of
the Protestant party, of which I have recorded instances in the foregoing pages.

There is a very important passage on this subject
in Warner, relative to the conduct of the Catholic
gentlemen of Munster. This is Warner's language:—

"There are many honourable testimonies of the
"care and preservation of the English by
"Lord Muskerry and his lady; not only in
"saving their lives from the enemy, but also
"in relieving them, in great numbers, from
"cold and hunger, after they had been
"stripped and driven from their habitations.
"Indeed, all the gentlemen in that part of
"the kingdom" [viz. Munster] "were ex-
"ceedingly careful to prevent bloodshed,

" and to hinder the English from being pil-
" laged and stript, although it was many
" times impossible."—*Warner's Hist. Irish
Reb.*

Yet, this Lord Muskerry was afterwards barbarously executed by the Cromwellians. It is said that
his lady shared his fate.

Another instance, in which the illustrious head
of the house of Mountgarret—the ancestor of the
present Earl of Kilkenny, figures in the character
in which one would naturally expect to find a member of his illustrious family.   A gallant soldier in
battle—humanity personified towards the unarmed
foe :—

" In the above-mentioned province of Munster,"
    says Carte, " Lord Mountgarret, by procla-
    " mation, strictly enjoined all his followers
    " *not to hurt any of the English inhabi-*
    " *tants either in body or goods ;* and he
    " succeeded so far in his design for their
    " preservation, *that there was not the least*
    " *act of bloodshed committed.*   But it was
    " not possible for him to prevent the vulgar
    " sort, who flocked after him for booty, from
    " plundering both English and Irish, Papist
    " and Protestant, without distinction.   He
    " used his authority, but in vain, to put a
    " stop to this violence ; till seeing one of the
    " rank of a gentleman, Mr. Richard Cant-

"well, (descended from Mr. Cantwell of
" Painstown, a man much esteemed in his
" country,) transgressing his orders, and
"plundering in his presence, he shot him
" dead with his pistol."—*Carte's Ormond.*

Now for a few instances of the manner in which
the Irish, when successful, treated their enemies
when in their power. Here is a remarkable instance :—

" 'I took,' says Lord Castlehaven, 'Athy by
" 'storm, with all the garrison (700 men)
" 'prisoners. I made a present of them to
" ' Cromwell, desiring him by letter that he
" 'would do the like with me, as any of
" 'mine should fall into his power. But he
" 'little valued my civility. For in a few
" 'days after he besieged Gowran, and the
" 'soldiers mutinying, and giving up the
" 'place with their officers, he caused the
" 'governor, Hammond, and some other
" 'officers, to be put to death.' "—*Castlehaven,* 107.

There is another instance which is still more
gratifying; as it shows how even the private soldiers of the Catholic party rivalled their officers
in their abhorrence of, and forbearance from,
cruelty :—

" The next day Rathfarnham was taken by storm,
" and all that were in it made prisoners;

"and though 500 soldiers entered the castle
"before any officer of note, *yet not one*
"*creature was killed;* which I tell you by
"the way, to observe the difference between
"our and the [Cromwellian] rebels making
"use of a victory."—*Lord Ormond's Let-*
ters, II. p. 408.

Thus it appears that even the Irish soldiery
ceased to shed blood, from the moment when resistance was at an end. I could easily multiply instances; but the few I select are so emphatic, that
more are unnecessary. I cannot however avoid
giving this. It is another proud honour to the
House of Mountgarret :—

"At the same time the said Lord Mountgarret's
"eldest son, Colonel Edmund Butler, taking
"possession of Waterford, none of the in-
"habitants, of whatever country or religion,
"was either killed or pillaged; and such of
"the British Protestants as had a mind to
"leave the place, were allowed to carry off
"their goods wherever they pleased."—
Carte's Ormond.

Contrast, now, the manner in which the Irish
Catholics performed the conditions of surrender,
with the mode wherein the Protestant party behaved
on similar occasions. This is the Catholic instance :—

"When Birr surrendered to General Preston,

"in January, 1642, the articles were faith-
"fully performed ; and the Earl of Castle-
"haven, his Lieutenant-General, conveyed
"the garrison and inhabitants, to the number
"of 800 persons, in a long march of two or
"three days together through the woods of
"Irregan and waste countries, safe to Athy."
—*Carte's Ormond,* vol. I.

There are many more instances of this kind—
highly honourable to the Irish party. I select the
following :—

"The towns of Clonmell and Carrickmagriffit,
"in Tipperary, and Dungarvan, were seve-
"rally surprised by Mr. Richard Butler, of
"Kilcash, second brother to the Marquis of
"Ormond ; and he had such an influence
"over his followers that he kept them not
"only from murder but even from plunder ;
"his great care and noble disposition being
"acknowledged even by his enemies."—
Carte's Ormond.

Here is another :—

"Callan and Gowran were seized at the same time
"by persons thereunto designed by Lord
"Mountgarret, *without any bloodshed:* some
"plunder, however, was there committed,
"though with less violence for fear of com-
"plaints, it being well confined to cattle
"of English breed which were stolen as

" well from the Irish who had any of that
" breed, as from the English."—*Carte's
Ormond.*

I give another instance more in detail:—

" James, Lord Dunboyne, hearing of the surprise
" of Fethard by Theobald Butler, and being
" chief commander of the barony of Myddle-
" thyrde, by special grants made to some of
" his ancestors for service performed to the
" Crown of England, repaired thither the
" next day, and took on him the command
" of the town, dispersing the rabble, and
" placing in it a garrison which he formed
" of the most substantial inhabitants of the
" place and neighbourhood. *He imme-
" diately set the English at liberty, restored
" them their goods, and sent them away in
" safety to Youghall, and other places,
" which they chose for their retreat.* Two
" of these were clergymen, of whom Mr.
" Hamilton was, at his request, sent with
" his family to the Countess of Ormond."—
Carte's Ormond.

Let the reader now compare the extracts I have
given descriptive of English Protestant cruelty, with
the chivalrous generosity of the Irish leaders and
troops : the English cruelties not being palliated or
relieved from their horror by any acts of generosity
or any traits of humanity.   But extermination was

the object, and unmitigated murder and slaughter
the means.

I think I cannot more appropriately close this
part of my illustrations of Irish history, than by
quoting from Bishop Burnet the following description of the treatment given by the Irish to the
Right Rev. Dr. Bedell, Protestant bishop of Kilmore; a most humane and worthy man. He was
in the hands of the Irish during the worst part of
the insurrection. The Irish not only did him no
harm ; but they took care of all those persons—
(being Protestants of course)—who came to him
for protection. In short they treated him with
kindness, and protected him whilst he lived; and
honoured him at his death. This affecting account
is taken from Burnet's *Life of Bedell* :—

" Doctor Bedell, Bishop of Kilmore, when a
" prisoner with the insurgents, who doubtless
" had many priests among them, was never
" interrupted in the exercise of his worship,
" although not only his house and all the
" out-buildings, but also the church and
" church-yard, were full of people that
" flocked to him for protection. So that,
" from the 23rd of October, to the 18th of
" December following, he, and all those
" within his walls, enjoyed, to a miracle,"
says Bishop Burnet, " perfect quiet. And
" when he died at the age of 71, the titular

" bishop of that diocese, though he had
" proselyted his brother, a popish priest, to
" the communion of the established church,
" suffered him to be buried in consecrated
" ground, the Irish doing him unusual
" honours at his funeral. For the chiefs of
" the insurgents having assembled their
" forces, accompanied his body to the
" church-yard with great solemnity ; and
" desired Mr. Clogy, one of his chaplains,
" to bury him according to the church offices.
" At his interment they discharged a volley
" of shot, crying out in Latin, ' *Hic requi-*
" *escat ultimus Anglorum !*'   May the last
" of the English rest in peace ! Edmund
" Farrilly, a popish priest, exclaimed at the
" same time, ' *O, Sit anima mea cum*
" *Bedello !*'   Would to God that my soul
" were with Bedell !"—*Bishop Burnet's
Life of Bedell.*

I have now concluded the quotations which
contrast the brutal ferocity of the English Protestant party, with the humanity and generosity of the
Irish Catholics during the civil war. And I shall
next proceed to a few further illustrations of the
conduct of the adverse party during that disastrous
period.

OBSERVATIONS,
PROOFS, AND ILLUSTRATIONS.

CHAPTER III.—PART V.

It is, I repeat it, singularly curious, that whilst the English party had the strongest inducements to calumniate the Irish Catholics, they yet should have preserved so many traits of humanity and mercy on the part of the Irish; while at the same time they have not attempted to state a single act of kindness, charity, humanity, or mercy amongst the leaders of the English Protestant party. Extermination of the Irish was their object. Accordingly, extermination was their practice. I cannot, after the most minute search, discover one single instance in which life was spared to combatant or non-combatant, being Irish; to Irish man, Irish woman, or Irish child. I do not believe there are any such instances—I *hope* there are such; because if there be, the publication of this work will assuredly induce somebody to hunt them out and bring them forward. It would be desirable to mitigate the horror arising from the atrocity of the blood-thirsty Protestant party of that day. It could be wished, for the sake of humanity, that the cruelties of the English should have *some* mitigation arising from at least one solitary act of virtue.

Let it not be supposed that I am ignorant that *even* Cromwell occasionally observed the faith of treaties; or that he sometimes carried into effect that quarter for which men in arms had stipulated before surrender. It was his best policy on some occasions to do so; and not to drive to utter despair all the armed Irish. But even these acts of justice were extremely rare. And some of them were liable to be impeached for base unfaithfulness. His first perfidious slaughter at Drogheda, leaves any person attempting to become his advocate, by reason of his *occasional* performance of stipulation, in a situation not the most enviable. The truth is, that a fiend so black with crime, so stained with blood, never yet exhibited in any country to compare with Cromwell and his gang of sanguinary biblical enthusiasts in Ireland.

The deep interest which the English party had in calumniating the Irish is manifest. The atrocious iniquity of falsely charging the Irish with crime, was calculated to give these advantages to the English :—

Firstly—These false charges would serve to mitigate the horrors, otherwise unpalliated, of the massacres committed by the English Protestant party. It would place these massacres in the light of a retaliation upon the Irish for *their* crimes. Although, in sad truth, retaliation by means of the slaughter of unoffending men, women, and children, would be a poor plea for such barbarous inhumanity. But yet it would be *some*, and it *could* be the *only* mitigation.

Secondly—It would serve (as it *did* serve) as an excuse for seizing all the estates of the Irish, and declaring them forfeited to the Cromwellian party.

Thirdly—It would serve—and it *did* serve—to enable the ungrateful Stewart family to leave in the hands of the Cromwellian soldiers, or to convert to their own use, the estates of the faithful Irish Catholics, who had fought and bled and suffered in the cause of Charles the First, and whose properties were left as a plunder to those enemies of that Monarch who brought him to the scaffold; a plunder participated in to the extent of eighty thousand acres by the Duke of York, afterwards the miserable and contemptible James the Second.

With such powerful motives to calumniate and to persevere in calumny, it will not be surprising to find, that all inquiry into the real facts was refused; either contemptuously or upon the most futile pretences. *The Irish repeatedly pressed for the fullest inquiry.* And when the King's necessities compelled him to offer them an amnesty; *the Irish actually refused to accept any amnesty for*

any person of their party who should be proved
guilty of murder, breach of quarter, or any inhu-
man cruelty. The following is the 19th proposition
addressed to the King, with a remonstrance on their
grievances, by the confederate Catholics who assembled at Trim in 1642 :—

> " 19thly. Forasmuch as your Majesty's said
> " Catholic subjects have been taxed with
> " many inhuman cruelties which they never
> " committed, your Majesty's said suppliants,
> " therefore, for their vindication, and to
> " manifest to all the world their desire to
> " have all such offenders brought to justice,
> " DO   DESIRE,   THAT   IN   THE
> " NEXT PARLIAMENT, ALL NOTO-
> " RIOUS MURTHERS, BREACHES
> " OF QUARTER, AND INHUMAN
> " CRUELTIES   COMMITTED   OF
> " EITHER SIDE, MAY BE QUES-
> " TIONED IN THE SAID PARLIA-
> " MENT, IF YOUR MAJESTY THINK
> " FIT ; AND SUCH AS SHALL AP-
> " PEAR TO BE GUILTY TO BE
> " EXCEPTED OUT OF THE ACT
> " OF OBLIVION, AND PUNISHED
> " ACCORDING   TO   THEIR   DE-
> " SERTS."—*Borlase*, p. 191.

The reader will not be surprised to hear that
this proposition was rejected at the instance of the

English Protestant party. This single fact of re- jection will be conclusive in the mind of every reasonable man as to the guilt or innocence of the parties respectively.

There was a peace made in 1643—termed "The Cessation"—between the confederated Catholics and the King's friends in Ireland, with the Marquis of Ormond at their head : and again a regular peace in 1648. Upon *both* these occasions the Irish Catholics refused to accept an indemnity for persons convicted of murder, breach of quarter, or inhuman cruelty. On the contrary, their leaders were desirous that every person who had shed human blood out of battle, should be condignly punished.

" In the two peaces concluded" [by the Irish Catholics] "with the Marquis of Ormond, " viz. those of 1643 and 1648, *they expressly* " *excepted from pardon all those of their* " *party that had committed such cruelties.* " And long before either of these peaces, " Lord Clanricard testified, '*that it was the* " '*desire of the whole nation that the actors* " '*of these cruelties should, in the highest* " '*degree, be made examples to all poste-* " '*rity.*'—*Carte's Ormond,* vol. III. And " the Marquis of Ormond himself confessed, " 'that those, assuming power among the " 'Irish, had long disclaimed them, and

" 'professed an earnest desire that they
" 'might be brought to punishment.' "—
Ibid.

In short, the Irish Catholics acted precisely as
innocent men would act : not seeking to screen any
of the idle or dissolute of their own party, who in
the wild license of civil war might have slain any
Protestant out of battle, or committed any other
murder. On the contrary, the Irish Catholics
sought anxiously to have all such offenders punished
without mercy. The following extract from the
Rev. Peter Walsh, tends further to elucidate these
transactions ; and *he* is confessed, by the Protestant
writers of his own and all subsequent periods, to
be a faith-worthy witness :—

" Not to dwell longer," says Mr. Walsh, " on
" particulars, the whole body of the Catholic
" nobility and gentry of Ireland did, by their
" agents at Oxford in 1643, petition his
" Majesty :

" ' *That all the murders committed on both sides,*
" ' *in this war, might be examined in a fu-*
" ' *ture parliament, and the actors of them*
" ' *exempted out of all the acts of indemnity*
" ' *and oblivion.* But this proposal the
" ' Protestant agents, then also attending
" ' the King **at Oxford,** wisely declined ;
" ' upon which it was justly observed that if
" ' it should be asked wherefore this offer of

" ' the accused Irish has been always re-
" ' jected or evaded by their accusers, (for it
" ' was more than once repeated afterwards,)
" ' there is no man of reason but understands
" ' it was, because the Irish were not guilty
" ' of those barbarous and inhuman crimes
" ' with which they were charged; and
" ' because those who charged them so exor-
" ' bitantly, found themselves, or those of
" ' their party, truly chargeable with more
" ' numerous crimes and murders, committed
" ' on the stage of Ireland, whereon they
" ' had acted, and yet but partly, their own
" ' proper guilt; for many of them had
" ' acted it on that of Great Britain too,
" ' even the most horrid guilt imaginable,
" ' by the bloody and most execrable murder
" ' of the best and most innocent of Kings.' "
—*Peter Walsh's Reply to a Person of Quality.*

All the official acts of the confederated Catholics were consistent with this pure and honourable principle; the principle of inquiry into the crimes actually committed at all sides; the principle of exonerating the innocent and punishing the guilty. And this principle of justice was repudiated and rejected by the Protestant party!

In every part of these transactions, there is something singular and striking. The confederated

Catholics were in possession of power from the year
1643 to the year 1649. They were in possession
of, and had the management of, nearly all Ireland,
with the exception of Dublin and a few other places.
In 1644 they were at the acme of their power.
Their General Assembly met at Kilkenny, enacted
laws, and carried on the government. This assembly was composed almost exclusively of Catholics;
the Executive were exclusively so. *Yet they never
were once accused of having made a single intolerant law ; or a single intolerant or bigoted regula-
tion or ordinance! They did not persecute one
single Protestant ; nor are they accused of any
such persecution.* This indeed is matter of which
the Catholics of Ireland may be justly proud.

I have already shown from extracts taken from
Protestant writers,* the admission that the confederated Catholics never persecuted a single Protestant.

Now if the reader will go back to page 283, he
will find the sanguinary orders issued against the
Irish by the English parliament ; the utter refusal
to give the Irish quarter. And especially in page
274, he will find the exterminating orders given in
Dublin by the Lords Justices, bearing date the
23rd of February, 1641 ; in which, by the bye,
there is a perfect gloating over every word descriptive of sanguinary cruelty ; and above all, *the*

---

* Parnell and Taylor.

*direction to destroy all towns wherein the rebels
had been relieved or harboured,* aṇd "*to kill and
destroy all the men there inhabiting capable to
bear arms,*" aye, although thoroughly innocent in
thought, word, or deed, of any crime !

The contrast afforded to this ineffable barbarity
by the conduct of the Catholic power is painfully
pleasing.   In May, 1642, the Catholic body—
clerical and lay—met in national Synod at Kilkenny.   *They wielded not only temporal authority,
but also the spiritual thunders of the Catholic
church, against all those who, during the war,
should commit any cruelty.*   I take the following
description of this Catholic body, from a Protestant
historian, Doctor Warner :—

"This was," says Dr. Warner, "a general Synod
"of all the popish bishops and clergy of
"Ireland.   Three of the titular archbishops,
"six other bishops, the proxies of five more,
"besides vicars-general and other dignita-
"ries, were present at this Synod.   And as
"these are the acts and ordinances purely
"of the Roman Catholic clergy of Ireland,
"represented in a general Synod, I suppose
"it would be allowed on all sides that
"whatever proceedings are here condemned,
"are to be placed to the account of the
"follies and vices of particular people ; and
"cannot fairly be charged on the Roman

faith."—*Warner's Hist. Irish Rebellion,*
p. 201.

I will now give three of the articles unanimously
agreed on at this Synod:

" Articles agreed upon, ordained, and concluded
    "in the General (Catholic) Congregation
    "held at Kilkenny, May, 1642.

" We declare the [present] war, openly Catholic,
    "to be lawful and just ; in which war, *if*
    "*some of the Catholics be found to proceed*
    "*out of some particular and unjust title,*
    "*covetousness, cruelty, revenge, or hatred,*
    "*or any such unlawful private intentions,*
    "*we declare them therein grievously to*
    "*sin, and therefore worthy to be punished*
    "*and restrained with ecclesiastical censures,*
    "if (advised thereof) they do not amend."
    —*Rushworth,* V. 516.

" We will and declare *all those that murder, dis-*
    "*member, or grievously strike ; all thieves,*
    "*unlawful spoilers, robbers of any goods,*
    "*extorters; together with all such as favour,*
    "*receive, or any ways assist them,* TO BE
    "EXCOMMUNICATED ; and so to remain until
    "they completely amend and satisfy, no
    "less than if they were namely proclaimed
    "excommunicated.

" We command all and every the generals, colo-
    "nels, captains, and other officers of our

" Catholic army, to whom it appertaineth,
" that they *severely punish all transgressors*
" *of our aforesaid command, touching mur-*
" *derers, maimers, strikers, thieves, and*
" *robbers ; and if they fail therein, we*
" *command the parish priests, curates, or*
" *chaplains, respectively,* to declare them
" interdicted ; and that they shall be excom-
" municated if they cause not *due satisfac-*
" *tion to be made unto the commonwealth*
" *and the party offended.* And this the
" parish priests or chaplains shall observe,
" under pain of excommunication on sen-
" tence given *ipso facto.*"—*Borlase,* p. 122 ;
and *Rushworth,* V. 520.

Thus, the public acts of the confederated Catholics, contrast as favourably with the public acts
of the Protestant party, as the generosity and
humanity of the Catholic Irish, armed and unarmed, contrast with the atrocities of the Protestant
English.

OBSERVATIONS,
PROOFS, AND ILLUSTRATIONS.

CHAPTER III.—PART VI.

From the quotations which I have made from various historians, he who has taken the trouble to follow me, must have perceived how completely the Cromwellian power had been established, through oceans of blood, and through scenes of fiendish and appalling cruelty. I shall now proceed to show how the survivors of the Irish were disposed of.

" The affairs of the confederate Catholics being
" now absolutely irretrievable, the Marquis
" of Clanricard in 1652 left Ireland, carry-
" ing with him the royal authority.—*(Bor-*
" *lase, Irish Reb.)* ' And within a twelve-
" ' month after, Mortogh O'Brien, the last
" ' of the Irish commanders, submitted to
" ' the parliament, on the usual terms of
" ' transportation; by the favour of which,'
" (adds Borlase,) ' twenty-seven thousand
" ' men had been that year sent away.'
" ' Cromwell,' says a late historian, ' in

" ' order to get free of his enemies, did not
" ' scruple to transport forty thousand Irish
" ' from their own country, to fill all the
" ' armies in Europe with complaints of his
" ' cruelty, and admiration of their own
" ' valour.'—(*Dalrymple, Mem. of Great
"Brit.* vol. I. part 2, p. 267.)"—*Curry's
Review,* p. 386.

I have given proofs enough to show, that the
design of the English Protestant party was totally
to exterminate the Irish people. For the purpose
of effectually clearing the country of the native
Irish, it was of course expedient to get rid of as
many persons of the military age as possible. It
was in this way that the 27,000 persons mentioned
in the last extract were disposed of. Several other
detachments, comprising from one to four thousand
men each, under the command of Irish officers,
were disposed of by Cromwell and his Government
to foreign princes.

But the enormities of the ruling tyrants did not
stop here. Those of military age who were spared
from the slaughter, to the amount, by a safe calculation, of more than forty thousand, were sent into
foreign service on the continent of Europe, especially to Spain and Belgium. The following note
will be found in Lingard :—

    " According to Petty, (p. 187,) six thousand
    " boys and women were sent away. Lynch

" (*Cambrensis Eversus*, in fine) says, that
" they were sold for slaves. Broudin, in
" his *Propugnaculum*, *(Pragæ*, anno 1669,)
" numbers the exiles at 100,000. Ultra
" centum millia omnis sexus et ætatis, e
" quibus aliquot millia in diversas Americæ
" tabbacarias insulas relegata sunt, p. 692.
" In a letter in my possession, written in
" 1656, it is said : Catholicos pauperes
" plenis navibus mittunt in Barbados et in-
" sulas Americæ. Credo jam sexaginta
" millia abivisse. Expulsis enim ab initio
" in Hispaniam et Belgium maritis, jam
" uxores et proles in Americam destinatur."
—*Lingard's England*, vol. X. p. 306.

Thus, we see from Broudin, that there were
more than 100,000 persons of every age and sex
banished ; of whom several thousands were, as he
says, sent to the West India islands. We also
learn from the original letter in the possession of
Dr. Lingard, that the vessels were crowded with
the poorer classes of Catholics and sent to Barbadoes and the other West India islands. " I believe,"
says the writer, " that already sixty thousand are
gone ; for the husbands being first sent to Spain
and Belgium, already their wives and children are
destined for the Americas." It would be indeed
idle to exclaim at any cruelty committed at that
time. Those unhappy exiles perished in hundreds

and thousands. Of the myriads thus transported, not a single one survived at the end of twenty years.

Was there any species of crime which was not perpetrated against the Irish by the barbarians of the English Governments ?

In Thurlow's correspondence, the formation of press-gangs to collect the male and female youth for transportation, is stated at length. Some have thought that the system adopted by the monster who now rules in Russia, of collecting young women from his Polish subjects to send to his military colonies, was an invention of his own! But there is no atrocity so great as not to have its prototype in the brutalities inflicted upon the people of Ireland by some of their English rulers. It is melancholy to read such a statement as the following :—

" After the conquest of Jamaica in 1655, the " Protector, that he might people it, pro- " posed to transport a thousand Irish boys " and a thousand Irish girls to the island. " At first, the young women only were de- " manded, to which it is replied, ' Although " ' we must use force in taking them up, yet, " ' it being so much for their own good, and " ' likely to be of so great advantage to the " ' public, it is not in the least doubted that " ' you may have such number of them as " ' you shall think fit.'—*Thurloe*, IV. 23.

" In the next letter, H. Cromwell says, ' I
" ' think it might be of like advantage to
" ' your affairs there, and ours here, if you
" ' should think fit to send one thousand five
" ' hundred or two thousand young boys of
" ' twelve or fourteen years of age to the
" ' place aforementioned. *We* could well
" ' spare them, and they would be of use to
" ' you ; and who knows but it might be a
" ' means to make them Englishmen, I mean
" ' rather Christians?' (p. 40.) Thurloe
" answers, ' The committee of the council
" ' have voted one thousand girls, and as
" ' many youths, to be taken up for that
" ' purpose.' (p. 75.)"

Sacred heaven! Thus it is that the English
" *did good*" to the people of Ireland! The young
women were to be taken by force from their
mothers, their sisters, their homes! and to be
transported to a foreign and unhealthy clime. " O,
but," said the English rulers, " it is all for their
own good ! ! !" Then again, look at the cold-
blooded manner in which Henry Cromwell proposes
to make " Englishmen and Christians."

" *Englishmen and Christians !*"..........

But no. Comment is useless.

All these things appear like a hideous dream.
They would be utterly incredible, only that they
are quite certain.

There remained, however, too many, to render possible the horrible cruelty of cutting all their throats. The Irish Government, constituted as it was of the superior officers of the regicide force, resorted to a different plan. Here is the account given by Lord Clarendon of their conduct :—

" They found the utter EXTIRPATION of
" the nation *(which they had intended)* to
" be in itself very difficult, and to carry in
" it somewhat of horror, that made some
" impression upon the stone-hardness of
" their own hearts. After so many thou-
" sands destroyed by the plague which raged
" over the kingdom, by fire, sword, and
" famine, and after so many thousands
" transported into foreign parts ; there re-
" mained still such a numerous people that
" they knew not how to dispose of : and
" though they were declared to be all for-
" feited, and so to have no title to anything,
" yet they must remain somewhere. They
" therefore found this expedient, which they
" called an *act of grace* ; there was a large
" tract of land, even to the half of the pro-
" vince of Connaught, that was separated
" from the rest by a long and large river,
" and which by the plague and MANY
" MASSACRES remained almost desolate.

" Into this space they required all the Irish
" to retire by such a day, *under the penalty*
" *of death;* and all who should after
" *that time be found in any other part of*
" *the kingdom, man, woman, or child,*
" SHOULD BE KILLED BY ANY-
" BODY WHO SAW OR MET THEM.
" The land within this circuit, *the most*
" *barren in the kingdom,* was, out of *the*
" *grace and mercy of the conquerors,*
" assigned to those of the nation as were
" enclosed, in such proportions as might
" with great industry preserve their lives."
—*Clarendon's Life,* vol. II. p. 116.

It would seem as if the English rulers of Ireland
had determined that there should be no species of
injustice omitted in the catalogue of their crimes
towards Ireland. For, certainly, a greater cruelty
than this "transplanting" (as it was technically
called) could not be committed upon human beings
who were allowed to live. This cruelty was refined.
For the tyrants took care to provide against the
contingent chance of the restoration of the royal
authority. They had the baseness to compel
the unhappy Irish gentry to execute releases of
their former property; releases which were used
for the worst of purposes by the profligate Monarch
who regained the throne, and by his more profligate
advisers.

Clarendon continues the account of the transplantation thus :—

" And to those persons, from whom they had
" taken great quantities of land in other
" provinces, they assigned the greater pro-
" portions within this precinct ; so that it
" fell to some men's lot, especially when
" they were accommodated with houses, to
" have a competent livelihood, though never
" to the fifth part of what had been taken
" from them in a much better province.
" And that they might not be exalted with
" this merciful donative, it was a condition
" that accompanied this their accommoda-
" tion, that they should all give releases of
" their former rights and titles to the land
" that was taken from them, in consideration
" of what was now assigned to them ; and
" so they should for ever bar themselves and
" their heirs from ever laying claim to their
" old inheritance. What should they do ?
" They could not be permitted to go out of
" this precinct to shift for themselves else-
" where ; and without this assignation, they
" must starve there, *as many did die every*
" *day of famine.* In this deplorable con-
" dition, and under this consternation, they
" found themselves obliged to accept or
" submit to the hardest conditions of their

" conquerors; and so signed such convey-
" ances and releases as were prepared for
" them, that they might enjoy those lands
" which belonged to other men."—*Clarendon's Life*, II. 116, 117.

The English usurpers now declared that Ireland
was pacified. It was literally in the words of
Tacitus,—

" Ubi solitudinem faciunt, pacem appellant."

They had made a solitude; but it was not of a
sterile waste; it was of a fertile and beautiful land.
They were glad to inhabit it, these officers and
soldiers! They brought over as many of their
companions, relations, and friends, as they could.

I now will insert a sketch of the manner in which
the Cromwellians divided Ireland among themselves:—

" On the 26th of September, 1653, the English
" parliament declared, that the rebels in
" Ireland were subdued, and the rebellion
" ended; *and thereupon proceeded to the
" distribution of their lands*, in pursuance
" of the Act of Subscriptions, 17° Caroli.
" ' This being notified to the Government of
" ' Ireland, Lord Broghill, afterwards Earl
" ' of Orrery, proposed at a council of war
" ' of all the chief commanders for the par-
" ' liament, that the whole kingdom should

" 'be surveyed, and the number of acres
" 'taken, with the quality of them; and
" 'then that all the soldiers should bring in
" 'their demands of arrears; and so, give
" 'every man by lot, as many acres as
" 'should answer the value of his demand.' "
—*Morrice's Life of Orrery.*

We shall now see what was done upon this proposal :—

" This proposal was agreed to, and all Ireland
" being surveyed, the best land was rated
" at only four shillings an acre, and some
" only at a penny."—*(Morrice's Life of
Orrery,* vol. II. p. 117.) " The soldiers
" drew lots in what parts of the kingdom
" their portions should be assigned them."
—*(Carte's Ormond,* II. 301.) " Great abuse
" was committed in setting out the adven-
" turers' satisfaction for the money they had
" advanced at the beginning of the war; for
" they had whole baronies set out to them
" in gross; and then they employed sur-
" veyors of their own, to make their admea-
" surements."—*Ib. id.*

I may here remark that the general survey
which was made in pursuance of Lord Broghill's
proposal, is the same which is known by the name
of " the Down Survey ;" in the making of which,
Sir W. Petty, the paternal ancestor of the pre-

sent Marquis of Lansdown, had a very principal part.

Amidst this rapine, it may excite a faint smile to see the choice that Cromwell made for himself ; although his premature death prevented the realization of his plan :—

" A good and great part (as I remember the
" whole province of Tipperary) Cromwell
" had reserved to himself, as a demesne (as
" he called it) for the State, and in which no
" adventurer or soldier should demand his
" lot to be assigned ; and no doubt intended
" both the State and it for making great
" his own family. *It cannot be imagined*
" *in how easy a method, and with what*
" *peaceable formality, this whole great*
" *kingdom was taken from the just lords*
" *and proprietors, and divided and given*
" *amongst those who had no other right to*
" *it but that they had power to keep it.*"—
Clarendon's Life, vol. II. p. 117.

It will be well to remember, when we come to treat of the reign of King Charles II., who *they* were that got the greatest share of the lands of the Irish royalists :—

" *No men had so great shares as they who had*
" *been instruments to murder the King.*
" What lands they were pleased to call un-
" profitable (which were thrown in gratis)

" they returned as such, let them be never
" so good and profitable."—*Carte's Ormond*,
II. 301.

" The lands held by the soldiers *as unprofitable*,
" and as such returned into the surveyor's
" office, amounted to 605,670 acres. In this
" manner was the whole kingdom divided
" between the soldiers and the adventurers
" of money."—*Curry's Review*, p. 388.

Thus was the slaughter and the robbery of the
Irish people complete.

But the iniquity was *not* complete. It could not
be so, without the intervention of what were termed
" Courts of Justice." I believe there is no instance
in English history of any villainy being perpetrated
upon the people of England, Scotland, and Ireland,
in which my lords the Judges had not their full
share of the crime. Accordingly, Cromwell instituted his " Courts of Justice" in Ireland.
They were familiarly called *Cromwell's slaughter-
houses*.

" HIGH COURTS OF JUSTICE IN IRELAND.

" About this time, a new tribunal, under the
" title of an high Court of Justice, was
" erected by the usurpers in different parts
" of both kingdoms, for the trial of rebels
" and malignants ; that is to say, of those
" who were still found faithful to the King.

" That which sat at Dublin in 1652, was
" besides* authorised ' to hear and deter-
" mine, all massacres and murders done or
" committed since the first day of October,
" 1641 ; that is to say, the actors, contrivers,
" promoters, abettors, aiders, and assisters
" of any of the said massacres or murders,
" or killing after quarter given.' From the
" iniquitous and bloody sentences frequently
" pronounced in these courts, they were
" commonly called ' Cromwell's slaughter-
" houses';† 'for no articles were pleadable
" in them : and against a charge of things
" said to be done twelve years before, little
" or no defence could be made; and that
" the cry was made of blood, aggravated
" with expressions of so much horror, and
" the no less daunting aspect of the court,
" quite confounded the amazed prisoners, so
" that they came like sheep to the slaughter."
—*Curry's Review of the Civil Wars in
Ireland*, p. 392.

The Irish Catholic party, as we have seen, repeatedly requested a full investigation of all the
murders committed during the war. But they demanded that it should be an inquiry into the crimes
of all parties—the Protestant as well as the Catholic.

---

* Borlase's Irish Reb.   † Hist. of Independency.

This inquiry the Irish pressed to obtain in 1642, in 1646, and again in 1648. But at each of these times the request was eluded or denied by the English Protestant party. And they acted wisely, in so denying it, for their own interests.

These repeated offers on the part of the Irish Catholics—these repeated refusals on the part of the English Protestants, can of course leave not a doubt on the mind of any rational man at the present day, of the innocence of the one, and of the deep guilt of the other.

Cromwell's courts, however, were quite unequivocal. Their examination was avowedly and exclusively confined to the crimes committed *by* the Irish party; and did not extend to any crimes committed *upon* them. Yet, such is the nature of a just cause, that even those tribunals confirmed the general innocency of the Irish party. Such was the indiscriminate and glaring injustice of these courts, that in various parts of Ireland they contrived to condemn about two hundred persons as guilty of murder, on forged, corrupt, or even upon *no* evidence :

" Yet," says Leland, " in the northern province, " which had been the great scene of barba- " rity, not one was brought to justice but Sir " Phelim O'Nial."—*Leland*, vol. III. 394.

The remark which Leland makes upon there being but one case in the northern province, would have assumed quite a different shape if he had been fair or candid. He should have said that when this active, energetic, and ambulatory tribunal of blood could find but one case in all Ulster, and when *that one* was the case of Sir Phelim O'Neill; and as Ulster was the province the most deeply and extensively charged with inhumanity and murder, it followed inevitably that the charges were most enormously exaggerated even against the people of Ulster; as we have in fact seen that they were. If there had been many murders in the rest of Ireland, surely this sanguinary tribunal would have found more victims than the number mentioned— about two hundred. Let it be recollected that even against the two hundred persons who *were* convicted, judgment was given either on *no* evidence, or on *corrupt or forged* evidence. To a thinking mind, there is no quantity of written or verbal authority that would so coerce a conviction of the innocence of the Irish Catholic party, as the result of the investigation of this sanguinary and energetic court. That court was ambulatory, and sat in almost every county in Ireland. They had to investigate the crimes committed *by* the Irish during an insurrection rendered hideous by the crimes committed *upon* the Irish. It was a court in which no defence was listened to. Men who had surrendered on the faith of articles of capitulation, and who had performed their own part of the stipulation, were deprived of the benefit of those articles. No faith was kept with the Irish—no justice was done. And yet—O ! astonishing !—*not more than two hundred victims could be found affording a shadow of pretext for putting them to death upon the allegation that they had committed crimes during the rebellion !*

Yet the Irish were made to endure the infliction of the most horrible calumnies, sustained not only upon *false*, but on the most *incredible* of all imaginable testimony, for nearly a century before they were allowed so much as to assert or defend their own innocence ! Such was the course and manner of English justice to Ireland.

I cannot proceed without giving one trait of the unhappy Sir Phelim O'Neill. There is no man of the Irish party so deeply stained with the crimes accompanying the insurrection. He was, in short, the worst of the Irish. Yet, at his trial, he was offered his life, if he would but charge the King with having authorised him to commence that insurrection. He utterly refused to accuse the King falsely. Accordingly, he was sentenced to execution. There is for this fact the authority of Dr. Sheridan, Protestant Bishop of Kilmore, who was present at the execution, and who asserts—

"That Colonel Hewson coming towards the "ladder, Sir Phelim made his public ac-"knowledgments to him in a grateful

" manner, for the civil treatment he had
" met with during the whole course of his
" imprisonment; and only wished that his
" life had been taken from him in a more
" honourable manner.   To this Colonel
" Hewson answered, that he might save his
" life if he pleased, only by declaring at that
" moment to the people, that his first taking
" arms was by virtue of a commission under
" the broad seal of King Charles the First :
" but Sir Phelim replied *that he would not*
" *save his life by so base a lie, by doing so*
" *great an injury* to that Prince.   'Tis true,
" he said, that he might the better persuade
" the people to come unto him, he took off
" an old seal from an old deed, and clapt it
" to a commission that he had forged, and
" so persuaded the people that what he did
" was by the King's authority ; but he never
" really had any commission from the King.
" This, adds Mr. Carte, the bishop told me
" he heard him say."—*Macpherson's Hist.*
Great Britain, III. 280 ; also *Leland*,
Book VI. chap. 2.

Thus, even amongst the worst of the Irish, do
we find a redeeming or a mitigating quality, that
will enable them to compete with the very foremost
of the English party.   And this I say without at
all palliating Sir Phelim's crimes.   All I say is,

that if he had a thousand crimes—yet, bad as he was, he had *one* virtue; whereas his enemies had none at all!

I have already quoted crimes enough committed by the English Protestant party, to satiate the most satanic disposition for cruelty; but not enough to satiate the English party.

The Irish parliament being suppressed, the usurped powers in Ireland legislated by proclamations. There was no other form. But these proclamations were perfectly efficacious, sustained as they were by the power of the sword.

I will give the first specimen :—

" In the same year (1652) the parliament com-
" missioners at Dublin published a proclama-
" tion, signed Charles Fleetwood, Edmund
" Ludlow, and John Jones; wherein the
" act of the 27th of Elizabeth was made of
" force in Ireland, and ordered to be most
" strictly put in execution. By this act,
" 'every Romish priest, so found, was
" 'deemed guilty of rebellion, and SEN-
" 'TENCED TO BE HANGED UNTIL HE WAS
" 'HALF DEAD; THEN TO HAVE HIS HEAD
" 'TAKEN OFF, AND HIS BODY CUT IN QUAR-
" 'TERS; HIS BOWELS TO BE DRAWN OUT
" 'AND BURNED ; *and his head fixed upon*
" '*a pole in some public place.*' "—*Curry's Review,* p. 392.

The only excuse for enacting this horrible and
barbarous law, was, that it was already in force in
England. But in England the Catholic priests
were comparatively few; in Ireland they were
many. Protestant intolerance found this method
of diminishing their number in Ireland; hanging
them till they were half dead, and then tearing out
their bowels. In the next proclamation these law-
givers exceeded even the English brutality. Here
is the specimen :—

" The punishment of those who entertained a
" priest, was, by the same act, confiscation
" of their goods and chattels, and the igno-
" minious death of the gallows. This edict
" was renewed the same year, with the
" additional cruelty of making even the
" private exercise of the Roman Catholic
" religion, a capital crime. And again
" repeated in 1657, with the same penalty
" of confiscation and DEATH to all those who,
" knowing where a priest was hid, did not
" make discovery to the Government."—
Curry's Review, p. 392.

Nor were these mere idle threats. They were
carried into full execution. The Protestant party
were triumphant; and no Catholic who fell within
their grasp was spared. Let others speak for me :—

" Of the strict execution of these barbarous edicts,
    " many shocking examples were daily seen

" among these unhappy people, insomuch,
" that, to use the words of a contemporary
" writer and eye witness, ' Neither the
" ' Israelites were more cruelly persecuted
" ' by Pharaoh, nor the innocent infants by
" ' Herod, nor the Christians by Nero or
" ' any other of the Pagan tyrants, than
" ' were the Roman Catholics of Ireland at
" ' that fatal juncture of these savage commis-
" ' sioners.'—*Morrison's Threnodia*, p. 14."

There was an awful pleasantry also in the cruelty
of these sanguinary wretches :—

" *The same price* (five pounds sterling) *was set*
" *by these commissioners on the head of a*
" *Romish priest as on that of a wolf;* the
" number of which latter was then very
" considerable in Ireland ; and although the
" profession or character of a Romish priest
" could not, one would think, be so clearly
" ascertained as the species of a wolf, by the
" mere inspection of their heads thus severed
" from their bodies, yet the bare assevera-
" tion of the beheaders was, in both cases,
" equally credited and rewarded by these
" commissioners."—*Curry's Review*, pp.
393—4.

Here let me pause amidst these scenes of horror
and desolation.   Here let me pause ; consoled and
soothed by the recollection of the glorious contrast

of the humanity and mercy exhibited by the Irish
Catholics, with the fiendish cruelty and barbarity
perpetrated by the English Protestants. The
documents put forth by each party fully establish
this contrast. On the side of the Irish there cannot
be quoted any letter, any writing, any document,
any general or particular order, edict, law, or
command; enjoining, suggesting, or palliating
murder or pillage—plunder or crime. No—*not
one!* I repeat it, NOT ONE! On the contrary,
every authentic document that has ever been produced as emanating from the Irish Catholics, sug-
gests lenity, forgiveness, and mercy. And, as in
the case of the act of the general Catholic confederacy in 1642, there are not only pains, just
pains and penalties denounced against all evil-doers,
plunderers, robbers, and murderers; but punishment is denounced in the strongest terms against
every person, no matter of what rank, who should
connive at crime, or endeavour to extend impunity
to criminals! And even going so far, that to the
inflictions by the tribunals of this world, there is
superadded the more awful judgment of excommunication. (See pp. 262—3.)

On the other hand, you can read the gloating
satisfaction with which the English Protestant Lords
Justices, the English parliament, English officers
in command, and English parliamentary commissioners in possession of legislative and executive

authority in Ireland, not only commanded but
enforced the perpetration of the most brutal barbarities and diabolical cruelties upon the Irish
people, by their public and private documents, their
proclamations, their orders to the military, their
ordinances, edicts, and laws. All, all steeped in
blood, and saturated with horrors.

Contrast the two. Recollect that, with a very
small exception, the entire of Ireland was in the
possession of the confederated Catholics for nearly
six years; that is, from about 1643 to 1649.
Recollect that during that period (and for the two
years preceding it) the utmost atrocities were perpetrated upon the Irish. Recollect all this—and
join then with me in blessing Providence who gave
the Irish nation a soul so full of humanity, a disposition so replete with mercy, that, excepting in the
actual civil war itself, the Irish shed no blood,
committed no crime, perpetrated no barbarity,
exhibited no intolerance, exercised no persecution.

When, O when! will justice be rendered to thy
sons, O loved fatherland? When, O when! will
mankind recognise the just title of the Irish to pre-
eminence in the most glorious virtues? to morality
of the purest order, domestic and public? Temperance of the most extensive and practical utility?
Tenacious religious fidelity, beyond the example
of all, or any, of the countries on the face of Christendom?

OBSERVATIONS,
PROOFS, AND ILLUSTRATIONS.

CHAPTER III.—PART VII.

I SHALL close the disastrous period embraced in this third chapter, by the insertion of some documents illustrative of the practices of the times. The first is taken from a note to Lingard's *History of England*, and shows the spirit that animated the popular party in England. I desire to show that it was not only the Protestant Government, but the Protestant *population of England*, that gloated over Catholic blood :—

"I have not been able," says Lingard, " to as-
" certain the number of Catholic clergymen
" who were executed or banished for their
" religion under Charles I., and under the
" Commonwealth. But I possess an original
" document, authenticated by the signatures
" of the parties concerned, which contains
" the names and fate of such Catholic priests
" as were apprehended and prosecuted in
" London between the end of 1640 and the

" summer of 1651, by four individuals who
" had formed themselves into a kind of joint
" stock company for that laudable purpose,
" and who solicited from the council some
" reward for their services. It should,
" however, be remembered, that there were
" many others engaged in the same pursuit,
" and consequently many other victims be-
" sides those who are here enumerated."
Lingard then proceeds to quote from his original
document as follows :—

" The names of such Jesuits and Romish priests
" as have been apprehended and prosecuted
" by Captain James Wadsworth, Francis
" Newton, Thomas Mayo, and Robert De
" Luke, messengers, at our proper charge;
" whereof some have been condemned, some
" executed, and some reprieved since the
" beginning of the parliament, (3rd Novem-
" ber, 1640,) the like having not been done
" by any others since the Reformation of
" religion in this nation :—

" William Waller, als. Slaughter, als.
" Walker, executed at Tyburne.
" Cuthbert Clapton, condemned, re-
" prieved, and pardoned.
" Bartholomew Row, executed at Tyburne.
" Thomas Reynolds, executed at Tyburne.
" Edward Morgan, executed at Tyburne.

" Thomas Sanderson, als. Hammond, exe-
" cuted at Tyburne.

" Henry Heath, als. Pall Magdalen, exe-
" cuted at Tyburne.

" Francis Quashet, died in Newgate after
" judgment.

" Arthur Bell, executed at Tyburne.

" Ralph Corbey, executed at Tyburne.

" John Duchet, executed at Tyburne.

" John Hamond, als. Jackson, condemned,
" reprieved by the King, and died in
" Newgate.

" Walter Coleman, condemned, and died
" in Newgate.

" Edmond Cannon, condemned, and died
" in Newgate.

" John Wigmore, alias Turner, con-
" demned, and reprieved by the King,
" and is in custodie in Newgate.

" Andrew Ffryer, alias Herne, alias
" Richmond, condemned, and died in
" Newgate.

" John Goodman, condemned, and died
" in Newgate.

" Henry Morse, executed at Tyburne.

" Thomas Worsley, alias Harvey, in-
" dicted and proved; reprieved by
" the Spanish ambassador and others.

" Charles Chanie (Cheney), als. Thomp-

" son, indicted and proved, and begged
" by the Spanish ambassador, and since
" taken by command of the Council of
" State, and is now in Newgate.

" Andrew White, indicted, proved, re-
" prieved before judgment, and ba-
" nished.

" Richard Copley, condemned, and ba-
" nished.

" Richard Worthington, found guiltie, and
" banished.

" Edmond Cole, Peter Wright, and Wil-
" liam Morgan, indicted, proved, and
" sent beyond sea.

" Philip Morgan, executed at Tyburne.

" Edmund Ensher, als. Arrow, indicted,
" condemned, reprieved by the parlia-
" ment, and banished.

" Thomas Budd, als. Peto, als. Gray,
" condemned, reprieved by the Lord
" Mayor of London and others, justices,
" and since retaken by order of the
" Council of State, and is now in
" Newgate.

" George Baker, als. Macham, indicted,
" proved guiltie, and now in New-
" gate.

" Peter Beale, als. Wright, executed at
" Tyburne.

" George Gage, indicted by us, and found
" guiltie, and since is dead.

> " JAMES WADSWORTH,
> " FRANCIS NEWTON,
> " THOMAS MAYO,
> " ROBERT DE LUKE.

" This catalogue," continues Lingard, " tells a
" fearful but instructive tale ; inasmuch as
" it shows how wantonly men can sport with
" the lives of their fellow-men, if it suit the
" purpose of a great political party. The pa-
" triots, to enlist in their favour the religious
" prejudices of the people, represented the
" King as the patron of popery, *because he*
" *sent the priests into banishment, instead of*
" *delivering them to the knife of the exe-*
" *cutioner.* Hence, when they became
" lords of the ascendant, they were bound
" to make proof of their orthodoxy ; and
" almost every execution mentioned above
" took place by their order in 1642 or 1643.
" After that time they began to listen to the
" voice of humanity, and adopted the very
" expedient which they had so clamorously
" condemned. They banished, instead of
" hanging and quartering."—*Lingard*, vol.
X. p. 428.

As a pendant to the foregoing, and to form a
kind of relief to the wholesale slaughters, I insert

.an extract of the translation of an exceedingly rare and curious tract, and published the year after Cromwell's death. The original is in Latin, and is entitled " MORISONI THRENODIA HIBERNO-CATHOLICA, sive Planctus Universalis totius Cleri et Regni Hiberniæ *de transcendenti Crudelitate Anglorum adversus Catholicos in Hibernia,*" Œnipont, 1659 :*—

" A CATALOGUE OF SOME OF THE CHIEFS AND NOBLES
    " SLAUGHTERED BY THE PROTESTANTS.

" CHAP. VI.

" I do not here enumerate any person slain in
" battle, although he might have fallen in
" the cause of his religion ; nor do I give
" the tenth part of the persons of quality
" who were murdered : but *only* the more
" illustrious, being chiefly those who were
" received into allegiance by the Protestants,
" after the amnesty had been made and
" actually entered on ; [a treachery] which

---

* " QUORUNDAM MAGNATUM AC NOBILIUM, AB HÆRETICIO
    SUSPENDIO NECATORUM, SYNOPSIS.

" CAPUT VI.

" Non recenseo hic ullum in bello occisum, quamvis causâ fidei occideretur, neque decimam partem nobilium, suspendio necatorum, sed *tantum* illustriores, eosque majori ex parte ab hæreticis in fidem receptos, post amnestiam factam, et fædus

" barbarians and infidels themselves would
" abhor and deem detestable.

" 1. Lord Hugh MacMahon, the chief of his
" illustrious race ; a brave and noble mili-
" tary leader, was, after two years' impri-
" sonment in London, half-hanged; and
" *ere life was extinct,* quartered; his head
" was then placed on an iron spike on Lon-
" don bridge to feed the ravenous fowls of
" the air; his four quarters were placed
" over four of the gates of London.

" 2. Cornelius Maguire, Lord Viscount Iniskil-
" len, a most devout and holy man, sole com-
" panion in captivity of the aforesaid Hugh
" MacMahon, underwent the same butchery
" about two months after the execution of
" MacMahon.

---

initum, quod ipsi barbari & æthnici abhorruerunt, & nefas putârunt.

" 1. Illustrissimus *D. Hugo MacMahon,* illustrissimæ suæ familiæ præcipuus, magnanimus, ac strenuus belli dux, *Londini* in Angliâ, post duorum annorum diram captivitatem, patibulo semi-suspensus, et semi-vivus, in quatuor partes dissectus, caput ipsius in spiculo ferreo appensum supra pontem Londinensem, in escam volatilibus cæli collocatum est; quatuor verò partes, ad quatuor portes urbis *Londinensis* appendebantur.

" 2. Illustrissimus D. *Cornelius Maguire,* Vice-Comes de Inis-killen, vir sanctissimus & devotissimus, necnon præfati *D. Mac-Mahon,* individuus captivitatis comes, *Londini,* duobus circiter mensibus post præfatum D. pari per omnia, Carnificio plecteba ur.

" 3. The illustrious Felix O'Neill (captured by
" Protestant device) was half-hanged in
" Dublin, A.D. 1652, and while yet alive
" was quartered. His head was stuck upon
" a great spike at the western gate of Dub-
" lin; and his quarters were sent to be stuck
" on spikes in four different parts of the
" kingdom.

" 4. Henry O'Neill, son of Eugene O'Neill;
" taken prisoner in battle, and, *notwith-*
" *standing plighted faith,* slaughtered, in
" Ulster, A.D. 1651.

" 5. Thaddæus O'Connor, (Sligo,) descended
" from the royal race of the last and most
" powerful monarchs of Ireland; a man of
" great goodness and innocence ; hung in
" the town of Boyle, in Connaught, A.D.

" 3. Illustrissimus D. *Fælix O'Neill,* (insidiis ab hæreticis
captus) *Dublinii* in Hibernia, an. 1652, patibulo semi-suspensus,
et semi-animis in quatuor partes dissectus ; caput ad occiden-
talem portam Dubliniensem, magnâ infixâ perticâ, appende-
batur, et quatuor partes ad diversa Regni loca similiter appen-
dendæ, mittebantur.

" 4. Illustrissimus D. *Henricus O'Neill,* filius illustrissimi
D. *Eugenii O'Neill,* in prælio captus, & post fidem præstitam
gladiis trucidatur, in Ultonia, anno 1651.

" 5. Illustrissimus D. *Thadæus O'Connor,* Sliego, ex ultimo-
rum, ac potentissimorum Hiberniæ monarchum prosapia satus,
vir miræ innocentiæ, ac bonitatis, post amnestiam cum toto

"1652, after the general amnesty had been
"made.

"6. Constantius O'Ruairk, taken prisoner in bat-
"tle, murdered in 1652, *notwithstanding*
"*plighted faith.*

"7. Theobald De Burgo, Lord Viscount Mayo,
"after truce had been made with all such
"persons in the kingdom as were not ac-
"tually in arms against the Protestants, and
"a general amnesty promised, was shot in
"Galway in 1651.

"8. Charles O'Dowd, of a most high and noble
"race, hanged A.D. 1651.

"9. The illustrious Donat O'Brien, descended
"of the royal race of the O'Briens, a most
"generous man, and of surpassing hospi-
"tality; after the Protestants had plighted

Regno factam, in oppido de *Boyle* in Conacia, suspendio
necatur, ann. 1652.

"6. Illustrissimus D. *Constantinus O'Ruairk*, in prælio
captus, & post fidem præstitam, gladiis trucidatus, anno 1652.

"7. Illustrissimus D. *Theobaldus de Burgo*, Vice-Comes de
Mayo, post fædus initum cum toto Regno (hoc est qui actualiter
non erant in armis contra hæreticos), & amnestiam promissam,
ab hæreticis capitur, & Galuiæ in Conacia globis trajicitur,
anno 1651.

"8. Perillustris ac generosus D. *Carolus O'Duda*, suspendio
necatur, anno 1651.

"9. Illustrissimus D. *Donatus O'Brien*, ex regali Brienorum
prosapia, vir liberalissimus, et incomparabilis hospitalitatis,

" to him their faith, and given him safe con-
" duct in order that he might become their
" tributary; an attack being made one day
" by the Protestants against the Catholics,
" he (O'Brien) relying on his having been
" received into their friendship, approached;
" when a certain Protestant knight shot him
" through the body. Unsatisfied with this
" cruelty, when the venerable old man (then
" aged about 64 years) had entered a hut,
" half dead, that he might in penitence com-
" mend himself to God, a soldier followed,
" set fire to the hut, and burned this noble
" old man—in Thomond, A.D. 1651.

" 10. James O'Brien, of illustrious lineage, ma-
" ternal nephew of the aforesaid Donatus
" O'Brien, a youth of high hopes and pros-
" pects, was murdered at Nenagh in the

---

postquam fidem, & salvum conductum, ei præstiterint hæretici,
& eorum foret tributarius, quodam die, irruentibus Hæreticis
contra Catholicos, occurrit ipse postquam jam in gratiam &
amicitiam hæreticorum adoptatus esset; quidam eques hæreticus,
cum globo trajecit ; nec satiatus hac crudelitate, cum venerabilis
senex (erat enim sexaginta quatuor, vel circiter, annorum)
quoddam tuguriolum semi mortuus intrasset, ut Deo, per
pœnitentiam, se commendaret, insecutus ipsum miles, tugurium
incendit, ac nobilissimum virum combussit, in Thomonia,
anno 1651.

" 10. Perillustris, ac nobilissimus D. *Jacobus O'Brien*, ex
magnifica parentela satus, et ex sorore nepos præfati D. *Donati*,

" Ormonds. They cut his head off and
" sent it to his uterine brother, Moriarty
" O'Brien, then their prisoner.

" 11. Bernard O'Brien, of the same noble family,
" a youth of equally fair prospects, was
" hanged in 1651.

" 12. Daniel O'Brien, first cousin of the said
" Bernard, was hanged, and his head cut
" off at Nenagh, 1651.

" 13. The illustrious Colonel John O'Kenedy, a
" man of the utmost integrity, was slain by
" the swords of the Protestants, after their
" faith had been pledged to him in battle.
" His head was then cut off and fastened on
" a spike in the town of Nenagh, A.D. 1651.

---

juvenis bonæ spei et magnæ expectationis, in oppido de *Nenach*
in *Ormondia,* caput abscissum, præsentârunt suo fratri uterino,
illustrissimo D. *Moriarto O'Brien,* in captivitate ibidem tunc
existenti.

" 11. Perillustris D. *Bernardus O'Brien,* ex eadem prosapia
satus, juvenis non minoris expectationis, ibidem pari suspendio
necatur, anno 1651.

" 12. Perillustris D. *Daniel O'Brien,* præfati D. Bernardi
frater germanus, in eodem oppido de *Nenach,* suspendio, et
abscissione capitis, vitam finivit, anno 1651.

" 13. Illustriss. D. *Joannes O'Kenedy,* colonellus, vir integerrimæ sinceritatis, post fidem in prælio præstitam, ab hæreticis
gladiis trucidatur, & caput abscissum in oppido de *Nenach,*
spiculo appenditur, anno 1651.

"14. James O'Kenedy, son of the aforesaid
"illustrious gentleman, a youth of great
"hopes, being deluded with a similar pledge
"of good faith, was hanged in Nenagh,
"A.D. 1651.

"15. The illustrious Sir Patrick Purcell, Vice-
"General of all Munster, noble hearted,
"and a most accomplished warrior, (re-
"nowned for his services in Germany
"against Sweden and France, under Ferdi-
"nand III. of Augustan memory,) was
"hanged after the taking of Limerick, his
"head cut off, and exposed on a stake over
"the southern gate (called John's gate) of
"the city of Limerick—A.D. 1651.

"16. The illustrious and most generous Sir
"Godfrey Barron, a sincere Catholic, of the
"highest fidelity, and of singular eloquence,

"14. *Jacobus O'Kenedy,* filius præfati illustrissimi domini,
juvenis magnæ spei, pari promissione fidei delusus in præfato
oppido de *Nenach,* suspendio ablatus est, anno 1651.

"15. Illustrissimus D. *Patricius Purcell,* totius Momoniæ
Vice-Generalis, magnanimus, et dexterrimus miles (in Germania
sub Augustæ memoriæ Ferdinando Tertio contra Suecum &
Gallum notissimus) post captam urbem *Limericensem,* patibulo
suspenditur, caput abscinditur, et perticâ infixa, ad portem
Australem (quæ porta S. Joannis dicitur) urbis *Limericensis*
appenditur, anno 1651.

"16. Perillustris, ac generossissimus D. *Galfridus Baronius,*
vir planè Catholicus, magnæ fidelitatis, & raræ eloquentiæ, qui

" who had been deputed by the confederated
" Catholics of Ireland as their envoy to his
" most Christian Majesty, was also hanged
" at Limerick.

" 17. The noble Sir Godfrey Galway, was like-
" wise hanged at Limerick, 1651.

" 18. The noble Thomas Stritch, Mayor of
" Limerick, and alderman, was, with the
" like cruelty, hanged at the same time with
" the rest. His head was then cut off and
" fastened to the city gate.

" 19. The noble Dominicus Fanning, ex-Mayor
" of Limerick, and alderman, a well known
" man, and of the highest integrity, who
" had been of great service to the confe-
" derated Catholics, and had laudably con-
" ferred much benefit on the kingdom as

à Confæderatis Regni Hiberniæ Catholicis, apud Regem Chris-
tianissimum oratorem egit, ibidem *Limerici* suspendio necatur.

" 17. Perillustris D. *Galfridus Galway,* eques auratus,
ibidem *Limerici* suspendio occiditur, anno 1651.

" 18. Perillustris D. *Thomas Strichæus,* urbis *Limericensis*
Archi-prætor, & Consul, eodem tempore cum reliquis, pari
crudelitate suspenditur, et capite plectitur, quod ad portem
civitatis appensum fuit.

" 19. Perillustris, ac generosissimus D. *Dominicus Fan-
ningus,* ejusdem urbis *Limericensis* Ex-prætor, & Consul, vir
notissimus, & integerrimæ fidelitatis, qui multa bona Confæderatis Catholicis præstitit, et multa munia laudabiliter ad
utilitatem Regni, et urbis, obivit, ibidem *Limerici* cum reliquis,

" well as on the city, was hanged at Lime-
" rick along with the rest, A.D. 1651.   His
" head was cut off and affixed to the gate.
" 20. Daniel O'Higgins, medical doctor, a wise
" and pious man, was hanged at the same
" time at Limerick, A.D. 1651.
" 21. The illustrious and Right Reverend Ter-
" ence O'Brien, Bishop of Raphoe, (of
" whom I have already spoken,) was hanged
" at the same time, and his' head cut off.
" He went gloriously to heaven, A.D. 1651.
" 22. The illustrious John O'Connor, Lord of
" Kerry and Iracht, on account of his adhe-
" sion to the Catholic party, and his efforts
" to draw to it not only his personal fol-
" lowers, but all with whom he had friend-
" ship, was, after having been seized upon
" by stratagem by the Protestants, brought

patibulo suspensus, vitam cum morte commutavit, anno 1651,
caput abscissum appenditur portæ.

" 20. D. *Daniel O'Higgins,* doctor medicinæ, vir sapiens,
et pius, ibidem Limerici suspendio necatur, anno 1651.

" 21. Illustrissimus & Reverendissimus D. *Therensius
O'Brien,* Episcopus Immolacensis (de quo supra) ibidem suspendio, & abscissione capitis, gloriosus migravit in cœlum,
anno 1651.

" 22. Illustrissimus D. *Joannes O'Conor,* Kieriæ, et Baroniæ
de Iracht, eo quod Catholicis partibus adhæserit, et sibi ad-
hærentes, ac amicitiâ conjunctos, eodem attrahere conabatur,
ab hæreticis, insidiis captus, *Traliæ* in ipsomet comitatu

" to Tralee in that county, and there half
" hanged and then beheaded, A. D. 1652.

" 23. The illustrious Lord Edward Butler, son
" of Lord Mountgarret, an innocent man,
" hanged, who had never taken arms, was
" at Dublin after the truce had been com-
" menced, and amnesty promised throughout
" the whole kingdom, A.D. 1652.

" 24. The illustrious and Reverend Bernard
" Fitzpatrick, priest, and descended from
" the illustrious lineage of the Barons of
" Ossory, who, flying for refuge from the
" fury of the Protestants to a cave, was
" pursued by them ; who there cut off the
" head of this most holy man (who was
" equally renowned throughout the kingdom
" for his life, his doctrine, and his lineage).
" They affixed his head to a spike over the

Kieriæ semi-suspendio, & capitis abscissione necatus est, anno
1652.

" 23. Illustrissimus D. *Edwardus Butlerus,* filius illustrissimi
D. de Montgarrett, vir innocens, qui nunquam arma offensiva
portavit, post fædus initum, et amicitiam in toto Regno promissam, patibulo suspensus est *Dublinii,* anno 1652.

" 24. Perillustris, ac Reverendissimus D. *Bernardus Fitz-
Patrick,* presbyter, ex familia illustrissimorum DD. Baronum
Ossoriensium, seu de Ossory, qui ad quandam speluncam, a
rabie hæreticorum confugiens, eum hæretici insecuti, sanctis-
simum virum (erat enim vitâ, doctrinâ, et prosapiâ conspicuus,
et in toto Regno notus) capite plexerunt in spelunca : caput in

" town gate to be meat for the fowls of the
" air, and left his flesh to be devoured by
" the beasts of the field.

" Nor was the inhuman fury of the Protestants
" satiated with this slaughter of men ; but
" they also drew their swords against women.

" Thus,—

" The noble Lady Roche, wife of Maurice, Vis-
" count of Fermoy and Roche, a chaste and
" holy matron, whose mind was solely occu-
" pied with prayer and piety, being falsely
" accused of murder by a certain ungrateful
" English maid-servant, (whom she had com-
" passionately taken when a desolate orphan,
" and supported and educated,) was hanged
" at Cork in 1654, although stricken in
" years, and destined in the course of nature
" soon to die.

---

porta cujusdam oppidi, infixâ perticâ,* *in escam volatilibus cæli* appenderunt, & *carnes* ibi pro *bestiis terræ,* reliquerunt.

" Nec hac virorum cæde, immanis hæreticorum rabies satiata fuit, set contra mulieres gladios strinxerunt.   Itaque,—

" Illustrissima D. *Rochæa,* uxor illustrissimi D. *Mauritii Roch,* Vice-Comitis, de *Farmoy* & *Rupe,* matrona prudens, & sancta, quæ nulli rei, nisi soli orationi intenta erat, a quadam sua ingrata ancilla Angla (quam orphanellam, derelictam, misericorditer enutrivit & educavit) notorio mendacio de homicido accusata, jam grandæva, et secundo cursū naturæ diu vivere nequiens, patibulo suspensa est, Corcagiæ, 1654.

* Hebr. xi.

" The noble Lady Bridget of the house of Darcy,
    " wife of Florence Fitzpatrick, one of the
    " Barons of Ossory, was hanged by the
    " Protestants at Dublin in 1652, without
    " the form of law or of justice.

" What shall I yet say ?   Time would fail me to
    " narrate the martyrdoms of chiefs, nobles,
    " prelates, priests, friars, citizens, and others
    " of the Irish Catholics, (whose purple gore
    " has stained the scaffolds almost without
    " end ;) who ' *by faith conquered kingdoms*
    " ' *and wrought justice.*' Of whom some had
    " trials in mockeries and stripes, moreover
    " also of chains and prisons.   Others were
    " stoned, cut asunder, racked, or put to
    " death with the sword. *(Heb.* xi.)   Others

" Illustrissima D. *Brigida,* ex familia Darsæa, conjux illustrissimi D. *Florenti Fitz-Patrick,* ex Baronibus *Ossoriensibus,*
absque forma juris aut rationis, ab Hæreticis patibulo suspensa
est, *Dublinii,* anno 1652.

" *Quid adhuc dicam ?** *Deficiet enim me tempus enna-
rantem* de Martyrio Magnatum, Nobilium, Prælatorum, Pres-
byterorum, Religiosorum, Civium, cæterorúmque Catholicorum
Regni Hiberniæ (quorum sanguine, infinita fere purpurata sunt
patibula) *qui per fidem vicerunt Regna, operati sunt justitiam;*
quorum, *alii ludibria, et verbera experti, insuper et vincula
et carceres ; Alii lapidati sunt, secti sunt, tentati sunt, in
occasione gladii mortui sunt.*   Alii *circuierunt* totum mundum,

* Heb. xi.

" have wandered over the world in hunger,
" thirst, cold, and nakedness ; being in
" want, distressed, afflicted ; wandering in
" deserts, in mountains, and in dens and
" in caves of the earth. And all these being
" approved by the testimony of the faith,
" without doubt received the promise.
" Amen."—(pp. 65—72.)

The conclusion of this chapter shall be the following extract from a pamphlet published in London
in the year 1647, and which passed through several

---

in fame, siti, frigore, & nuditate, *egentes, angustiati, afflicti,*
in solitudinibus errantes, in montibus, & speluncis, et in
cavernis terræ, et hi omnes testimonio fidei probati, procul-
dubio, acceperunt repromissionem. Amen."—pp. 65—72.

The above long extract is copied verbatim from an exceedingly
scarce and curious tract, written by a Catholic Priest named
Maurice Morison; and which is entitled, " THRENODIA HIBERNO-
" CATHOLICA, sive PLANCTUS UNIVERSALIS TOTIUS CLERI ET
" Populi Regni Hiberniæ. In qua veridicè et sincerè recensetur
" epitome inauditæ & transcendentis crudelitatis, qua Catholici
" Regni Hiberniæ tyrannicè opprimuntur ab Anglo Antheistis
" sub Archi-tyranno *Crumuello,* trium Regnorum, nempe *An-*
" *gliæ, Hiberniæ,* & *Scotiæ,* usurpatore et destructore. PER
" F. M. MORISONUM, ORDINIS Min. strict. Observantiæ, S.
" Theologiæ Lectorem. Præfatæ Crudelitatis testem ocularem.
" —ŒNIPONTI, 1659."

This very curious account of the *Persecution of the Irish*
Catholics by Cromwell is extremely rare.

editions.   It serves to show what the sentiments of
the English people were, and what the topics were
that excited their interest, and obtained their approbation :—

" THE SIMPLE COBBLER OF AGGAVAM IN AMERICA.

" BY THEODORE DE LA GUARD.

" A word of Ireland : not of the nation univer-
" sally, nor of any man in it, that hath so
" much as one haire of Christianity or hu-
" manity growing on his head, or beard; but
" only of the truculent cut-throats, and such
" as shall take up armes in their defence.
" These Irish, anciently called *Anthropophagi*,
" man-eaters, have a tradition among them,
" that when the devil showed our Saviour
" all the kingdomes of the earth and their
" glory, that he would not show him Ireland,
" but reserved it for himself.   It is most
" probably true, for he hath kept it ever
" since for his own peculiar ; the old fox
" foresaw that it would eclipse the glory of
" all the rest : he thought it wisdome to keep
" it for a boggards for himself and all his
" unclean spirits employed in this hemis-
" phere, and the people to do his son and
" heire, I mean the Pope, that service for

" which *Lewis* the Eleventh kept his barber,
" *Oliver*, which makes them to be so blood-
" thirsty. THEY ARE THE VERY OFFAL OF
" MEN, DREGGES OF MANKIND, REPROACHE
" OF CHRISTENDOME, THE BOTS THAT CRAWLE
" ON THE BEASTE'S TAILE. I wonder *Rome*
" itself is not ashamed of them.

" I beg upon my hands and knees that the expe-
" dition against them may be undertaken
" while the hearts and hands of our soldiery
" are hot, to whome I will be bold to say
" briefly : Happy is he that shall reward
" them as they have served us; and *cursed*
" *is he that shall do the work of the Lord*
" *negligently.* CURSED BE HE THAT
" HOLDETH BACK HIS SWORD
" FROM BLOOD: YEA, CURSED BE
" HE THAT MAKETH NOT HIS
" SWORD STARKE DRUNK WITH
" IRISH BLOOD; that doth not recom-
" pense them double for their hellish trea-
" chery to the English; that maketh them
" not heaps upon heaps, and their country a
" dwelling-place for dragons, an astonish-
" ment to nations ! Let not that eye look for
" pity, nor that hand be spared, that pities
" or spares them; AND LET HIM
" BE ACCURSED THAT CURSETH
" THEM NOT BITTERLY."—*London,*

*printed by J. D. and R. I. for Stephen
Bowtell, at the sign of the Bible, in Pope's-
Head Alley*—1647.

There is no person who will read this work, but
must exclaim with me, that no people on the face
of the earth were ever treated with such cruelty as
the Irish.

The pamphlet I have last quoted contains, in fact,
a short development of the spirit which animated
the conduct of the English Government towards
the people of Ireland.